EVERYDAY LAW MADE SIMPLE
NEW REVISED EDITION

EVERYDAY LAW
MADE SIMPLE

NEW REVISED EDITION

BY

JACK LAST, LL.M.
MEMBER OF: Bar of New York State, United States District Court,
United States Court of Claims, United States Immigration and Naturalization,
United States Court of Appeals

Revised and Expanded
by
DOUGLAS B. OLIVER
J.D., Columbia Law School
Member of the Bar of New York State

and
BETSY B. MCKENNEY
J.D., Columbia Law School
Member of the Bars of the States of New York and New Jersey
and the Bar of the United States District Court

MADE SIMPLE BOOKS

DOUBLEDAY & COMPANY, INC.

GARDEN CITY, NEW YORK

Library of Congress Cataloging in Publication Data

Last, Jack, 1910–
Everyday law made simple.

(Made simple books)
Includes index.
1. Law—United States—Popular works. I. Oliver,
Douglas B. II. McKenney, Betsy B. III. Title.
KF387.L36 1978   340'.0973
ISBN: 0-385-12921-1
Library of Congress Catalog Card Number 77–15164

Copyright © 1954, 1960, 1978 by Doubleday & Company, Inc.
All Rights Reserved
Printed in the United States of America

349.73
L349e

ABOUT THIS BOOK

Modern living has become a very complicated affair. The everyday activities of average citizens are regulated by laws that constantly multiply and change. There are laws regulating your work, your domestic arrangements, laws about every conceivable relationship you can enter into.

Most people know that when they buy a house, sign a contract, form a partnership or a corporation, draw a will, and so on, as well as when they are summonsed in a court action, they need the advice of a lawyer. Few people are aware, however, that in many of the everyday acts of their lives, what they do and how they go about it affect the outcome of some future litigation.

When they marry, buy a car on time, make a sale, sign a check, or in one of the hundreds of other things they may be called upon to do in the course of a day, they may unwittingly start something that will wind up in a courtroom. The law applies with equal weight to these acts as it does to the formation of a corporation or the transfer of real estate.

This book aims to explain the law, without technical "mumbo-jumbo," as it applies to you in situations you are likely to encounter in the course of your private and business life. However, it does not undertake to enable you to dispense with a lawyer's services on the occasions when you need one.

The knowledge of law required in the situations when a lawyer has to be consulted can never be gotten out of one book. Remember that a legal education takes from three to five years of post-graduate study and continues all through legal practice.

This book is intended to help you in legal well-being, to make you aware of your legal rights and responsibilities in everyday life, and to recognize the situations when you should seek professional help.

—JACK LAST

CONTENTS

CHAPTER ONE

THE NATURE AND SCOPE OF THE LAW

CHAPTER TWO

THE LONG REACH OF THE LAW

CHAPTER THREE

CONTRACTS

Contents

CHAPTER FOUR

SALES

CHAPTER FIVE

NOTES, DRAFTS, AND CHECKS

CHAPTER SIX

PRINCIPAL AND AGENT, EMPLOYER AND EMPLOYEE, MASTER AND SERVANT

CHAPTER SEVEN
PARTNERSHIPS

CHAPTER EIGHT
CORPORATIONS

CHAPTER NINE
REAL PROPERTY

CHAPTER TEN
MORTGAGES

x   *Contents*

CHAPTER ELEVEN

LANDLORD AND TENANT

CHAPTER TWELVE

DEBTORS AND CREDITORS

CHAPTER THIRTEEN

PATENTS, COPYRIGHTS, TRADEMARKS, TRADE NAMES

CHAPTER FOURTEEN

WILLS: THE INHERITANCE OF PROPERTY

CHAPTER FIFTEEN

WILLS: INTESTACY AND OTHER INHERITANCE PROBLEMS

CHAPTER SIXTEEN

CIVIL WRONGS

CHAPTER SEVENTEEN

CIVIL WRONGS: OTHER THAN NEGLIGENCE

CHAPTER EIGHTEEN

DOMESTIC RELATIONS: ENGAGEMENT AND MARRIAGE

CHAPTER NINETEEN

DOMESTIC RELATIONS: ANNULMENT, SEPARATION, DIVORCE

CHAPTER TWENTY

CRIMINAL LAW

CHAPTER TWENTY-ONE

PRACTICE IN THE COURTS: PREPARING THE CASE

CHAPTER TWENTY-TWO

PRACTICE IN THE COURTS: JURIES AND EVIDENCE

Contents

CHAPTER TWENTY-THREE

CIVIL RIGHTS

CHAPTER TWENTY-FOUR

LABOR AND MANAGEMENT

CHAPTER TWENTY-FIVE

THE LEGAL PROFESSION

LIST OF FIGURES AND TABLES

INTRODUCTION TO THE NEW REVISED EDITION

The law is not static. It undergoes continuous change just as our society undergoes change. Granted: Certain principles remain as constants; but others modulate to meet the needs of the time and new concepts come into being in order to deal with new problems. It is to keep abreast of the development of the law that this book has been revised.

The purpose of *Everyday Law Made Simple* has always been to survey the basic principles of the law in an uncomplicated fashion, and we have always kept this in mind in our work of revision. The reader should get a sense of his legal rights and responsibilities in the various situations in which he is likely to find himself. We have tried to show the reader what's required of him, and what he has a right to ask of others. But this book is *not* intended to replace the services of a lawyer; it will point out when you have a legal problem, but your lawyer will tell you how to deal with that problem.

In addition, *Everyday Law Made Simple* can help you arrange your affairs so that problems do not arise. Because the law is such a basic element of our society, the more you know about "the way it is," the fewer headaches you'll have in the future. An ounce of prevention is truly worth a pound of cure.

Douglas B. Oliver
Betsy B. McKenney

EVERYDAY LAW MADE SIMPLE
NEW REVISED EDITION

CHAPTER ONE

THE NATURE AND SCOPE OF THE LAW

In this continuously changing world of ours, customs, relationships and ideas are in flux— and the law evolves and changes with them. That is why legislatures and courts must continue their sessions. And, as modern life brings new complexities into human relationships, the laws that regulate them—that determine what is right and wrong—grow ever more complicated.

NOT AN "EXACT" SCIENCE

It would simplify matters if the law were a science like physics and chemistry; if it dealt, as they do, with measurable quantities and energies; if the interactions of people could always be predicted, like the interactions of chemicals. But law deals with that disconcerting "variable," human beings, in their ever altering relationships to each other, and to the community; and with human emotions for which no yardstick has yet been found—if it ever will be. In addition, law deals with value judgments a society makes as to what is right or wrong, or what is to be aimed for. These value judgments periodically change, too. For instance, Prohibition has come and gone, the way we treat criminal defendants has changed drastically over the past decade, and there has been a lot of legislation lately dealing with environmental concerns.

So we must resign ourselves to the fact that the law is still an inexact branch of knowledge. That is why our courts are so overburdened with litigation. That is also why there are split decisions and eminent judges who disagree with each other.

However, it is an exact science in the sense that the principles have been formulated and tested, and decisions and interpretations have been recorded. Where it can give no immediate, precise answer to a problem, it can provide a means for arriving at an answer.

Certain guiding principles underlie our laws through all the changes. These, we hope, are made clear in this book. We'll now analyze some of the distinctions between the main categories of law—Common Law and Statute Law, Civil Law and Criminal Law, Constitutional Law, Federal Law, State Law, and International Law.

STATUTORY LAW AND COMMON LAW

Each of the fifty sovereign states of the United States has its own legislature and its own system of courts. On top of this we have the federal Congress and the federal courts. The Constitution of the United States is the source from which the powers of both the federal and state legislatures are derived and by which their scope is limited.

Law is made by the state in two ways: by enactment in legislatures—statutory law; and by decisions in the courts—common law, sometimes also called "case law."

Common Law. The basic law of most of the United States is the common law of England, brought over by colonists and later adopted in the early constitutions of the states as they were formed. The outstanding exception is the state of Louisiana, where the "code" system prevails as a result of prior French influence. Statute law, rather than case law, is the basic law of that state.

Common law is often referred to as "unwritten law." This is inaccurate, since the decisions or precedents are well recorded and organized for reference. It is only "unwritten" in the sense that it is not written by the legislature, but comes down to us through use and custom by way of the courts.

However, although the common law can be found in written reports of judicial hearings, in a technical sense this record is not the law. It is only evidence of what the law is. The technicality is an important one because, if we regarded a particular decision as *the law*, rather than as evidence of how the law is applied in a given case, the common law would become rigid. It would lose the elasticity that makes it adaptable to changing times and conditions.

Statute Law. The laws enacted by the legislatures of the various states, and those passed by Congress, constitute our statutes, or "written law." The function of statutes is to modify the common law to suit changing times, to replace it if necessary, and to provide for situations not covered by the common law.

How the common law has been modified by statute may be seen in the Jones Act. Under the common law, a seaman injured through the negligence of the master of a vessel could recover nothing beyond his wages and medical care. The Jones Act changed this; it permitted injured seamen to claim damages.

Effect of Decisions on Statute Law. Often enough, the language used by our lawmakers leaves its meaning and intent in doubt. Even lawyers skilled in the interpretation of obscure and ambiguous passages find themselves in disagreement on the precise meaning of some statutes.

In such a case, the meaning is left in question until it becomes the subject of litigation. The courts are then given the task of interpreting the statute. So cases and decisions involving statutes have the same value as cases and decisions based on the common law.

CIVIL LAW AND CRIMINAL LAW

Civil Law. When this term is used to distinguish between civil and criminal actions, it has to do with the right of one party against another, in claims for the recovery of property, or for damages for injuries sustained through assaults, negligence, fraud, libel, etc. Thus, civil law (sometimes called "private law") has to do with wrongs done, not to society, but to an individual, who resorts to the court for redress.

Criminal Law. Criminal law defines "crimes"—offenses against the community—and provides punishment. It has a public rather than a private character, and is therefore sometimes called "public law." The action is brought in the name of the state, or the people of the state, against the wrongdoer. The crime is wrongdoing against society, even if the victim is one person.

When Both Apply. Suppose that, in the course of your business, someone makes a payment to you by check. The check turns out to be of the rubber variety—it is drawn on a bank in which no funds are on deposit. The maker of the check has wronged you, and you have the right to bring a civil action against him to recover the amount of the bad check.

At the same time, and by the same act, he has wronged society, since issuing a fraudulent check is a larceny. If you institute an action, the district attorney will bring a criminal action against the wrongdoer. If he's found guilty, he will be given a jail sentence.

As a practical matter, in dealing with offenses like passing bad checks, criminal prosecution is usually speedier and more effective than instituting a civil suit. The district attorneys and police have the power to arrest the wrongdoer and bring him to trial in courts that are often not as congested as the civil courts. Both types of actions can proceed, although magistrates will often suspend sentence, or withdraw or dismiss the case if restitution is made.

Actually, law enforcement officers don't like the idea of acting as collection agents for complaining citizens. Theirs is the duty of prosecuting offenders and they sometimes resent the withdrawal of charges when the offender makes good.

INTERNATIONAL LAW

This special form of law exists even though there is no international legislature with power to enforce its acts, and no international courts with power to enforce their judgments. The laws in this area have been formulated by international treaty, by general principles established through the decisions of our own courts, and principles set down by scholars and experts on the subject. These are constantly referred to.

The problems dealt with in the area of international law belong to four general categories:

Disputes between nations;

Disputes between the citizens of one nation and the government of another nation;

Disputes between the citizens of different nations;

Disputes between the citizens of the same nation in which principles of international law are involved.

The League of Nations, following World War I, and the United Nations, after World War II, made significant progress toward the establishment of a World Court where litigation between sovereign nations could be heard. However, the parties must go to the Court of their own free will. The World Court is more in the nature of a court of arbitration than a court of law as we have come to know it in the United States.

International law deals with questions of nationality, the right of individuals to the protection of the nations of which they are citizens; the right of nations to make laws affecting their own citizens; the nationality of ships on the high seas; the immunity of diplomats from local laws and local prosecutions; neutrality; recognition of new governments which

by revolution, absorption or war replace former governments.

Problems in the area of international law arise because countries have their own interests, which often conflict with those of other nations. For example, the question of how far from shore a nation can control fishing rights is one that is being argued today. Treaties between nations, perhaps with some give and take in other areas of common interest, are often the only way to solve such conflicts.

FEDERAL, STATE AND LOCAL LAWS

Federal Laws. The Constitution of the United States specifically reserves to Congress the right to make laws regarding interstate and foreign commerce, provide for the common defense, coin money, regulate immigration, and deal with all matters having to do with interstate or foreign relations.

Although most of the laws that affect states are state laws, in recent years, because of the expansion of business across state lines, almost everybody is engaged in some form of interstate commerce. So almost every business has become affected by federal law. The use of this power has become necessary in order to provide uniform treatment throughout the United States, even in areas only tangentially related to commerce. For instance, the federal government can impose certain sanctions against businesses engaged in interstate commerce if they violate federal directives regarding civil rights.

State Laws. Under the Constitution of the United States, legislative power not expressly delegated to the federal government, and not prohibited by the Constitution, is reserved to the states. Consequently, most of the laws relating to the health and general welfare of a community and its citizens are passed by state legislatures within limitations set by the federal and state constitutions. Unless a federal question is involved, or a question in which citizens of different states are involved, litigation belongs in the state courts.

Local Laws. Laws passed by cities, towns,

villages, or counties derive their authority from the state constitution or the state legislature. When a city passes a traffic ordinance, for example, it exercises the police power of the state, by specific authority of the state.

LAW ENFORCEMENT AGENCIES

The division of authority among federal, state, and local governments becomes a little clearer when we look at the activities of their law enforcement agencies.

State and Local Police. In most of the states the responsibility of law enforcement is part of the executive power of the governor. Law enforcement authority is usually delegated to localities, so it is the local police who have jurisdiction over and responsibility for maintaining the peace within their precincts. The governor appoints prosecuting attorneys, called "district attorneys" or "state's attorneys," who represent the state in actions against individuals. The states are divided up into counties, and the responsibility of each district attorney is usually confined to the county assigned to him.

Cities and towns usually have their own police forces and, often, local courts of justice. It is the duty of the state police to handle law enforcement in areas outside the jurisdiction of city police, as in rural areas or along highways.

The Federal Bureau of Investigation. The FBI is a police arm of the United States Department of Justice. Its authority to investigate and enforce extends only to federal matters. The FBI cannot, for example, investigate a larceny committed within a particular state. But if an automobile is stolen in one state and transported to another, an interstate or federal crime has been committed. The FBI then has the right to investigate the crime and apprehend the criminal.

ADMINISTRATIVE LAW

One other source of law should be mentioned—administrative agencies are creations of the legislature, and they promulgate rules and regulations that affect everyone. Agencies can "fill in" a statute, and their amendments have the force of law; they can also issue interpretations of statutes which are usually deferred to by the courts. This rulemaking power is quasi-legislative in that the rules are prospective—that is, they apply to events in the future rather than just to a specific situation in the present. The rulemaking process includes certain safeguards in order to prevent a misuse of power. There must be notice to and consultation with interested parties, a testing period, and an adherence to legislative guidelines. In addition, the legislature can supervise the agency as it goes about its business. Generally, the basic procedures and rights of any trial must be respected by an agency.

There can be judicial review of an agency decision, but the reviewing authority generally considers only the agency's authority and the substantiality of the evidence on which the decision is based. (For this reason, the agency's findings of fact should accompany its decision.) If the agency's decision has a rational basis and is consistent with prior rulings, it is usually allowed to stand.

Before agencies take formal action, a detailed procedure must be followed. There must be hearings on the subject, although this may be dispensed with in informal proceedings, and, *in all cases,* interested parties must be given notice and an opportunity to be heard. The final order must be based on the entire record of the proceedings. The hearing takes place before an impartial presiding officer, and there must be an opportunity to present all the evidence and to cross-examine the opposition. Examples of this type of proceeding are hearings on environmental projects, with buinessmen and their experts testifying as to the need for construction and what its effects will be on an area, while others testify on the unique qualities of the land and its animals, and the nonindustrial uses that the land offers, as well as on the harm that construction will cause.

Dealing with agencies is a complex process and should be done with the help of an attorney well versed in the proper procedures. However, one shouldn't feel powerless in the face of bureaucrats and agency action. Judicial review will be available if there has been a violation of due process—which, in simple terms, is basic fairness to all interested parties—along the way to a decision. Courts often defer to agency decisions, however, since the agency is acting for the legislature that created it. That is not to say that agencies are allowed to go beyond the bounds of the power given them, or to act in an arbitrary manner or without considering all the pertinent information.

Freedom of Information Act. To oppose agency action effectively, you must have the information on which an agency has based its decision. The Freedom of Information Act makes government records available for public inspection. The agency has the burden of showing why information shouldn't be released to the public (i.e., because of pressing reasons for its remaining secret), and courts will review an agency's decision not to make its documents available. This Act gives "watchdog" groups the ability to keep track of what agencies are doing. Similarly, the Act allows individuals to find out what information about themselves the government has in its records.

Sovereign Immunity. This term refers to the government's freedom from being sued for liability for acts arising from its governmental functions. Now, it is difficult to sue the government—be it federal, state, or local—but it can be done. Ordinarily, you must proceed on one of two grounds: Either the statute giving the government agency its authority is unconstitutional, or an individual officer acted outside the bounds of his lawful authority. You probably won't be able to sue the government for errors a government employee makes *within* the bounds of his authority. However, other roads to recovery against the government are open. Often, the government allows itself to be sued. And if property is taken by the government, compensation will be paid to the complaining party.

Sometimes the protection given to government to allow it to do its job conflicts with Constitutional protections of the individual. In such a case, the government can be sued. For example, when federal law enforcement agents arrested an innocent man after illegally searching his home, the injured party was allowed to sue the agents for their excesses. There is no immunity against violations of the Constitution; the discretion to act that government agents have. is always restricted by the constitutional protections each American enjoys. The federal civil rights acts make suits against government agents easier in instances where the power of the state is used in violations of civil rights.

CHAPTER TWO

THE LONG REACH OF THE LAW

The purpose of this chapter is to show, in a general way, how in our society law applies to us even before we are born and after we die. It covers and regulates almost every human activity and relationship in whatever capacity we act. No matter what our status or calling, we are subject to the law and governed by it for our own protection, the protection of those we deal with, and the good of the community.

BEFORE BIRTH

Law begins for a person in our society even before birth—at least to some extent. States may pass laws regulating a woman's access to an abortion in the final three months of her pregnancy, which means, in effect, that some rights of the unborn can be recognized before birth. In addition, these rights may be recognized in accident and injury cases. Parents-to-be have been awarded damages if it can be shown that a miscarriage resulted from someone's misdeed or negligence, and the child may win a judgment if such acts affect him after birth.

AT BIRTH

A whole set of rights and responsibilities comes into being along with a newborn child.

His right to care and support is recognized by the state. If, for some reason, his parents are incapable or unfit to care for him, if they abandon him, or if he becomes orphaned, custody of his person is awarded to others through a legal proceeding in which the state exercises its authority as his guardian.

He becomes a dependent for tax purposes.

He acquires the right to own property, to buy and sell through legal guardians, and to sue and be sued. The law can be invoked to protect him against persons who might take advantage of his youth.

Obligations he incurs as a child are legally voidable by him when he becomes an adult.

His property must be handled by his guardian in ways that are prescribed by law to prevent any losses through deceit or through unwise or speculative investments.

Most states require him to be educated at least through grammar school, and have regulations laid down by their education or labor laws regarding children who work.

Debts of Children. Until he is "of age," legally, a child cannot be held to a contract and cannot be made to pay for anything except the necessities of life: food, clothing, medical treatment, etc. The definition of "necessities" will vary according to the financial station of the child. But it is a good idea, regardless of his wealth, to extend credit to a child only for the basic necessities of life.

Debts to Children. If you owe a child a sum of money, you should make sure you pay it to the one who has the right to receive it for the child—the guardian of the child's property, who, in most cases, is his father (although that position might be open to argument today). Paying the child does not discharge the debt. You may have to pay all over again.

Earnings of Children. A child's earnings are controlled by his parents. Many states have laws to ensure that the child's earnings are not misused by his parents. A child who is completely self-supporting is generally entitled to the fruits of his labors.

The Age of Consent. Just to make things complex, a person comes of age at different times for different purposes, and the ages differ in the various states.

The tables in this books will show, among other things, at what age a person can marry without parental consent; at what age a person can make a valid will, buy and sell realty and, generally, enter into valid contracts as a fully responsible adult.

Legal Capacity. In addition to children, there are certain other persons to whom the rules of law affecting adults don't apply. Such persons can't make a contract, marry, sue or be sued without the consent or assistance of a guardian or legal representative. Such people are said to be "without legal capacity."

These include insane persons—or, to be more accurate, persons who have been adjudged insane or incompetent. Sometimes people of full age and sound mind are temporarily without legal capacity. That could occur when, for any reason, they are deprived of the power to give knowing consent.

For instance, if you are compelled to sign a document at the point of a gun, you can hardly be said to be consenting to whatever the document says. Later, when the gun is removed, you can legally repudiate the document, and your signature on it won't bind you, if you can prove the compulsion which forced you to sign it.

The persuasive force need not be anything as dramatic as a gun. It can be a threat or act of domination that deprives you of the freedom to give or withhold your consent. It might even be whiskey applied with disabling generosity.

In the discussions that follow, we shall assume that our characters are sane, competent, over the age of consent, and reasonably sober.

THE LAW AND THE ADULT

As a person reaches his majority, now usually eighteen, the law withdraws from him the special cloak of protection extended to minors. At this age, he becomes responsible for all his acts and/or omissions. First, as a member of the political community, he must observe the laws enacted in his and the community's behalf. These are the laws to protect the peace, health, property, and general welfare of the public of which he is a part. These may be called public laws. Second, there are the laws governing his dealings with other individuals. Included among "other individuals" are corporations, partnerships, and other legal entities.

If he decides to get married, the law requires that he obtain a license, which constitutes the consent of the state. The marriage ceremony itself must be performed only by persons authorized by the state, after delays prescribed by law, and sometimes only after blood tests or physical examinations.

Now let's look at laws governing the individual's rights and obligations to others. The marriage ceremony, for instance, is in reality a formal entry into a contract in which each party undertakes obligations to the other.

In marriage, the husband generally becomes liable for the wife's support. Each has the right to expect from the other a course of conduct which, if departed from, can be the subject of civil litigation in the courts.

If the ceremony was performed by an officer without authority, the marriage is void, except in states that still recognize common law marriages. In states that don't, neither of the parties need bring an action to declare the marriage void. If, however, the ceremony itself was legal, but the husband had obtained the wife's consent to the marriage by a material fraud or deception, the marriage can be ended by an action brought by the wife.

As a Parent. Being a father or a mother also brings into play the public laws as well as the laws governing individual relationships. If a father should fail to support his child, he may be punished by the state. At the same time, the child, through a special guardian, may bring a civil suit against the father to compel support.

As a Property Holder. As the owner of a

dwelling, one is under legal obligations to the state and to the community. They require that the construction of the house comply with certain minimum standards; that it be fit for occupancy for its intended use; that the electrical work pass certain standards; that the building doesn't violate any local zoning restrictions, etc.

But the owner may have more than the public authorities to consider. Individuals and their rights must also be respected. His building, garage, driveway, and improvements must not encroach on a neighbor's land or his enjoyment of it. And when the owner buys the property, his lawyer will have to search the title to ascertain that it is clear and valid, to make sure that the owner's rights are secure.

As a Businessman. The law affects businessmen every day in all types of transactions which are contractual even though they aren't in writing. A businessman is both a creditor and a debtor. He uses negotiable instruments such as checks, notes and bills of exchange. He is an employer, a taxpayer, an owner or tenant of real property, and a shipper or receiver of transported goods. If he does business outside his home state, he is engaged in interstate or foreign commerce, and enters a new area of legal regulation. The laws that affect him overlap and are sometimes in conflict with one another. But in all of his capacities, actions and relationships, the law lays down the rules of the game. These rules protect the community on the one hand, and the businessman and the people he deals with on the other.

AT AND AFTER DEATH

The death of a person doesn't end the law's interest in him. The public laws require that a certificate of death be filed by the attending physician, giving the cause, date, time and place of death, and identifying the deceased. The law also regulates how one's remains may be disposed of. The undertaker must be li-

censed under the law, etc. Most states allow their citizens to say, during their lives, how their remains should be disposed of after death. Recently, some states have allowed terminally ill patients to refuse certain life-prolonging medical treatment. Under certain circumstances, the law permits post-mortem examinations to determine the cause of death.

After death, of course, comes the disposition of the property left by the deceased. This is strictly regulated by the law, and it is possible for the law to be concerned with the estate for years after death.

We've touched only lightly in this chapter on such subjects as marriage, wills, real estate, and others that are dealt with in detail elsewhere in the book. Their mention here was to show the scope of the law's coverage. We have had to leave unmentioned countless situations in which law affects the individual. Many of these you will find in the chapters that follow.

AGE OF MAJORITY

The age of majority is the age at which the infant generally assumes the obligations of an adult in the eyes of the law. The chart that follows indicates the law in the various states.

It should be remembered, however, that in many states there are exceptions to these rules. Marriage will relieve a minor of his or her legal disabilities. In many states, a court may remove the disabilities of infants regarding real property rights. And it is common for there to be a higher age limit in regard to the use of alcoholic beverages. The reader should remember that these laws governing the age of majority are modified by state laws dealing with the right to make a will, and the age at which people can marry without parental consent. And while the age of majority, according to state law, has been lowered from twenty-one to eighteen in most cases, it remains twenty-one for certain federal tax provisions.

Table 1—COMPULSORY EDUCATION CHART

	Age of Compulsory Attendance	Exceptions		Age of Compulsory Attendance	Exceptions
Alabama	7—16	A-B-C-D-F-G	Montana	7—16	A-B-C-E-G-Y
Alaska	7—16	A-C-F-G-K	Nebraska	7—16	A-C-D-F
Arizona	8—16	A-B-C-D-H-T	Nevada	7—17	A-B-C-D-E-F-G-V-Y
Arkansas	7—15	A-C-E-T-V	New Hampshire	6—16	A-C-H-T-Y
California	8—16	A-B-C-D-G	New Jersey	6—16	A-B-C-D-E
Colorado	8—16	A-B-C-D-E-T-Z	New Mexico	6—18	A-C-D-F
Connecticut	7—16	A-B-C-D	New York	7—16	A-B-C-D-F
Delaware	6—16	A-B-C-E-Y	North Carolina	7—16	A-B-C-T-Y
D.C.	7—16	A-B-C-Z	North Dakota	7—17	A-C-E-G-V
Florida	7—16	A-B-C-D-G	Ohio	6—18	A-B-C-D-T-V
Georgia	7—16	A-C-F-T	Oklahoma	7—18	A-C-F-T
Hawaii	6—16	A-B-C-D-G-T	Oregon	7—18	A-B-C-D-F-G-Y
Idaho	7—16	A-C-Y	Pennsylvania	8—17	A-B-C-D-F-G-T-Y
Illinois	7—16	A-C-D	Rhode Island	7—16	A-B-C
Indiana	7—16	A-C-D-Y	South Carolina	7—16	A-D-Y-Z
Iowa	7—16	A-B-C-D-E-T	South Dakota	7—16	A-B-C-E-N-T
Kansas	7—16	A-B-C-D-E	Tennessee	7—16	A-C-F-G-T-Y
Kentucky	7—16	A-C-F	Texas	7—16	A-C-G
Louisiana	7—16	A-C-G-T	Utah	6—18	A-B-C-D-E-F-G-V-Y
Maine	7—17	A-B-C-H	Vermont	7—16	A-B-E-T-V
Maryland	6—16	A-B-C-G-N-P-Y	Virginia	7—16	A-B-C-G-N-T
Massachusetts	7—16	A-C-D-G-J	Washington	8—17	A-C-D-J-T
Michigan	6—16	A-C-G-P	West Virginia	7—16	A-B-C-D-F-G-N-V
Minnesota	7—16	A-B-C-Y	Wisconsin	7—16	A-B-C-T
Mississippi*		A-C-D-Y	Wyoming	7—16	A-C-N-T-V-Y
Missouri	7—16	A-B-C-D			

*Compulsory school attendance law repealed in 1956.

FOOTNOTES

Exceptions are permitted under the following conditions:

(A) Where the child lacks physical or mental capacity.

(B) Where the child is receiving similar competent private or home tuition.

(C) Where the child is receiving similar competent instruction at a private or a parochial school.

(D) Where the child is legally employed, as provided by state child labor laws. These laws vary. In some states the child must be at least fourteen years old; in others the minimum age is higher. In most of the states which permit the child to leave school while employed, the law requires attendance at part time classes until the maximum age is reached.

(E) Where the child has completed at least the eighth grade, though under the required age.

(F) Where the child has completed high school although under the required age.

(G) Where the pupil resides at a distance from the school and no transportation is provided. The distance varies in the many states, generally in excess of two miles.

(H) Where the child has completed grammar school although under the required age.

(I) Where the child has completed at least two years of high school although under the required age.

(J) Where the child has completed the ninth grade although under the required age.

(K) Where the child has completed the highest grade taught in the school district which has jurisdiction over him.

(N) Where there is a serious illness in the immediate family making presence at home an actual necessity; or presence in school a health menace to other pupils.

(P) Child is employed as a messenger or page in the state legislature.

(T) The State Board, superintendent or similar officer has authority to make exceptions in their discretion (generally in cases of emergencies, distances, sickness, or seasonable labor requirements in the community).

(V) Where the child must work to support the immediate family.

(Y) Where the child's attitude and conduct demonstrate that further education would not be to the best interest of the child or the state. These laws vary. Most of these states apply this exemption only to children above the age of 14 or to those who have completed the eighth grade.

(Z) Where a child between the ages of fourteen and sixteen has completed the eighth grade and is employed.

Table 2—AGE OF MAJORITY

Alabama 19	Montana 18
Alaska 19	Nebraska 19
Arizona 18	Nevada 18
Arkansas 18	New Hampshire 18
California 18	New Jersey 18
Colorado 18	New Mexico 18
Connecticut 18	New York 18
Delaware 18	North Carolina 18
District of	North Dakota 18
Columbia 18	Ohio 18
Florida 18	Oklahoma 18
Georgia 18	Oregon 18
Hawaii 18	Pennsylvania 21
Idaho 18	Puerto Rico 21
Illinois 18	Rhode Island 18
Indiana 18	South Carolina 18
Iowa 18	South Dakota 18
Kansas 18	Tennessee 18
Kentucky 18	Texas 18
Louisiana 18	Utah 18
Maine 18	Vermont 18
Maryland 18	Virginia 18
Massachusetts 18	Washington 18
Michigan 18	West Virginia 18
Minnesota 18	Wisconsin 18
Mississippi 21	Wyoming 19
Missouri 18	

Note: In many states, the marriage of a person
below the age of majority is deemed to
terminate his minority, and the age of
majority is greater in regard to alcoholic
beverages.

CHAPTER THREE

CONTRACTS

In practically every transaction you have with other people, every day of the week, you enter into or perform a contract of some kind. The fact that you don't sign your name to a formal document doesn't change the character of the transaction. It is still a contract, provided that an offer is made, the offer is accepted, and some "consideration" passes or will pass between the parties.

THE NATURE OF A CONTRACT

When a waitress in a restaurant offers you a menu which has as one of its items "Ham and Eggs . . . $1.50," and you order ham and eggs, you've entered into a legal contract. The offer to you was to serve ham and eggs at the stated price and the acceptance was your order. When the waitress serves you the ham and eggs, the restaurant has performed its part of the contract and you are legally bound to make payment of $1.50. The "consideration" passing between the parties is the food on the one hand, and the promise to pay money on the other.

Now this is, of course, the simplest of transactions. But let's see the variety of problems that may arise in connection with it.

Reasonable Value: No Price Mentioned. Assume that the menu doesn't show the price of each item. The menu simply lists a variety of dishes, one of which is ham and eggs. Without asking the price, you give your order.

You get the bill, and the price is $7.50. You say that's outrageous, that you never agreed to pay that much, and you refuse to pay. The manager says that $7.50 is the usual charge in

his restaurant for ham and eggs, and he insists that you pay the bill. How is this resolved legally?

The rule is that when people enter into a contract without mentioning price, the purchaser has obligated himself to pay the reasonable value of what has been delivered to him. The reasonable value of ham and eggs in a restaurant isn't easily fixed—it depends on the circumstances. The important thing to remember, however, is that when the price is not mentioned, it cannot be set later by either party. The only obligation is to pay the *reasonable value*.

IMPLIED TERMS

Fitness for Use. Although the entry on the menu simply read "Ham and Eggs . . . $1.50," words that weren't there actually formed a part of the contract. These words are "fit to be eaten by human beings." If the food you are served is foul, you have no obligation to pay for it. The restaurant cannot say, "You ordered ham and eggs. We served you ham and eggs. Pay the check."

The unwritten words on the menu constitute what is known in the law as an *implied warranty*. It is as much a part of the contract as though printed on the menu. The warranty of fitness for use is perhaps the most common of the implied warranties.

Commonly Accepted Meaning of Words. Suppose the waitress serves you two ostrich eggs with your ham. You complain, and the manager says to you, "Eggs is eggs. It says eggs on the menu and we gave you eggs. Pay up."

Maybe if you were traveling in some remote region where the word "eggs" commonly referred to ostrich eggs, the management's position would be sound. However, where the word "eggs" usually means hen's eggs, you aren't required to accept any other type. The principle involved here, although somewhat exaggerated, is that the words of a contract, unless they deal with a highly technical subject, are always to be understood in their commonly accepted meanings.

Timely Delivery. Suppose you enter the restaurant during the regular lunch period, order your ham and eggs at about 12:30, and when 1:15 rolls around, you still don't have your food. You start to leave and at the cashier's desk you're stopped and asked to pay for the food which, you are told, is being prepared to your express order. You explain how long you've waited, and say you're due back at work.

The manager comes up and says there's nothing on the menu that says that your food would be delivered to you within so many minutes. You agree that nothing has been said but insist that you expect reasonable delivery. You add that delivery has been decidedly unreasonable and that you cancel your order. Your position is perfectly sound. Since you went into the restaurant at the conventional lunchtime, it's reasonable that your food should be served to you promptly.

You see, then, that the simplest of transactions can become quite complicated. Thus, the simple item, "Ham and Eggs . . . $1.50," really reads something like this: "We offer to deliver to you, within a reasonable time, a dish of ham and the eggs of a hen which shall be clean, pure and fit for human consumption." Actually, the phrase could be expanded much further to cover the general responsibility of the restaurant to protect you and your property while you are there, etc. But such matters will be dealt with elsewhere.

At this point, let's go over some important aspects of a contractual offer. Generally, an offer must contain limitations as to the amount of goods involved and the parties who can accept the offer. (A newspaper ad "Shirts on sale for $5.00" is not an offer.) Only those to whom the offer is addressed can accept, and acceptance must be in accord with the terms of the offer. If the acceptance is conditional, it's a counteroffer. Terms implicit in the offer can be made explicit, and additional terms are often seen as suggestions for agreements beyond the present pact. Offers and acceptances are determined objectively: If you're joking, you can still be bound by your words if the other party reasonably believes you and acts on your words. A contract must be sufficiently definite to permit an appropriate remedy in the event of a breach. As we've seen, terms such as price, time of performance, or color or size of goods may be written in by the courts.

An offer is terminated by the offeror's revocation before acceptance, impossibility of performance, lapse of a stated time period, or a rejection or counteroffer by the offeree.

Bases for Enforcement. Generally, a promise is enforceable if it's supported by consideration, which can be another promise or actual performance. (A diner promises to pay his check at the meal's end; at a bar, one often pays as the drink arrives.) Consideration may be a "peppercorn"—that is, of nominal value. But "past" consideration is not good—a promise to pay someone a pension for work done in the past is not enforceable. Often, the reliance of one party on another's promise serves to make a contract, if there would otherwise be a loss. And sometimes a court will "make" a contract when one party confers a benefit on another, even though there wasn't a proper contract regarding payment.

COMMON REMEDIES

Though the subject is too complex to cover in this space, there are some general rules for dealing with a contract that's gone wrong. If there has been a mistake by both parties, if performance has become impossible, or if one party has used fraud or physical or economic duress on the other, the remedy is often *recission* of the contract or of the offending provisions. The same is true for unconscionable clauses—provisions that take unfair advantage of the unsuspecting, particularly in consumer cases. In rare instances, a court will order specific performance of a contract if no other remedy offers a fair solution.

Damages. The most common remedy is money damages, which should serve to redress the breach rather than to punish the party breaching the contract. The most often used measure of damages is the "benefit of the bargain"—the injured party is awarded an amount which will leave him as if the contract had been performed. The damages are limited, however, to what the defendant could reasonably foresee as the probable result of his breach. And the injured party has a duty to mitigate his loss whenever practical. There are special rules for contracts involving builders. If a builder does less than he's promised, the owner is entitled to the difference in value between the agreed-upon standard and what was provided—or, rarer, to the cost of remedying the defect. If the owner violates the contract, the builder gets, at least, his expenses plus a pro rata share of his anticipated profits.

A claim for damages arises only after a *material* breach of the contract—the materiality of the nonperformance depends on its importance to the other party. If the breach goes uncured for more than a reasonable time, the contract is no longer enforceable. It's necessary, then, to determine which party is obliged to perform first. (Generally, simultaneous performance is favored, although a builder, for example, often has to finish his work before he's paid. These rules are subject to contrary agreement, though.) Beware of nonperformance after the other party has failed to act—his failure may not be material, and then you'll be liable for damages.

For construction and service contracts, if there has been substantial performance of the contract, the owner must pay the agreed-upon price less damages for the nonmaterial work not done. And an act which implies that future nonperformance is assured, gives the other party the right to sue immediately for damages for a total breach. This is true for sales contracts, as well.

WHEN A CONTRACT MUST BE IN WRITING

In order to bind the parties, a contract needn't be in any particular form. It can be oral, although it's best if it is written. A contract can be contained in an exchange of letters. It can even be contained in a combination of oral statements, memoranda, and the acts of the parties.

Statute of Frauds. However, by statute, *certain contracts must be in writing* if they are to be enforced by the courts. The exact characteristics of the agreements that must be in writing vary from state to state. They are usually specified in a law called the "Statute of Frauds." Table 3 briefly gives these characteristics state by state.

To assist the reader in the use of the chart, take the state of New Jersey as a typical example. There, a contract must be in writing when the term set for the performance exceeds one year; or if it provides for the lease of real property for more than three years; or for the sale of goods worth more than $500. Even if there is the *possibility* that a contract will fall into these categories, the statute's requirements must be met. This doesn't mean that such contracts are in themselves illegal if not in writing. It does mean that they are not enforceable in the courts.

Certain types of contracts uniformly require a writing and so are not represented in the table. As a rule of thumb, agreements that deal with real property (especially transfers), that relate to provisions in wills or trusts, or that concern one party answering for the debts of other parties, must be written. Generally, contracts that aren't to be performed within one year must be in writing unless both parties can freely terminate them. So a promise to work for five years must be written.

It should be noted, however, that in most states there are many exceptions to the general rule. Thus, courts can be appealed to in disregard of the rule where the contract is performed by one party and not by the other. This is also true in the case of the sale of goods valued in excess of $500, where such goods have been delivered to and accepted by the party refusing payment. In some states, if the goods have been manufactured especially for the buyer and cannot be sold to others, the buyer cannot reject them on the grounds that the contract was not in writing.

New York's statute of frauds offers a good example of the types of agreement that should be written. A contract that's not evidenced by a writing is unenforceable if it is:

not to be performed within one year (or completed by the end of a lifetime),

a promise to establish a trust or make a testamentary devise,

made in consideration of marriage (except for mutual promises),

a guarantee to answer for another's debts,

a promise to pay for negotiating a loan, or for the purchase, sale, exchange, rental, or lease of real property or a business (except as to lawyers, auctioneers, or real estate brokers),

a promise of an executor or an administrator to pay a debt of the decedent,

a contract for the sale of goods for a price of $500 or more (with limited exception).

Why Make a Written Contract? Many people like to have it said about them that "his word is as good as his bond." They prefer, they assert, one handshake to ten contracts in writing.

That is, of course, commendable from a moral point of view. Too often, however, the handshake deal winds up in the courts. Or, more frequently, it brings a loss to one of the

parties of a kind that he feels he can't take to the courts.

There are many reasons for breaches of handshake contracts. Chief among them is the fact that a man's honor is sometimes better than his memory. He may not have the slightest intention of going back on his word, but there may be a difference of opinion about what his word was.

Sometimes it's his health or his luck that's not as good as his word. He may have every intention of performing his part of the bargain, but before he can do so, he is struck down by an illness or an accident, and dies. Then the person who handles his estate, even if he knows about the deal, can't use the handshake alone as the basis for paying off a claim out of estate funds.

Besides, people can change. The sweet guy you made an oral deal with last week can sour after someone else reneges on a deal with him later. The man who followed the golden rule yesterday may tomorrow switch to the dog-eat-dog way of life. You are then left, after a handshake, holding the bag.

WHAT THE WRITTEN AGREEMENT SHOULD CONTAIN

When you sit down to write a contract, you have already reached an understanding with the other party. What you write, then, should be an accurate statement of what you have already agreed upon. All the terms of your oral understanding should be clearly set out in the written contract. From it alone, anyone should be able to gather what are the obligations of each of the parties. This is the minimum.

When the contract is of some importance, either because it involves a large investment of money, labor, or materials, or for other reasons, it is advisable to make provision for every event you can foresee that may effect its validity or performance under it. Then the document itself determines the parties' rights and obligations in any circumstance that can reasonably be foreseen.

Names and Dates. The complete contract

Table 3—AGREEMENTS WHICH REQUIRE A WRITING

State	Contracts not to be performed within period specified	Leases for a period longer than years indicated	A sale of goods in the amount specified	State	Contracts not to be performed within period specified	Leases for a period longer than years indicated	A sale of goods in the amount specified
Ala.	1 (year)	1 (year)	$500	Neb.	1	1	500
Alaska	1	1	500	Nev.	1	1	200
Ariz.	1	1	500	N.H.	1	(c)	500
Ark.	1	1	500	N.J.	1	3	500
Cal.	1	1	500	N.M.	1	3	(b)
Colo.	1	1	500	N.Y.	1	1	500
Conn.	1	1	500	N.C.	No Requirement	3	500
Del.	1	1	500	N.D.	1	1	500
D.C.	1	1	500	Ohio	1	(c)	500
Fla.	1	1	500	Okla.	1	1	500
Ga.	1	1	500	Ore.	1	1	500
Hawaii	1	1	100	Pa.	No Requirement	3	500
Idaho	1	1	500	R.I.	1	1	500
Ill.	1	1	500	S.C.	1	1	500
Ind.	1	3	500	S.D.	1	1	500
Iowa	1	1	500	Tenn.	1	1	500
Kan.	1	1	500	Tex.	1	1	500
Ky.	1	1	500	Utah	1	1	500
La.	No Requirement	(d)	(a)	Vt.	1	(c)	500
Maine	1	(c)	500	Va.	1	1	500
Md.	1	1	500	Wash.	1	1	500
Mass.	1	(c)	500	W. Va.	1	1	500
Mich.	1	1	500	Wis.	1	1	500
Minn.	1	1	50	Wyo.	1	1	500
Miss.	15 months	1	500				
Mo.	1	1	30				
Mont.	1	1	200				

FOOTNOTES

(a) A contract for the sale of goods is enforceable without any writing.

(b) A contract for the sale of goods in any amount must be in writing to be enforceable.

(c) All contracts concerning land must be in writing.

(d) Louisiana recognizes oral leases.

begins with the date on which it is entered into and describes the parties by name and precise address. If any of them are not acting in their individual capacity, the true capacity must appear—for example, "Adam Jones, as executor for the estate of Abigail Jones." If one of the parties is a corporation, its full corporate name should be written out, together with the state where it is incorporated, the law under which it was organized and is doing business, and its principal place of business.

Who, What, Why, Where, How, When. There should follow a complete and precise statement of the understanding of the parties. The document should provide the full answers to *who* the parties are; *where* they live; *where* the contract is being made; *where* it is to be performed; *where* payment is to be made; *where* delivery is to be made if the contract calls for delivery; *where* notices are to be given (if provided for in the agreement); *why* the parties are making the agreement; *what* the agreement seeks to accomplish; *what* each of the parties is to do, to furnish, to pay, or to receive; *what* the parties assume, if anything, as to the basis of their agreement; *how* the parties are to discharge their obligations to each other; *how* they will deal with such events as strikes, shortages of materials, the death of one of the parties, bankruptcy, or delays that are the fault of neither.

It's possible to make a one-paragraph contract that will be as binding and as legal as a twenty-page document covering the same transaction. It's possible that the one-paragraph agreement will be performed without incident. However, in general, a complete statement of the understanding of the parties is preferable. This tends to avoid disputes and costly litigation.

It is important to remember that the more one writes, the more possibilities there will be for dispute and various interpretations unless the document is very clear and is prepared with skill. An important document that is to serve a legal purpose should always be drawn or examined by a lawyer.

CHAPTER FOUR

SALES

The housewife in the supermarket and the manufacturer of automobiles are engaged in transactions that are basically the same . . . they are SALES. Big or small, whatever the nature of the property, if ownership changes hands for a price, the deal is a sale. When does ownership actually pass from seller to buyer? What is the meaning of F.O.B., C.O.D., and C.I.F.? Who bears the loss when goods are lost in shipment? How is the average consumer protected? These questions and others are discussed in this chapter.

Uniform Commercial Code. Because there are so many sales each day, because sales are the basis of our commercial life, and because so many sales transactions cross state lines, it would be a real obstacle to business if the law governing them differed in every state. Therefore, the Code—a uniform sales act—has been adopted by most states, and in the rest it is followed almost to the letter.

A Sale Is a Contract. An agreement whereby the seller transfers goods to the buyers for a price, is a sale. A sale has two parts—the contract to sell, and the subsequent delivery of the goods. There is a difference between a contract to sell in the future (an executory sale) and a present sale (an executed sale). Whether a sale is executory or executed depends on when the transfer of ownership between buyer and seller takes effect. When the price is paid makes no difference. If there's no delivery, we have only a contract to sell.

The Risk of Loss. Regardless of when the property is paid for, the seller must bear all

risks related to it until title is transferred to the buyer. This means that the seller must suffer the loss if the property is stolen, destroyed by fire, damaged by the elements, etc. When title passes, generally, the risk of loss passes with it. (More specifically, if the seller is a merchant, the risk of loss passes when the buyer takes possession of the goods; if the buyer is not a merchant, the risks shift upon tender of delivery.)

Transfer of Title. When the title to property passes is a matter that can be agreed upon by the parties. Where the parties don't make any specific provision fixing the time, their intention must be gathered from all the facts and circumstances. These include the nature of the sale, the type of merchandise, terms of delivery, customs of the trade, means of transportation, who pays for transportation, and other factors. No single one of these factors will determine passage of title.

Suppose you order a quantity of lumber from a yard in Syracuse with which you have open credit, to be delivered to your plant in Buffalo. The terms of the sale are "F.O.B. Syracuse" and you have named the trucker who'll deliver the goods. When your lumber has been segregated from the yard's stock and placed on board the truck, the title has passed to you.

The term "F.O.B." means "free on board." This means that the price agreed upon by the parties covers no transportation beyond the point mentioned after the term "F.O.B." The freight from Syracuse to Buffalo is for you to pay. In the event the shipment is lost after it

has been loaded on board the truck, the loss is
yours to bear. But if the term is "F.O.B.
Buffalo," the seller bears the costs and risks
prior to delivery.

Suppose, instead of naming the trucking
company, you said, "Ship fastest way" or "Ship
cheapest way." Title would then pass to you as
soon as the goods, consigned to you, were
placed on board the means of transportation.

If the delivery of the goods fails to conform
with the contract, the risk of loss rests with the
seller until the default is corrected or the
goods accepted. However, if the buyer repu-
diates or otherwise breaches the contract, he
bears the risk of loss for a reasonable time
thereafter, even if the risk hasn't otherwise
been transferred to him.

To Retain Title Until Payment. The simplest sale is a cash sale where the seller bears
all the burdens until he surrenders the goods
for cash and where the buyer is free to inspect
the goods before purchase. Arrangements that
differ from this mode must be bargained for.
It is possible for a seller to retain title and
control over the shipment after it has left his
plant. This is usually done as a means of secur-
ing payment before the merchandise is actually
delivered to the control of the buyer.

In such a case, the seller consigns the load
of lumber (in our example) to himself or to an
agent of his in Buffalo. With the goods go instructions to deliver the merchandise to you, or
to deliver to you a bill of lading or document
of title only after you have paid for the merchandise or given some document promising
to pay for it. The terms of such a sale could
still be F.O.B. Syracuse, but the meaning of
the term here would simply be that you, the
consignee, would have to pay the freight
charges from Syracuse to Buffalo. Title in such
a case would pass when delivery is made, and
that would be when the document of title or
the merchandise itself is delivered to you in
Buffalo.

What's the benefit of all this? The seller is
assured of payment when he gives up the
goods, and the buyer is assured of control of
the goods once he pays. But the buyer can't inspect the goods unless the contract permits it,
and it's a wise move to get that right.

But it must always be remembered that the
parties, by agreement, can arrange for the passage of title and the assumption of risk at any
point in the transaction. As we have seen, title
can be made to pass as soon as the merchandise you order is separated from the seller's
stock and identified in some manner as being
consigned to you.

**Rules for Ascertaining the Intent of the
Parties in Transferring Title.** The importance
of determining the exact time when title in
goods passes from the seller to the buyer is
such that rules for finding the intention of the
parties are laid out in the Uniform Commercial
Code.

RULE I. Where there is an unconditional
contract to sell specific goods, in a deliverable state, title to the goods passes to the
buyer when the contract is made. It is immaterial whether the time of payment, or the
time of delivery, or both, are postponed.

RULE II. Where there is a contract to sell
specific goods, but the seller is bound to do
something to the goods for the purpose of
putting them in a deliverable state, the title
doesn't pass until that is done.

RULE III. 1. When goods are delivered to
the buyer "on sale or return," or on other
terms indicating an intention to make a present sale while giving the buyer an option to
return the goods instead of making payment,
title passes to the buyer on delivery. But he
may revest the property in the seller—that
is, pass the title back to the seller—by returning or tendering the goods within the
time fixed in the contract or, if no time has
been fixed, within a reasonable time. The
costs of returning the goods are the buyer's.

2. When goods are delivered to the buyer
"on approval" or "on trial" or "on satisfaction," or on similar terms, title passes to
the buyer:

(a) When he signifies his approval or acceptance to the seller, or does any other act

confirming the transaction (but testing the goods isn't acceptance);

(b) If he does not signify his approval or acceptance to the seller, but retains the goods, without giving notice of rejection within a time fixed for the return of the goods or, if no time has been fixed, on the expiration of a reasonable time. What is a reasonable time depends on the circumstances.

The costs and risks of returning goods "on approval" are the seller's.

RULE IV. Where there is a contract to sell unascertained or future goods by description, and goods of that description and in a deliverable state are unconditionally set aside and identified as the property of the buyer, either by the buyer with the assent of the seller, or by the seller with the assent of the buyer, title in the goods then passes to the buyer. Such assent may be express or implied, and may be given either before or after the identification of the goods is made.

Identification of the goods as those to which a contract refers occurs if the seller delivers the goods to the buyer, or to a carrier or other bailee (persons to whom the goods are committed in trust), whether named by the buyer or not, to be held for or transmitted to the buyer. This presumption is applicable even though by the terms of the contract the buyer is to pay the price before receiving delivery of the goods, and the goods are marked with the words "collect on delivery" or their equivalent.

RULE V. If the contract to sell requires the seller to deliver the goods to the buyer, or at a particular place, or to pay the freight or cost of transportation to the buyer, or to a particular place, title does not pass until the goods have been delivered to the buyer or have reached the place agreed upon.

Goods Not Yet in Existence. It is not possible to have a sale of merchandise that is not in existence. It is possible, however, to enter into a contract of purchase and sale of goods that will be manufactured or of crops that will be harvested. But the sale itself cannot be made and the title cannot pass until the property has actual existence, although that existence may be the conception of a calf, for example, or the sowing of crops.

Goods Destroyed Before Passage of Title. If you contract to buy *specific* goods at some future time—for example, if at planting time you agree to buy a crop of cotton from the grower and the crop is destroyed by the elements or some other accident before it is harvested—how does that affect the obligations of the parties?

(a) The seller is excused from his obligation to deliver the cotton.
(b) The buyer is relieved of his obligation to pay.
(c) If the buyer made part payment at planting time, he can claim a refund.

When Origin of Destroyed Goods Is Not Specified. If you contract with a broker to purchase a quantity of cotton without specifying the particular farm from which it is to come, the fact that the cotton he'd intended to buy to meet your order was destroyed does not change his obligation. He should have found a cover source for such an event.

FAILURE TO DELIVER

Rights of the Buyer. If the seller fails to deliver the purchased merchandise to the buyer, the latter may sue the seller to recover whatever damages he's suffered. These damages are either the cost of substituting like goods or the difference in market price of the goods between the date of the contract and that of the breach, plus incidental and consequential damages. (The buyer has no obligation to effect a cover—that is, to buy like goods from someone else.) If title to the merchandise has already passed, the buyer may, by legal action, force the seller to deliver the merchandise to him. He may sue to recover both the goods and the damages resulting from the breach of contract.

Sometimes even if title has not already passed, the buyer may compel the seller to deliver the specific goods that were the subject of the sales contract. This applies when the merchandise is of a peculiar or distinctive character, and where money damages wouldn't give adequate relief to the buyer. A piece of real estate or an important work of art would fall within this category.

FAILURE TO PAY

Rights of the Seller. If the buyer refuses to pay for the goods, the remedies open to the seller depend entirely upon who has physical possession of the goods. If the seller still has them, he can withhold delivery until payment is made (or he may halt a delivery that is in progress); he can cancel the contract entirely; he can resell the goods and sue the buyer for the difference between the contract price and the lower resale price, or he can hold the goods and sue the buyer for damages. This figure usually is the difference between the contract price and the lower market price, less expenses saved as a result of the breach, but may be measured by the profit anticipated by the seller. It is rarer for the seller to sue directly for the price of the goods, as that can occur only if the goods have been damaged or can't be resold after a reasonable effort. In all these situations, related damages may be added in to what the defaulting buyer must pay. Once delivery of the goods has been made to the buyer, the only remedy open to the seller is to sue for the purchase price. He cannot recover the merchandise unless delivery was made pursuant to a conditional sales contract, as explained later, or unless the buyer received the goods while insolvent.

SOME IMPORTANT TERMS

C.O.D. These initials are among the most frequently used in commerce. They mean "collect on delivery." The buyer is not entitled to possession of the goods until he pays for them. From this it would seem that title does not pass until payment is made. However, that isn't always the case.

Let's apply the rules. If you, in Chicago, send to a paint dealer in New York an order as follows, "Herewith is my order for 12 gals. of paint your catalogue No. 46 at $5.00 per gal. Terms C.O.D.," when the dealer has packed the paint to fill your order, properly addressed the shipment to you, and delivered it to a carrier for transportation, the title has passed to you. The obligation to pay the freight is yours, and the shipping arrangements were made by the dealer for your benefit. You have no right to inspect the goods before paying. But if you had specified that the price of the shipment was to be $60, delivered to your plant in Chicago, freight prepaid, title would not have passed until delivery.

F.O.B. This designation, followed by the name of a place, indicates where and when title will pass. Its meaning is "free on board." If the terms are F.O.B. Chicago, freight charges will be paid by the shipper only to the point of loading onto a carrier at the factory siding. All charges and responsibilities for the shipment, from that point on, are the buyer's. If the terms are F.O.B Chicago, freight charges and responsibility continue to be the seller's until the shipment reaches Chicago, and the buyer is free to inspect the goods before paying for them.

F.A.S. Used often in foreign commerce, this term means "free alongside." It indicates that the price quoted by the seller includes transportation to a dock, but not the cost of loading the merchandise on board a vessel.

C.I.F. This means that the price quoted by the seller includes "cost, insurance, and freight" to the named destination. However, under this type of contract, the buyer doesn't have the right to inspect the goods before payment. Both F.A.S. and C.I.F. should be used only with the name of a place: as F.A.S. Liverpool, or C.I.F. New York.

Waivers. You can give up, or "waive," certain rights by an express provision in a contract. Or you can do it by implication—by failing to take advantage of rights reserved to you in a contract. Suppose a sales contract allows you ten days to examine merchandise and to return it if not found satisfactory. Should you fail to open the package within the given period, but wait for twenty days to pass, and then find that the merchandise isn't satisfactory, you lose the right to return the goods, by waiver. However, you still have the right to sue for damages for breach of contract if the merchandise is not as ordered, or possibly for breach of warranty.

Another example: You manufacture table radios. Your plastic cabinets are supplied by an outside supplier under a contract that contains a delivery schedule. Before the first delivery is made, the supplier informs you that he is unable to procure the plastic material he needs. You say that you will get the material for him, since you have good sources. You get the plastic, but not in time to allow the cabinet man to meet the delivery schedule to fulfill his obligation to you. By your actions, you have consented to a delay and have waived whatever rights you may have had in the event of a default in delivery.

WARRANTIES AND REPRESENTATIONS

Express Warranties. Statements made by the seller which are relied upon by the buyer in making his purchase are called warranties or representations. Not every statement is a warranty. A certain allowance is made for the natural exaggeration of the salesman, which is called "puffing," or for his opinion. When a man praises his product as being superior to the products of his competitors, he isn't making a warranty. If, however, he says that a certain gauge of steel, for instance, has gone into his product, he *is* making a warranty. If he states that the product is the only one of its particular kind in existence, that too is a warranty. If it turns out that the steel is of a different gauge than that represented by the salesman, the seller has committed a breach of warranty for which the buyer can claim damages.

An express warranty needn't be a statement —production of a model or a sample is a warranty that the whole lot conforms to it. Express warranties cannot be disclaimed.

Implied Warranties. There are certain warranties that need not be expressed orally or in writing, but are implied in every transaction.

One is the warranty of *fitness for use*. In order for this warranty to be implied, the use to which the merchandise is to be put should be known to both parties. If one purchases a food freezer, there is no doubt in anyone's mind as to the use to which the property will be put. There, the implied warranty is that the equipment can be used for freezing food. If a buyer asks for an item by its brand name, this lessens his reliance on the seller.

Another implied warranty is that the quality of the goods meets generally accepted standards of quality unless the sale is made "as is," or if the price is lower than usual. (In such cases, it is the responsibility of the buyer to make a thorough inspection of the goods before accepting delivery.) This warranty arises only if the seller is a merchant of such goods. Common defects (say, bones in fish chowder) may be allowable without there being a breach of warranty. These two implied warranties can be disclaimed or modified only by a conspicuous, written notice on the item.

Warranty of Title. Every seller warrants that he owns or at least has the right to sell the property in question. Example: *A* sold a used car to *B*, who sold it to *C*, who sold it to *D*. *X* came along with a policeman and identified the car as having been stolen from him. Because no one can obtain good title from one who does not have it to give, the car is restored to *X*. *D* sued *C* for a breach of the implied warranty of good title, and he got his money back. *C* sued *B* and *B* sued *A*. All were bound by, and had the benefit of, the implied warranty. (Trouble arises if one chain in the link disappears. Then the party nearest to the thief must suffer the loss.) This warranty cannot be disclaimed.

Who Benefits from a Warranty? It used to be

that one could benefit from a warranty only if there was "privity of contract"—that is, if there was a contractual relationship between the claimant and the seller. That's no longer true. You can sue the manufacturer of a product for damages resulting from defects, even though your only contact is with a middleman. And someone—say, a family member—injured by a product you bought can sue, if their use of it was to be reasonably anticipated, even though their connection to the manufacturer is more remote. The same is true for employees and passengers of the purchaser.

The notion of anticipated use of a product has been taken even farther. For example, a remote purchaser can sue for a breach of an *express* warranty against a manufacturer who induced the purchaser to buy by representations of quality in mass advertising and on tags attached to the goods. The doctrine has also been extended to cover those who rescue someone injured by a defect in an impliedly warranted product, and even, in certain cases, to bystanders injured by the warranted article.

The manufacturer or seller of goods has a duty to warn the consumer of any risks related to the use of the product that aren't easily ascertainable. So to recover for injuries caused by latent defects, the plaintiff must prove that the product was defective when it left the manufacturer's (or seller's) control, that the defect caused the injury, and that he didn't know about the defect. No proof of fault is needed if the action is based on express or implied warranties.

Restrictions on Remedies. Generally, a seller can limit the buyer's remedies to return or replacement of the goods, or repayment of the price. But limitations on consequential damages for personal injury in regard to consumer goods aren't enforceable. (However, a manufacturer or seller isn't liable for breach of warranty if, for example, someone is unusually sensitive to his product—as with a perfume that causes a skin irritation for a small minority of people.) Generally, the statute of limitations for an action for breach of warranty is

four years, although this may be lowered to one year by agreement.

CONSUMER PROTECTION

One of the greatest sources of protection for consumers is the warranties we've discussed. However, states and localities have created pro-consumer agencies and enacted legislation, all to help the consumer in specific situations. Unit pricing in supermarkets has become widespread, and laws now require that food packagers and canners list the ingredients of their products. These requirements help consumers to know exactly what they are buying. Those with questions or complaints about products can take them to local consumer protection groups, in or out of government. And, as manpower allows, these groups do much investigating on their own. Plans are being formulated for a federal bureau of consumer affairs, but it has still not been decided just how much power this agency will have.

The consumer does get a good deal of help from the federal government now, however. Food and drugs, as well as nonedible products, are monitored by appropriate agencies to ensure that they are safe for use. Recent examples of federal protection are the banning of certain products because of cancer-producing agents. The consumer is also protected by federal regulations that govern just what can be claimed in advertising about products offered to the public.

Home Solicitation Sales. Many states safeguard consumers from buying merchandise in their homes which they really don't want. The purchase of items or services for personal or household purposes, payable over four installments at least, may be canceled up to three days after a contract has been signed. Then the seller might be able to keep a part of the money paid as a fee, and the goods and the balance of the money are returned within ten days.

Unconscionability. This is a rapidly growing concept. If a sales contract is one-sided or oppressive, or if it contains traps for the unwary, courts can declare it (or offensive parts of it) to be unconscionable, and therefore unenforceable. This doctrine is most often invoked to aid poor, uneducated consumers who have no bargaining power in regard to contract terms. So if a consumer who buys furniture on time must pay the whole bill before she owns any individual piece, with total repossession possible up to the last payment, that's unconscionable—but maybe it wouldn't be to a well-informed consumer. Courts consider all the facts of a given situation before deciding if the contract should be voided. Probably the two most common grounds for having a contract declared unconscionable are excessively high prices and situations where the seller restricts the buyer's remedies or in some other way expands his power at the other's expense.

Conditional Sales. This is an area in which the consumer should be careful. Installment sales, deferred payment plans, or time payment plans, all of which have about the same meaning and play so important a part in our economy, have been greatly facilitated by a device postponing the actual passage of title until full payment has been made. Here are the features of the transaction: a) Delivery of the merchandise is made to the purchaser; b) The seller retains title to the goods; c) The buyer and seller agree upon the conditions under which title will pass from the seller to the buyer; d) In the event that the buyer fails to fulfill the conditions, the seller may repossess the property. (Of course, the doctrine of unconscionability applies to such sales.)

Filing of Contracts. Conditional sales contracts are common in the sale of major purchases: stoves, refrigerators, furniture, automobiles. Such contracts are binding between the buyer and seller even if they aren't filed in the place prescribed by law. However, filing is necessary in order to safeguard the rights of the seller against parties who know nothing about the original transaction.

For example, you need a new refrigerator and buy a recently purchased one from your neighbor, Jones. Some weeks later a man from the local appliance store calls on you and says that the refrigerator is his. It appears that Jones had purchased the refrigerator on the installment plan in accordance with a conditional sales agreement. If he made regular payments until the full purchase price was paid, title would pass to him. But Jones had failed to make his payments. The dealer traced the refrigerator to you and now demands repossession. Can he take it from you? Yes, if the conditional sales agreement was properly recorded in the county clerk's office. No, if the agreement was not recorded.

This example illustrates a basic principle of the law of sales. It is not possible to transfer good title to something you don't own. And it is not possible to acquire good title from someone who does not have the right to sell. Sometimes, however, actions, or the failure to act, on the part of the person who is the true owner can deprive him of the right to claim his property. This would be the case if the dealer had failed to record the conditional bill of sale. And that's because he allowed Jones to have all of the appearances of the right to sell and failed to give you notice, which is the effect of the recording. Consequently, he would lose the right to reclaim the property.

If the conditional bill of sale had been properly recorded, you would be seen as having constructive notice of the fact that the refrigerator was not Jones's to sell. Actually, all you acquired from Jones were such rights as he had in the property. As a practical matter you would be allowed to keep the refrigerator if you fulfilled Jones's obligations and completed the installment payment. Of course, you would have a right of action against Jones.

CHAPTER FIVE

NOTES, DRAFTS, AND CHECKS

Commercial paper—checks, notes, drafts—
is essential to our way of life. If all bills were
paid in cash, if all debts required individual
contracts, and if our checks and notes were
not easily transferable, business would slow
down to a walk. But what makes paper negotiable? What are the rights of the holder? . . .
the bearer? . . . the maker? . . . the endorser? In this chapter we deal with everyday
problems that arise under the Uniform Commercial Code.

NEGOTIABILITY

A client tells the following tale of woe: "My
cousin Joe and I have been doing some business together and there is alway some kind of
open balance between us. Either I owe him or
he owes me. Yesterday Joe came around and
said that I owed him about a thousand dollars.
He asked me for a check right away because he
needed the money. Without questioning Joe,
I took out my checkbook and wrote out a
check payable to him for a thousand dollars.

"After Joe went off with the check, I began
to think about the deals we had together, and
the more I thought, the more I became con-
vinced that I owed him, at the most, only a
few hundred dollars. I went over my accounts
and, sure enough, the amount I owed Joe
turned out to be a hundred and seventy-five
dollars.

"I thought it odd that Joe should make a
mistake like that, and I tried to contact him
but couldn't. This morning when I finally got
through to him, he admitted that he knew the

figure wasn't quite a thousand, but that was
the amount he needed to meet an obligation,
and he didn't think I'd mind.

"I blew my top. I told him I didn't like his
shady methods and that I wanted him to return the check. He told me it was too late; he'd
already endorsed it over to somebody else.

"Now tell me, Counselor, can I stop payment on the check?"

To that question the lawyer's answer was:
"Yes, you can always stop payment if the bank
hasn't already charged your account. But you
may have to pay the thousand dollars anyway."

As a practical matter, when the holder of
the check finds that the check has been dis-
honored at the bank, he will immediately get
hold of Joe and try to collect from him. But if
that's not successful, the client is responsible
for the full amount, because the check had
been **negotiated** and was now in the hands of a
holder in due course.

If the check were still in Joe's hands, the
client could resist payment and raise all the
questions that exist between him, the maker,
and Joe, the payee. But once the check has
passed, for value, to an innocent party who
knew nothing about the dealings between the
cousins, the defenses that were good against
Joe can't be used against the innocent holder.

At this point we ought to strike a gong or
send up a flare because the case of the client
and his cousin Joe—and the law that applies
to it—will illustrate a number of important
points.

First, take the fact that when Joe passed
the check on, it became a stronger document

Figure 1
FORM OF PROMISSORY NOTE

$100.00

_____3 months_____ after date I promise to pay to

the order of _____Paul Payee_____

_____One hundred_____ 00/100 _____Dollars

Value received   Martin Maker

A note is an unconditional promise to pay a sum of money to another, or to his order, or to the bearer, at a fixed or determinable future time or on demand.

than when he had it himself. This is an exception to the legal axiom that no man can transfer to another what he does not himself possess. To say it in a more legal fashion, an assignee can generally acquire no greater rights from the assignor than the latter had. But if the client can refuse to pay Joe but cannot refuse Joe's assignee, Joe has been able to give more than he, himself, had.

POINT ONE: The law extends special protection to certain holders of negotiable paper. It makes negotiation safe by removing most risks (not all) from the circulation of checks, notes, and drafts. Obviously, if payment could be refused by the maker because the payee owes him something, or for any other reason (and there can be many) arising out of his transactions with the payee, nobody would take paper.

The essential quality of checks, notes, and drafts (also called bills of exchange) is *negotiability*. Without negotiability, our commerce would be stymied—and without the kind of protection the law gives to holders in due course, we could not have negotiability.

POINT TWO: The Uniform Commercial Code is an excellent example of the modification of the common law by statute. Before the Code and its forebears were enacted, when a note

was presented for payment by a holder, the maker could refuse to pay the face amount, simply stating that he no longer owed that money to the payee.

POINT THREE: The Uniform Commercial Code is a prime example of the development of the law to serve the ends of commerce. Each of the fifty states has its own set of laws. If the laws of each state differed with respect to negotiable paper, you would have to do a research job everytime you were offered an out-of-state check. Happily, most of the states have passed the uniform law, and the others have laws that vary only rarely from it. Here, unlike marriage, divorce, and other human relationships regulated by law, we don't have to consult the statutes of fifty individual legal entities.

What Makes Paper Negotiable? The following are the six elements of negotiability:

1. SPECIFICATION OF TIME WHEN PAYMENT IS TO BE MADE. If a note is made Payable "on demand," or after a stated number of days, weeks, months or years, the time of payment can be calculated and the note is negotiable. If no time is mentioned, the note is presumed to be payable on demand and is ne-

Figure 2
FORM OF BILL OF EXCHANGE

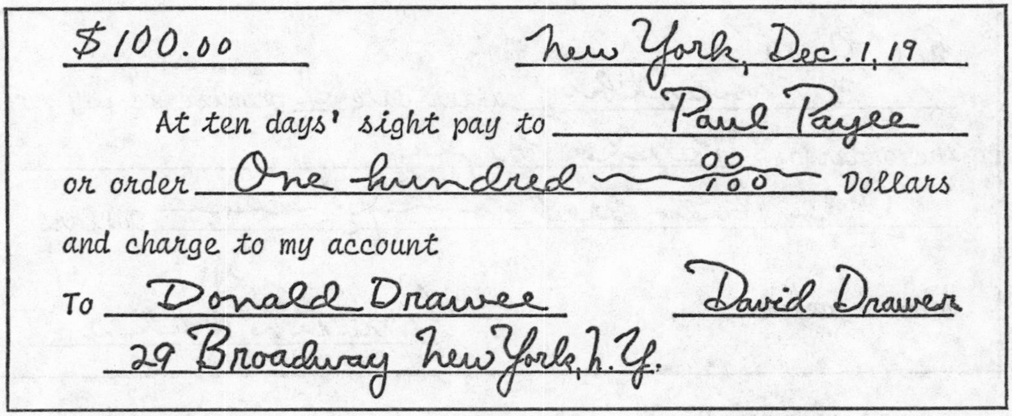

$100.00   New York, Dec.1,19

At ten days' sight pay to ___Paul Payee___

or order ___One hundred ~~ 00/100~~ Dollars

and charge to my account

To ___Donald Drawee___   David Drawer
___29 Broadway New York, N.Y.___

A bill of exchange, or draft, often used for collection of debts owed to the drawer by the drawee, is an order addressed by one person to another, requiring the addressee (drawee) to pay on demand, or at a fixed or determinable future time, a certain sum of money, to the payee, or to his order, or the bearer.

gotiable. It isn't essential that the time be fixed precisely, as long as the day is sure to come.

A note that promises to pay a sum of money "ten days after my marriage" is not good, because the marriage may never take place. On the other hand, a note payable "ten days after my death" is negotiable, because that event, death, is sure to happen. As long as a definite time for payment is fixed, there may be a clause allowing acceleration of payment if the holder feels insecure. Clauses allowing most extensions of the time of payment are also permissible.

2. THE PROMISE OR ORDER TO PAY MUST BE UNCONDITIONAL. "I promise to pay Joe Brown or bearer the sum of $100 on condition that the New York Yankees win the World Series." The condition in this promise kills negotiability. To be negotiable, a promise must be absolute.

3. THE AMOUNT PAYABLE MUST BE DEFINITE AND CERTAIN. The promise to pay "$100 and additional sums as may be due" is not definite, and not negotiable for that reason. But a note that promises to pay "$100 with interest" is

definite, even if the rate of interest is left blank, because, if the rate is not specified, the legal rate (the maximum allowed by law) applies. Negotability is not affected if a note is made payable in installments, or if it specifies the amount "plus costs of collection or an attorney's fee."

4. PAYMENT MUST BE MADE IN MONEY. A note or draft that promises or orders payment in goods, stocks, or services is not negotiable. It is essential that the instrument provide for payment in the lawful money of the country. The sum may be stated in foreign currency and, if so, is satisfied in the dollar value of that currency on the day of payment.

5. THE PAPER MUST BE IN WRITING AND SIGNED. The maker or drawer may use any writing instrument. It need not be pen and ink. Pencil, crayon, chalk, a typewriter, a printing press—even a lipstick—anything that can produce writing can be used. The signature may be any symbol a party adopts and may appear anywhere on the paper—not necessarily at the bottom—to comply with the law.

6. PAYABLE TO ORDER OR TO BEARER. An

Figure 3
FORM OF CHECK

NEW YORK _Dec. 1,_ 19___ No. _114_

BANK & TRUST COMPANY $\frac{1-1}{23}$

BROADWAY OFFICE

PAY TO THE ORDER OF _Paul Payee_ _100.00_

One hundred $\frac{00}{100}$ _____ DOLLARS

David Drawer [10]

A check is a bill of exchange drawn on a bank and payable on demand.

instrument is payable to *order* when it is payable to any person. To negotiate it requires the endorsement of the person named, plus physical delivery. An instrument is payable to *bearer* if it is payable (1) "to bearer," (2) to a specified person or bearer, or (3) to cash. This type of instrument can be negotiated simply by physical delivery. Basically, it is just like cash.

The Effect of Non-negotiability. If any one of the essentials of negotiability is lacking, the draft or note doesn't lose its value entirely. It does lose its character as a "negotiable instrument" and the holders are deprived of the advantages of the Uniform Commercial Code. The promise contained in the paper—the obligation itself—is still valid and even transferable from one person to another.

But each holder takes such a paper in the same way he would take assignment of an ordinary contract—that is, subject to all the rights of the original parties. If the payee of a non-negotiable note comes to you and asks you to accept it for its face value or less, you have to inquire about all the circumstances of the original transaction, because all of the defenses and counterclaims that the original maker has against the original payee will be good against you.

Defenses Against Payment. There are circumstances in which the maker of a note can refuse to pay. Different rules apply, depending on who presents the note for payment. If a holder in due course is the one demanding payment, only the so-called "real defenses" may be asserted against him. They are:

(a) Lack of contractual capacity—that is, the maker was a minor child or an insane person, etc.

(b) Want of consent—that is, the maker of the instrument didn't freely consent to the transaction. This occurs if, for any reason, he did not know what he was doing, he was coerced to sign, the note was forged, or if someone, finding a piece of paper with his signature on it, composed a note over the signature. Mere fraud on the part of the payee is not a real defense.

(c) Illegality. For example, in New York, a note or check in payment of a gambling debt is void. This means that it is without value even in the hands of a holder who knows nothing about the original transaction. The same applies to usurious transactions where more than the maximum legal rate of interest has been charged. If state law doesn't make a transaction void, the defense is not good.

Defenses when the Original Payee Demands

Payment. If the party who presents the note, check, or other draft for payment is the same party whose name appears on it as the payee, payment can be refused if:

(a) The maker was induced to sign the paper by fraud or under some threat of harm.

(b) There was no consideration for the paper—that is, the maker received nothing from the payee in exchange for the note, or what the maker received was not what the payee warranted it to be.

(c) The consideration was illegal—for example, a note given in payment of a bribe or in payment for the services of a prostitute.

(d) The payee took advantage of a mistake or ignorance on the part of the maker.

(e) The note was properly made but the delivery was conditional on an event that didn't occur. EXAMPLE: Brown sues Jones for $500. After some negotiation, they agree to settle their differences for the sum of $250, which Jones is to pay Brown. Jones gives Brown his note for $250 with the understanding that Brown will discontinue his suit and give Jones a general release. When Brown presents the note for payment Jones can refuse to pay because the case was not discontinued.

Responsibilities of Endorsers. Negotiable checks and notes often pass through many hands before they are presented for payment. Each person through whose hands the instrument has passed has some liability for payment of the obligation if, after due presentation for payment, there is a default. The nature and the extent of the liability of each depends on how he passes it on to the next person.

Jim Easy is your next-door neighbor. He drops in one evening and asks you to cash a $100 check for him. The check is made out to the order of Jim Easy and signed by Hans Smith. You don't know Smith and there is nothing on the face of the check that would give you any hint of the fact that he is a horse player and that the check is to pay Easy off on a bet. To oblige Jim, you give him the $100 in cash. He endorses his name on the back of the check and gives it to you.

Later that evening you drive into town. Stopping at Frank Water's gas station you find that if you pay him for gas and oil, you'll be short of cash for the evening ahead. You trade regularly with Frank, so you don't hesitate to ask him to cash the $100 check Jim Easy gave you. Frank takes his gas money out of the hundred and gives you the balance.

This leaves Frank a little short when his wife comes by to pick up some marketing money. Frank gives her the check, which she passes on to Paul Candle, the grocer. Paul asks Mrs. Water to sign the check on the back, takes his grocery money out of it, and gives her the balance in cash. Next morning, Paul Candle deposits the check in the bank with the day's receipts.

So far, so good. Everyone has gotten value for the check and has passed it on. The fun begins when the check is presented for payment at Hans Smith's bank. It seems that Mrs. Smith has found out about Hans's gambling. She has found out about the check, too, and she forces Hans to stop payment on the check at the bank.

The bank calls Paul Candle, the grocer, and tells him that payment has been refused. Paul is acquainted with Hans, so he calls him and asks him why the check has not been honored. Hans tells him why. Paul is seemingly stuck with a worthless piece of paper.

But he isn't worried. On the back of the check are the names of Jim Easy and Mrs. Frank Water as endorsers. When they endorsed the check, they said to every subsequent holder or endorser, as a matter of law: "This is a good check. If you make a proper and timely demand of the maker and payment is not made, I will pay it."

You happen to be the only one in the chain who did not sign the paper, so Paul can't look to you for payment. This doesn't mean that you are free of liability because, if Paul makes Water pay, as he probably will, Water, to whom you negotiated the check by simple delivery, can look to you. You, of course, can claim the full amount from Jim Easy. So Jim is the one left holding the worthless paper. Problems arise if any one link in the chain drops out of sight. If, for example, Jim leaves town, you could be left with the worthless check to remember him by.

FORGERY AND ALTERATION OF CHECKS

The basic rule to remember here is that the party closest to the wrongdoer almost always suffers the loss. (This assumes the forger can't be made to pay up.) If someone draws a check in your name, your bank is liable if it pays the check, and the party who received the forged check is liable if your bank dishonors the check. If the endorsement of a good check is forged, the party who received the check from the forger bears the loss—unless the forger can be forced to pay up. If a check written to you is stolen, and your endorsement is forged and the check is cashed, you and the check's maker are not charged with the loss—the maker's bank is.

Now suppose the amount of a good check is altered upward. If the original maker's bank honors or pays the check as altered, the maker is liable only for the original amount of the check, and the party who first received the altered check is liable for the rest—unless, of course, the wrongdoer is apprehended and can make good his alteration.

Drawer's Fault. Generally, the drawer doesn't bear the risk of his check's being forged or altered, or having forged endorsements. But if he substantially contributes to the wrongdoing, he will suffer the loss. So beware of leaving blank checks around or of not filling in checks completely, so that there is room for changes to be made. Those with checking accounts should also go over their account statements promptly so that any wrongdoing doesn't continue unnoticed.

"Stale" Checks. Remember that a check is always payable on demand, and that demand should be made a "reasonable time" after the check's date. In the ordinary course of affairs, *no delay* is contemplated. Ordinarily, transactions by check are completed in days.

Some delays do occur, however, and can be explained by distance. A check drawn by someone in New York to the order of a payee in Seattle may be a week old or more by the time the payee is ready to deposit or negotiate it. Such a delay won't affect the check or the rights of any of the parties—the "reasonable time" for cashing the check varies with the facts of each situation.

There are some limits, however. The "reasonable time" can extend up to thirty days after issuance of the check. If you take a check after that period, you risk some trouble in collecting on the check because it has become "stale." That period also defines the time the maker is liable on the check, unless he specifies a longer period. After seven days, the endorser's liability on the check ends.

But if you are asked to accept a check made and dated weeks or months ago, the age of the check itself is notice to you that something is wrong. It is "stale" in the sense that, for some reason, it wasn't presented for payment within the usual time.

The effect of this is to change the rights of the parties. You are no longer an "innocent" party. The maker, if he has any defenses he could make against the original payee, may be able to refuse payment to you.

The moral of this is: Don't accept old checks and don't delay in depositing checks you receive.

CHAPTER SIX

PRINCIPAL AND AGENT, EMPLOYER AND EMPLOYEE, MASTER AND SERVANT

The most common relationship in our business community is that of principal and agent. We are constantly acting for the account of others or authorizing others to act for us. This relationship carries with it duties and responsibilities not only between principal and agent, but also to third parties.

HOW AN AGENCY IS CREATED

By Agreement. When one party authorizes another to act for him, subject to his control, in any matter or transaction, and the other agrees, an agency is created. The person giving the authority is the principal, and the person receiving the authority is the agent. The authority may be expressed in a simple letter of instruction or a formal power of attorney. In many cases, the agency can be created verbally, or even without words if the agent can reasonably infer the principal's intent. An agent's authority may be withdrawn at any time although the principal may be liable for damages.

By Operation of Law. An agency may be implied by the words and conduct of the parties, or by the existence of certain relationships, without separate authorization.

For example: (a) In a partnership, each partner, as a matter of law, acts as agent for the others within the apparent scope of the partnership business at the same time he is acting as a principal for himself;

(b) Since a husband is responsible for the maintenance and support of his wife and children, a wife's purchases of necessities for the family are made as agent for her husband, and he is responsible.

By Ratification. If someone having no authority to do so acts for you in a way you could have authorized, and you accept the benefits of his action, you have ratified his authority. For example, if you employ a chauffeur to drive your car and to purchase gasoline for you, his authority does not extend to trading in the car, and an automobile dealer who makes a deal with him to sell you a new car cannot hold you responsible. However, if you knowingly accept the new car when the chauffeur brings it around, you have ratified his act and his authority, and you will be obligated to fulfill the terms of the contract he made for you. You cannot retract a ratification.

TYPES OF AGENTS

Capacity. Any person can act as an agent, but an under-age or incompetent principal can void any obligation entered into for him by his agent.

Special Agent. A special agent is one whose authority is limited to specific acts performed under well-defined instructions. You may, for example, appoint a real estate agent in connection with a particular piece of real estate you own, with authority to maintain it, collect the rents, execute leases or sell it. Despite his wide authority, he is a special agent with limited powers restricted to the one piece of property in connection with which you have authorized him to act in your behalf.

General Agent. A general agent is authorized to do all that you could do yourself in connection with your business where you could act for yourself. Whether or not he is to act in your name or in his name is to be specified in your arrangement with him.

Master and Servant. Generally speaking, a servant is the agent of his master, but is restricted by the terms of the relationship. A principal dictates the objectives an agent seeks while a master controls the details of attaining that end, as well. The same is true of the employer-employee relationship.

When Formal Document Is Required. If you are traveling out of state and will be absent when transactions will take place involving your property or interests, it is best to leave your agent a document of authority. A good rule to follow is that the document should be at least as formal as the documents he may be required to sign in your behalf. For example, if he will be required to sign a deed which will have to be notarized and under seal, the document giving him his authority (which will, in such a case, be a power of attorney) will have to be signed before a notary and also under seal. (See definition of **seal** in glossary.)

LIABILITIES OF THE PARTIES

Principal to Agent. The principal is obligated to compensate the agent according to the terms of their arrangement, and to refund to the agent all of the disbursements and expenses lawfully incurred by him in carrying out the terms of the agency. He is also obliged to indemnify the agent where, in the course of acting for the principal, he has incurred any liability or loss which was not his own fault.

For example, an agent, acting on instruc-

tions from his principal, charters a certain boat which turns out to be unseaworthy and, as a result, some cargo is lost. The agent has to pay the shipper's claims. The principal, in such a case, would have to indemnify the agent.

Agent to Principal. The agent is obligated to the principal to carry out the instructions given him; to use the same skill, prudence and diligence that he would use in his own affairs; and to keep regular accounts and to report at reasonable intervals to his principal. He must not take advantage of the relationship or violate his position by representing adverse interests, and must avoid confusion between his own interests and those of his principal. One who is the agent of another for the purpose of selling a piece of property cannot himself become the buyer while remaining the agent of the seller.

To Third Parties. As long as the agent acts within the scope of the authority granted to him by the principal, the latter will be bound to meet all of the commitments made by the agent. If the agent has made false representations in certain of his acts as agent, and the principal has accepted the benefit of the acts, the latter will be held responsible for the false representations even if he has not authorized them. The principal might even be held responsible for an agent's acts in excess of actual authority if a third party had a right to believe the agent was within his authority, and the third party would otherwise sustain a loss.

Undisclosed Principal. When an agent acts in his own name without disclosing the name of the principal, and without disclosing the fact that he is acting as an agent, he is committing himself and not the principal. But when he acts in his own name and discloses the fact that he is acting in behalf of another, he is obligating his principal, except in the case of negotiable instruments. Often a third party is free to hold either the agent or the undisclosed principal liable if the agreement is violated.

PURPOSE OF AGENCY

In general, anything we can lawfully do ourselves may be done for us by an agent appointed by us. There are, of course, exceptions.

First among them are certain acts that are essentially personal in nature and are subject to one's judgment or discretion. Voting, for example, is such a personal act and no agent may vote for a principal without special authorization. A trustee, a guardian or an executor of a will cannot delegate his duties involving personal discretion unless he has been specially empowered to do so. Merely ministerial or mechanical powers (i.e. selling property after the decision to sell has been made by the executor), however, may always be delegated. In addition, statutes require that certain acts be performed personally. Thus, a notary cannot appoint another to administer an oath for him, etc.

The appointment of an agent to do an illegal or immoral act is itself illegal. Suppose a public officer is offered a bribe by an agent. The principal will be held responsible for the crime. But if the agent sues the principal for his compensation, the courts will not enforce the contract, because the agency agreement was itself illegal.

TERMINATION

Ordinarily, a principal may revoke his agent's authority at any time, but he may be liable for breach of contract. Personal notification by the principal to third parties is advisable if there has been a history of dealing with the agent. An agency is terminated immediately on the death of the principal even before notice is given to the agent or a third party.

AGENTS AND INDEPENDENT CONTRACTORS

It is often necessary to analyze relationships in order to establish who is responsible when a worker is injured or commits a wrong. When you are in business, you often appoint an outside company to do certain acts for you. You may appoint an independent sales organization to represent you in certain territories; you may engage a contractor to build a house for you; or you may hire a trucking company to handle your deliveries.

A principal, or a master, is responsible for the acts of an agent or servant if they are committed within the scope of employment. Thus, if an outside company acts entirely under your control, with you supervising the details of the work and the hiring and firing of help, then you may be held responsible for all its acts. Its workmen will be considered to be yours. However, you will not be liable for acts or injuries that occur during any deviation from the scope of employment.

You aren't responsible for the acts of independent contractors. So if you hire workmen to achieve a desired result and leave the details, the method, and the means to them, allowing them to hire and fire their own employees and supervise their own work, they are reponsible for their own acts, except in regard to certain inherently dangerous activities or duties.

The presence of agents in different states can make a business taxable and suable in those states. And a car owner who drives out of state opens himself to suit in the state where he commits any damage, by impliedly appointing a state official as his agent for the service of related court papers.

CHAPTER SEVEN

PARTNERSHIPS

By combining their work, money and talents, two or more people as "partners" can do what one could not do alone. But there are many pitfalls. There must be the highest degree of mutual trust and confidence. In this chapter we discuss the essential elements of a partnership as a legal relationship, the rights of the partners as against each other, and the responsibilities of each to the other and to outside parties.

GENERAL NATURE OF A PARTNERSHIP

Al and Frank have known and trusted each other for a number of years. They decide to go into business together as partners in a filling station. They find a suitable location and prepare to start up under the name of A&F Service Station.

They go to a lawyer and ask him to draw up partnership papers "as simple as possible," and to do what is necessary to register the name of their new business. He draws up a partnership agreement in which they state their intention to do business as partners, describe the business, its starting capital, and how much each will chip in, and stipulate that they will jointly manage the business and give it all their time and labor. They are to own the business jointly and share equally in its profits and losses.

They both sign the agreement and another document, called a "certificate of doing business as partners," which their attorney files for them in the county clerk's office. Now they have a working arrangement with each other.

(Some states do permit less formal arrangements.) The paper filed in the county clerk's office serves notice to the world that the A&F Service Station is owned and operated by Al and Frank as partners.

At this point many lawyers would say, "Bless them, for they know not what they do." While the partnership form of doing business can produce excellent results in many cases, there are so many hazards attached to it that persons contemplating it should be advised to pause and consider certain aspects of the relationship.

Of course there are hazards and pitfalls in any form of business relationship, and a certain degree of mutual trust and confidence is necessary whenever people decide to embark on a venture with others. But in a partnership the degree of mutual trust and confidence has got to be very high. Why? Let's go further into the case of Al and Frank.

In personality and temperament the men were very different: Al was cautious and conservative while Frank was impulsive. The difference became a source of trouble in business.

The first thing that bothered Al was that Frank seemed always to be in debt personally. He was behind in his payments on his car, his furniture and his house. Then Al objected to the way Frank purchased equipment and merchandise for the business. He was an easy mark for salesmen and a pushover for new gadgets. To top it off, Frank found it hard to refuse credit to customers.

The partners had words. Frank resented

Al's criticism of the way he conducted his personal affairs. He said his personal debts were his own business. As far as his business practices were concerned, he felt that they would make for success in the end. He saw all business as a gamble and felt that the partners had only invested so much and that was all they stood to lose. Al disagreed, so they asked their lawyer for advice. This is what they were told.

Partnership Property Is Not Protected Against the Creditors of One Partner. If Frank's personal debts grow so large that they cannot be satisfied out of his private assets, his creditors can go after his share of the partnership property. In such a case the partnership would be terminated first.

Each Partner Is the Agent of the Other. In conducting the affairs of the partnership, all partners are bound by the acts of one of them, if the acts are within the apparent scope of the partnership business. If Frank should give an order for expensive equipment, possibly beyond the means of the partnership, Al as well as Frank is obliged to pay the bill. If there is not enough money in the business to pay the bill, the partners will have to dig into their personal funds to pay it.

Any knowledge one partner possesses is imputed to the partnership unless the partner is committing fraud on the partnership. However, one partner cannot, on his own, dispose of the good will of the business, add a new partner, or do anything that would make it impossible to carry on the partnership business.

No Limited Liability. The amount that the partners originally agreed to invest in the business has no effect on their liability for obligations. If the business incurs debts that are larger than their personal investment, the partners are personally responsible to creditors after all of the partnership property has been exhausted. An incoming partner is liable for partnership debts contracted before his entry, but only to the extent of partnership property.

Wrongful Acts of Partners. If one partner, while acting in behalf of the partnership, should cause loss or damage to other people,

the other partners are equally responsible for the loss, and are liable for damages.

"So you see why you must manage your personal as well as your business lives with the greatest of care," says the lawyer. "You may be made to pay partnership debts out of your personal funds and your personal debts out of partnership funds."

Partnership Property. Generally, all property acquired with partnership funds is partnership property, as is all property brought into the partnership. Most often, each partner shares equally in the business's profits and in its management, but is not paid for his services. So each partner has an equal voice in dealing with partnership property. That property can be transferred only if all the partners act together, and it is immune from attachment or execution on individual debts. However, a mere interest in partnership profits can be assigned by each partner without dissolving the partnership. This interest may be reached by creditors of each partner.

Silent Partners. Even if a partner is not active in the business and is not generally known to be a partner, a man who extends credit to the partnership may, when he learns of the existence of the "silent partner," hold him accountable for the debt if the partnership property is not sufficient to satisfy it.

Partners by Estoppel. Suppose that Al and Frank were not able to get credit from their suppliers on the basis of their own names and responsibility. They go to Frank's uncle, a substantial real estate man, for a loan. He says he is not in a position to lend them a large sum of money but would get credit extended to them by announcing that he has entered the partnership. Under such conditions, even if the uncle has no interest in the business, he might be held responsible as a partner if credit has been extended to the partnership on his statement that he is a partner.

Dissolution. Ordinarily, a partnership must be terminated and must wind up its affairs when one partner dies, withdraws or becomes bankrupt, or when a partner sells or assigns his partnership interest, or when there is a breach of the partnership agreement. When the partners get notice of a dissolution, they can only act to wind up partnership affairs and complete transactions. However, conditions under which the partnership business can be carried on after such events can be included in an appropriate partnership agreement. Actually, most of the usual partnership troubles can be anticipated and provided for in a carefully drawn contract.

Upon dissolution, the partnership assets are distributed, with nonpartnership creditors having priority. If one partner leaves a partnership, he should notify parties whose rights may be affected by his departure.

Taxation. A partnership is not a legal entity for most purposes. The partnership, unlike a corporation, does not pay taxes on its profits. However, each partner pays income tax on his share of the partnership's profits.

Limited Partnership. There is a way of investing money in a partnership without becoming liable as a partner for partnership debts. To achieve this, the law provides a procedure for the creation of "limited partnerships." An essential feature of this business form is public announcement, through publication in a newspaper or the filing of a certificate, of the terms of the limited partnership agreement. Thus, in theory at least, the whole world knows how the limited partners will be compensated and that they are not to be held accountable for more than their original investment. Another important feature is that the limited partners must not participate in the management of the partnership business. If they do, they lose the special protection given them by the law.

This is not a very widely used business form since the aim of limited liability is easily attained by the use of the corporation. But there are cases in which the creation of a corporation is either not sanctioned by law or impractical. Limited partnerships are often used by stock brokerage firms and on Broadway when companies are formed to produce a play. In the typical producing company, the actual producers and managers of the production are the general partners, while the investors who provide most of the money, the "angels," are the limited partners.

CHAPTER EIGHT

CORPORATIONS

There are sound reasons why the corporate form has been adopted by thousands of businesses large and small. This chapter discusses and explains some of the advantages, and also explains how corporations are formed and how they operate.

Many people think of corporations only in connection with big business. The "corporation lawyer" was pictured as having an office on Wall Street amid the tycoons, one of a handful familiar with the mysteries of corporate organization and finance. While there are some areas of corporate work that are specialized and intricate, today every practicing attorney should be familiar with corporation law, the corporate form having been adopted by hundreds of thousands of going concerns, large and small. Why? Because there are so many conveniences and legal advantages in the corporate form that even the smallest of businesses often finds that the trouble and expense of incorporation are justified.

HOW CORPORATIONS ARE FORMED AND HOW THEY FUNCTION

McDonald is a farmer, with his own acreage, machinery, cattle, and some money in the bank. He and his neighbors, farmers like himself, have for some time been dissatisfied with the marketing arrangements available to them for their dairy products. He has decided to invest most of his money and part of his land in a milk processing and bottling plant. He has just told his lawyer of his intention. Let's listen in.

"This new business is going to take as much money as I have. Maybe a lot more. The way I see it, I could afford to build the plant and buy the machinery, but that won't leave me any money for operating. Now I know two or three farmers hereabouts who are willing to go into this thing with me if we can work out a good way of protecting everybody. Mike Adams is willing to invest ten thousand dollars, my brother George will put up five thousand, and so will Sam Sykes. They all want to be partners, but the point is that I will be putting in more than all of them together, so we can't all be equal partners."

The lawyer answers promptly: "That doesn't seem like much of a problem. What you want to do is form a corporation. Each investor will get shares in proportion to his investment. If your business needs a hundred thousand dollars to start and you put up half of it, then you get half the shares. If Mike Adams puts up ten thousand, he gets ten per cent of the shares and owns ten per cent of the business."

"Yes," says McDonald, "but what about management of the business. The other investors are three to my one. They would be more powerful than me, and yet there will be more of my money in it than theirs."

"That's not so. A corporation acts through its board of directors. The directors are elected by the shareholders at a meeting where every share of stock has a vote. If you own fifty shares, you have fifty votes. Mike has ten shares; he gets ten votes. George's five shares give him five votes."

McDonald is satisfied that this method of dealing with ownership and control is fair. He asks, "What would we have to do to form this corporation? Is it expensive? Is it a lot of trouble? Does it take a lot of time?"

"Once you decide how much money the company will need and what kind of business it will conduct, you can leave the rest to me. It's not very expensive. You'll have to pay a fee to the state for recording a corporate charter. You'll have to buy and open a set of books. I can do that for you. I will also order certificates of stock from the printer and a corporate seal. We may get this done within a week."

It's as easy as that. But, of course, there is a great deal more to it. The case of Farmer McDonald runs along traditional lines because, in his case, the reasons for his interest in corporations were the reasons that explain the origin of corporations.

The Corporation as an Independent Being. The corporation is primarily a device whereby a group of people band together and create an independent and artificial being that can do something that the members of the group couldn't do individually. (Like individuals, however, it can incur debts, enter contracts, and be sued.) A corporation is created and largely controlled by state law, and some states—Delaware, for example—have fewer restrictions, which makes incorporation there favorable. A corporation organized in one state can function elsewhere, although there should be some ties to the state of incorporation. Since a corporation is a creature of the state, state law should be consulted and followed rigorously.

The Corporate Charter. This is often called the "certificate of incorporation." It is a grant by the state issued to the incorporators (usually at least three) whose names and addresses must appear on the application or in the certificate itself. The charter describes the purposes for which the corporation is being formed, how it is to be capitalized (number and value of shares, special rights the shares have, etc.), its name, the number of directors

and the names of the original directors, their addresses and the address of the corporation, as well as how certain important procedures of corporate management are to be carried out. These are the general requirements. Some states require more, some less. Special types of corporations like banking, insurance, and transportation companies are required to file special certificates.

After the certificate is filed, the incorporators adopt by-laws which tell how the corporation is to be run. These bylaws can generally be amended or repealed by the shareholders.

The Corporate Name. In general, the incorporators may use any name they fancy if it has not already been taken by some other firm in the state, if it does not too closely resemble the name of an existing firm, or if it doesn't suggest that the corporation is a government instrument. The Secretary of State of each state keeps an index of corporate names. Lawyers communicate with his office to make sure the proposed name is available before any work is done on corporate papers.

But even if the Secretary of State clears a proposed name and issues a charter, it doesn't always give the new firm an absolute right to use it. Why? Because he is only concerned with the corporations in his own state. There may be an out-of-state corporation bearing your proposed name which does business in the same areas where you intend to operate. Your use of the name, even if approved by proper authority, may create confusion, may be damaging to the other firm, and the courts may enjoin your use of it. Your lawyer has services available to him at moderate cost, which can, in a short time, conduct a coast-to-coast investigation into the possible prior use of your proposed name.

The name must include some word to indicate that the firm is a corporation. The word "company" isn't enough. The name must include "corporation," "incorporated," or "limited" (or their abbreviations). Why the public must be apprised of the corporate character of the business will become clear when we discuss the matter of *limited liability*.

State law sets the procedure for changing a corporation's name, as well as the fee.

Perpetual Existence. A corporation can be organized for any length of time—even perpetually. The life of a corporation doesn't end upon the death of any of its officers, directors, or stockholders; the corporation continues until it is dissolved by legal means. This is true even of the so-called "one man corporation" in which all of the stock is held by one individual. His death would not terminate the life of the corporation. His shares of stock would descend to others as his personal property.

Limited Liability. One of the most important features of the corporation is the protection given to investors with respect to the debts and obligations of the business. If the business turns bad and the debts go higher than the assets of the company, the creditors may not look to the individual owners (stockholders) of the corporation. Only the capital of the corporation is available for the payment of its debts. If McDonald Milk, Inc., turns out to be a failure, the most each of the stockholders can lose is the amount of his original investment. (But all profits belong to the stockholders without limitation as to amount.)

Each of them must, however, be responsible to that extent. This means that if any of them had not fully paid for his shares, he is responsible to the creditors for the unpaid balance.

If McDonald had decided to go into the milk-processing business as an individual, or in partnership with his neighbors, he would be personally responsible for the business debts. The amount he had decided to invest would have no bearing on his obligations because the people he dealt with trusted him personally. He would stand to lose all of his property, including his farm, if his business debts were large enough.

The limited liability might not be recognized if the corporation didn't have adequate initial financing or if it was organized to avoid an existing obligation or to defraud.

The Board of Directors. The responsibility for management rests with the directors. Their number is usually set in the bylaws of the corporation, adopted at the first meeting of the stockholders. There usually is a minimum of three. The directors occupy a position of trust and are responsible to the stockholders, who elect them and who can remove and replace them. It is improper for a director to be interested in any business that competes with the corporation, or even with an outside business that has transactions with the corporation, unless all the facts are known to the stockholders, and they approve.

The Officers. The President, Vice President, Treasurer, and Secretary (and other officers the particular corporation may require) are appointed by the board of directors. They are employees of the company. They need not be stockholders. Their compensation, duties, and conditions of employment are fixed by the directors.

Meetings. The bylaws of the corporation provide when, where, and how meetings of the stockholders and of the board are to be conducted. Meetings should occur at least annually. Often (and especially in closely held corporations) the meetings are just formalities conducted in the office of the company's lawyer. With larger corporations, special requirements must be satisfied regarding notice of the meeting, the necessary quorum, etc.

Dividends. When there are profits to be distributed, a dividend is declared by the board of directors. The total amount to be distributed is divided by the number of outstanding shares and the dividend is expressed in terms of dollars per share.

Whether or not to declare a dividend is a business decision for the directors to make. It isn't required by law that a corporation declare dividends if it earns profits. The directors may decide that the profits should be used in other ways—kept in the business, used to buy back some of the corporation's own stock, used for expansion or to provide bonuses for employees, etc. This is often the source of discontent on the part of minority stockholders, i.e. stockholders who don't control the management of the corporation. When it can be shown that the failure to declare dividends is arbitrary and part of a scheme to deprive certain stockholders of their fair share of the profits, a suit can be brought to compel a distribution of dividends.

Voting Rights. It is by casting his votes at annual meetings that the stockholder exercises his right to participate in the management of the corporation. Votes are cast only at meetings, but if a stockholder can't be present, he can vote by proxy. Corporations whose shares are held by large numbers of investors sometimes have active contests to decide who shall manage the corporation. Those who desire control will solicit the proxies of stockholders, usually by mail. Often the management will enclose proxy forms with annual reports of the company. When shares are widely held, it's possible for a relatively small percentage—5 or 10 per cent of the shares, voting together—to acquire management control.

Stockholders can contract with each other as to how they'll vote their shares; stock can also be transferred to a trustee who will vote it. These methods can quell fears about certain stockholders changing their minds.

Protection for the Small Investor. When forming a new corporation, it's possible, by agreement and by appropriate provisions in the bylaws, to make sure that the company is not dominated by the majority at the expense of the minority.

For example, the stockholders may agree among themselves that the minority shall be represented on the board of directors. In New York and several other states, it's possible to include in the certificate of incorporation that the number of votes necessary for conducting any business at stockholders' meetings be larger than a simple majority. For example, you can provide that your corporation can act only upon the vote of 75 per cent of the outstanding shares so that control of management isn't necessarily in the hands of those who own 51 per cent. There are other, more complicated, voting methods which can ensure minority representation. A lawyer can tailor these procedures to suit the needs of the minority stockholders.

All shareholders generally have the right to inspect the corporation's books and records. With this information, a shareholder can sue the corporation to enforce his rights as a shareholder. Or, in a more complex action, he can sue on behalf of the corporation, as when the management is working at cross-purposes from the best interests of the corporation. Strict regulations have to be met to institute this type of action, and they vary from state to state.

Fiduciary Duties. Wrongdoing by management can always be the subject of a suit because management is obligated to act in the *corporation's* best interests. Suppose that McDonald, who is president and a director of McDonald Milk, Inc., and owns 75 per cent of its shares, should have the opportunity to buy the majority interest in the trucking company that carries the McDonald Milk products to market. If he should buy the trucking interest for himself, his corporation might rightfully complain that the opportunity didn't belong to him personally but to the corporation. There are many instances of what is called the usurpation of corporate opportunity by directors, and some cases where there are conflicts of interest between the majority and minority.

Similarly, controlling stockholders have a duty to act in good faith so that corporate control isn't used solely for their own benefit. All corporate officers and directors must exercise care in the performance of their duties and must comply with fiduciary standards—that is, they must consider the welfare of everyone concerned with the corporation. Self-interest and laziness, for example, can make them open to shareholder actions.

CHAPTER NINE

REAL PROPERTY

The law of real property affects almost everyone in some way at some time. As an owner or tenant of a home, land, or business property, your rights are governed by this important branch of the law. Here we discuss the various factors involved in buying and selling, title questions, and the mechanics of a real estate transaction.

WHAT IS REAL PROPERTY?

In the past, a distinction was made between the two kinds of property: *real property* and *personal property*. This was based on the type of legal action one had to institute in order to recover property from someone who had taken it away from the rightful owner.

If, for example, the property was a horse, the suit would either be for the horse or *for its value in money*. But if the property was land, the claimant didn't seek money; he wanted *the land itself*, the *real* property. This is the origin of the term. In addition to land, real property includes everything that is erected on land (often called improvements), everything growing on it, and everything affixed to it.

Personal property is everything else capable of being owned. But it may be important— sometimes troublesome—to make the distinction between real and personal property, as in disputes between landlords and tenants.

For example, a tenant has the right to remove all his *personal* property from the *real* property that he has rented. However, if the property should have installations of a kind that cannot be removed without damage to the property, those installations are "affixed" to the realty and have become part of it. If improvements are custom built, installed flush or cemented to a wall, or the like, they are presumed to be affixed.

On the other hand, if the property is removable, like a refrigerator or a stove, it is called a domestic fixture and is personal property. Barring an agreement to the contrary, the tenant may take his additions to the property away with him even if the landowner objects, as long as they're not affixed. The use of nails and similar things doesn't make an object affixed to realty.

Of course such questions can be and usually are covered in advance, in the terms of the lease. But when they're not covered, or when the terms aren't clear, a test must be applied. Is it attached to the realty in such a way as to become part of it? Can it be removed without damage to walls, floors, etc? What was the intention of the one who installed it? When additions are installed by the owner himself, doubtful questions are decided in his favor.

The question of whether property is real or personal may also cause trouble in the settling of a deceased person's estate. The question may arise, for example, when real property is willed to one heir and personal property to another.

What Makes Real Property "Real"? Every piece of real property is unique. It is the only one in the world with that particular location. Since each piece of realty differs from every other piece, the law recognizes that this uniqueness involves obligations in transactions for its sale that are different from those affecting other property—a truck, for example.

If you refuse to deliver a truck, the buyer can get another one just as good. And if he has suffered damages, he can sue you. An award of money damages can adequately compensate him.

But if you fail to deliver real property you have contracted to sell, the court (in this case, sitting as a court in equity—see definition in glossary) will compel you to deliver that particular piece of property. It will compel you to do so even if it will cost you more than the agreed-upon price.

EXAMPLE: Landowner Jones advertises his property for sale. The first man to respond to the ad meets his price of $2,000. They draw up a contract of sale and fix a time for the transfer of title.

In the meantime, another purchaser comes along. He represents a large corporation which wants the lot for a new plant. He offers $20,000. Jones decides to ignore the first deal, thinking that even if he has to give the first buyer substantial damages he will still come out ahead of the game.

This may prove to be a miscalculation. He can be compelled to deliver the property to the first bidder with whom he has contracted to sell it, even if he has completed the sale to the corporation and received the $20,000.

Origin of Real Property Law. Since our laws are derived from England (except in Louisiana), it will help our understanding of the subject to review briefly the development of the English laws regarding land, rights in land, and transfer of title.

Originally, all land was considered royal property. The king allowed his henchmen the use of parcels of real estate for stated periods of time, or for as long as it pleased him. In exchange, those who received the land owed the king services which, at first, were purely military. Later, a portion of the crops or rents had to be paid to the king.

Under this system—the feudal system—the nobleman who received the grant from the king usually divided it into parcels which he distributed to *his* followers. Later the grants became grants for the life of the nobles; later

still they were made permanent. As of 1660, during the reign of Charles II, all landholders became absolute landowners.

Land Tenure in America. The colonists never brought the feudal system to America with them, although vestiges of it remain in our legal terminology relating to real property.

When, for instance, a property owner dies leaving no heirs—no one with a rightful claim to the land—the state, replacing the king, assumes ownership. We say that the property "escheats," a term used in the feudal system. And we still use the term "fee" to describe the absolute right to land, a word directly descended from the word "feud."

The original royal land grants were only for the life of those who enjoyed their use. The land would "revert" (go back) to the king when the holders died. Even after the feudal system ended, it was assumed that a land transfer from one owner to another was only for the lifetime of the grantee or purchaser, and that upon his death the right would revert to the original owner or to his heirs.

For this reason, when transferring real property today, we still use terms like ". . . to the purchaser, his heirs and assigns forever." This indicates that the property is being transferred absolutely, that the seller or grantor is surrendering all of his rights to the property and expects nothing to revert to him. Such language really isn't necessary any more to convey absolute title, but it is still used because it makes the intent of the parties clear. Today, a deed that transfers real property "to John Jones" passes absolute title, and if a life estate is all that's desired, it's necessary to spell out "to John Jones for life."

Rights in property for a term or for life have by no means disappeared. They are, in fact, quite common. So too are "reversions"— the right to receive back property after it has been used by someone else. Such rights, usually called "estates," are often set up in wills.

For example, a man may "devise" (a word used for the gift of real property by will) a house to his brother for life, and upon the brother's death, to his sister. His brother has what is known as a "life estate" in the house; upon his death, the sister will own the "fee" absolutely.

Real property of an intestate (one who leaves no will) "descends" to that person or persons who, by state law, have the right to receive it. Sometimes it is one person; sometimes it is a class of persons (children, nieces, nephews).

All these complications explain why the business of buying, selling, renting, and mortgaging real property is so technical, and why professional help should be sought by those who are buying or selling, or entering into any other transaction involving real estate.

BUYING REAL ESTATE

Suppose you are in the market to buy a house and lot. You see the property you want and strike a bargain with the owner. To bind the sale, you leave a deposit with him and arrange for a subsequent meeting to sign the sales contract. On that occasion, you arrange a time when title will be transferred. Each of these steps is normal and usual. Yet each is surrounded by technicalities; each has become the subject of litigation. A sales contract is a very formidable document when it relates to real property.

Today, sales often involve a broker. The prospective buyer first signs an offer to purchase which he gives to the broker along with a small deposit ($50 or so). This document contains the basics of the sales contract, but can contain more technical clauses which make the sale contingent on the purchaser getting certain types of financing. The seller then has three to five days to accept the offer. If he does, the buyer must then make the initial deposit. The buyer can usually cancel the deal, however, if the property is found to be less than was represented.

The Deposit. The question has often arisen whether the receipt given for the deposit, or "earnest money," may be considered a sales contract. That depends on its terms. A receipt for such a deposit will often contain such

words as "subject to approval by owner or by owner's attorney," or "subject to the execution of sales contract," or other stipulations that leave the owner the right to return the deposit if he changes his mind about the sale.

So you see, the binder given on receipt of a deposit may be tricky. It should be examined by an attorney before it's signed. But you don't take lawyers house-hunting with you, so binders are usually signed without legal advice.

CAUTION: The buyer, if he signs the wrong kind of binder document, may find himself obligated to buy a property despite unfavorable facts turned up by a later search—he may be committed to terms not satisfactory to him. In general, he should avoid signing a binder. If he gives a money deposit, it should be small in relation to the full purchase price, and he should get a receipt from the owner containing language like, "This deposit is returnable immediately if investigation, contract terms, survey, or title search reveals facts unsatisfactory to the buyer or his attorney." Reliable real estate brokers have forms available which are fair to both parties.

There are no provisions for second thoughts in the sales contract. Once it is signed, the parties are committed to a purchase and sale of the property, barring the violation of provisions in the document.

Searching a Title. When your attorney has the sales contract in hand, after overseeing the negotiations and execution of the contract, he will make a title search, or order one to be made for you. This is essential to ascertain, first of all, whether the seller actually has the right to sell. To determine this, the land records in the county where the property is located are thoroughly examined to establish the chain of title over a long period of years.

All too often it is discovered that the occupant who believes himself the true owner of a house with absolute right to sell, has what is known as a "cloud" upon his title. A right in the property held by someone else has not been extinguished.

Let's assume that Jones, the seller, bought

the property from McCann, who had purchased the property, after the death of Dickens, from Dickens' three children. When the land was conveyed to McCann, one of the three Dickens heirs was overseas, and didn't sign the deed. To remove the cloud on the title it will be necessary to get a deed from the missing Dickens, or from his heirs.

It's also possible that when the land you are about to buy was first subdivided from a larger tract, the original seller imposed a condition to which all of his buyers agreed. That may still be in existence, and you may not wish to buy the property under those conditions.

The search will also reveal the existence of any zoning regulations or restrictions, liens on the property for labor, services, taxes, assessments, water and sewage rates, the owner's debts, etc.

Obviously, you have no desire to buy property burdened with an accumulation of claims, mortgages, liens, other people's rights, etc. The purchase of real property may be the most important single transaction of your lifetime. Because of the many pitfalls, it's unwise to proceed without a thorough title search, even if it involves some expense.

Furthermore, no bank or lending institution will advance money with the house as security, without making a title search. So if you have to give a mortgage on the property in order to raise part of the purchase price, the title search should be made, simultaneously, for the purchaser of the property and the lender of the money.

Actually, the title company, if one is engaged to perform the search, will often render two separate reports: one to the purchaser and one to the lender. Separate reports are made because each desires the title organization to be responsible to him.

The Title Policy. In most areas of the country it's possible to insure your title. (Sometimes attorneys provide the service.) The insurance company is usually the same organization that makes the search and renders the report. The policy you receive guarantees the report and undertakes to make good your loss in money in the event that any defect in your title should turn up.

Most such policies contain exceptions. For example, if the title company finds that the local telephone company has acquired the right from a previous owner to string lines across your property, they won't insure you against the stringing of those lines.

Title policies should be read very carefully. Purchasers who feel that a title policy makes it possible for them to do without the services of an attorney should bear in mind that it often requires the skill of an attorney to analyze the policy itself. In many cases, the bank involved in the transaction supplies an attorney who acts for the buyer as well.

How Title Passes. Title is a means by which rights in real property are held and transferred. Long ago, the transfer of property was accomplished by a formal ceremony: the seller gave a twig or a clod of earth to the buyer as they stood on the land. This was called "livery of seisin."

Today title to property passes by *deed*. A deed is a formal document in which every word has significance. Every phrase in a deed has been the subject of litigation.

Several types of deeds are in common use throughout the United States. All serve to transfer title from the grantor to the grantee. The difference lies in the nature of the responsibility of the grantor to the grantee.

Types of Deeds. A "quit-claim" deed merely surrenders to the grantee all that the grantor has. There's no warranty of good title.

A "bargain and sale" deed adds a description of what the grantor is transferring, and usually contains a clause stating that he has done nothing to impair his title to the property. But there's no warranty against defects in the title, arising from prior owners.

A "full covenant and warranty" deed is, in effect, an undertaking by the grantor that the title is good, that there are no defects in it. The grantor is obliged to meet any costs incurred in removing clouds on the title that surface after the sale. It's advisable for buyers to try to get a full warranty and covenant deed, but the type most commonly in use is the bargain and sale deed.

Title Through Inheritance. Title can also pass through inheritance. This can occur by the terms of a will or in accordance with the state laws covering the descent of real property when there is no will.

Adverse Possession. It is possible to acquire title to real property without actually owning it, provided you maintain actual, open and continuous possession of the land, under claim of title in defiance of the owner, for at least ten years. (Some states require longer periods of possession.) Examples of a claim of title are cultivating or improving the property, occupying it, or enclosing it. Public lands can't be acquired this way, but land owned by state or local governments in a proprietary capacity can be—although the time period is generally longer. For tenants, the period for establishing adverse possession doesn't begin until, in New York as an example, ten years after the lease expires.

Identity of the Seller. Be sure to verify that the person you're dealing with is the rightful owner of the property. A title search will reveal the name of the owner and you must ascertain that the person you deal with is that person. If he's known by people in town and has in his possession the old deeds, title policy, insurance policy, tax bills, etc., you can be pretty sure you're talking to the rightful owner.

Description of the Property. Your contract, deed, title policy, and mortgage should each contain an accurate description of the property. This description should be identical, word for word, on all documents. Early in the negotiations, the description should be taken from the owner's old deed or title search, and if he has a survey, this should be borrowed from him.

The survey is important where the property is surrounded by other buildings, where buildings are close together, or where there are walls, fences or driveways shared by two owners. The survey will reveal possible encroachments upon the property by the owner

of the adjoining property, or, conversely, possible encroachments by the buildings being sold, or by its fences, driveways, or shrubs, upon the property of a neighbor, or upon a public street.

In the description, you should spell out any *exceptions* which exclude from the transfer what would otherwise pass to the new owner. Any *reservation* (such as an easement), which creates a new right in the property, should also be stated here. Exceptions and reservations can't be in favor of third parties.

Easements. These are certain rights, like rights of way over property, which can be created by deed, by agreements (covenants contained in deeds or separately entered into by neighboring landowners), or simply by usage. This last is a special case, as easements can't be created orally under normal circumstances. They do sometimes arise by implication if they are necessary for the enjoyment of the property and are already in existence, unofficially.

Here's an example of a more normal easement. John Price owns five acres between a lake shore and a highway. He decides to keep the shore frontage for himself, divides the rest into four one-acre parcels, and sells them separately. To retain access to the highway and to provide access to the lakeshore to the four other owners, he inserts a covenant into each of the deeds that gives each owner the right of way over the property of the others, to the lake.

Each owner possesses an easement in the property of the others. These easements that concern the very use of the land are said to attach to the land. No owner can destroy the easement on his own property, although the dominant party can release his rights. Every subsequent owner buys the property subject to the easement. However, if someone later buys all five parcels, he can terminate the easement on one or more of the parcels.

When the right of way is used, without a formal covenant, deed or some form of permission, but with the knowledge of the owner, over a long period of time (up to twenty years) which depends on the law of the state where the property is located, an easement comes into existence. This explains why, from time to time, a temporary fence will be put up across a private road which the owner usually allows his neighbors or the general public to use. By closing it off for a time, the owner preserves his exclusive right to the road as his property.

The easements we have considered pertain to specific pieces of property. Certain easements, however, can belong to individuals, but they are not assignable.

A right to enter another's land to remove something—sand, for example—is a *profit*. It requires a writing and is assignable. A *license* allows one to enter another's land for some purpose that's usually specified. It is not an interest in land and so may be granted orally. It isn't assignable and it ends with the death of the licensee. It may be revoked at any time. An "easement" without a writing is, in effect, a license.

Restrictive Covenants. A covenant may also forbid certain actions. For example, a man can restrict a neighbor's right to build too close to their common boundary, if such a power is granted in the man's deed. Or the deed to your property may bar you from building anything but a single-family residence on it. These powers are enforceable against a property owner's successors, too. They are presumed to have knowledge of any restrictions that are on record and can be discovered by a proper search. Any restriction against the occupancy of premises on the basis of race is unenforceable.

A municipality can enact zoning regulations to govern property use within its borders, irrespective of covenants in individual deeds. Zoning has frequently been challenged as discriminatory, but has been consistently upheld if its principal aim is shown to be nondiscriminatory.

Sales Contract. Next to the deed itself, the contract of sale is the most important document in a real estate transaction. It must be in writing, and it must be signed by both parties,

who should be accurately identified within the document.

In the contract the respective rights and obligations of the parties are "frozen." The obligation to deliver a deed on a certain day must be signed by all the parties whose signature will be needed on the deed itself. If a piece of property is owned by husband and wife, both should sign the sales contract as sellers.

The contract should describe the property and state the purchase price and the terms of payment. If there is an unpaid mortgage debt which the buyer is to assume as part of the purchase price, this must be stated. If there are covenants, easements, or restrictions, they should be spelled out and the sale made subject to them, provided they don't interfere with the intended use of the property. The buyer should insist on a representation by the seller that there are no violations of zoning or other ordinances, or that he will remove them before closing.

All contracts for the sale of realty contain a warranty of marketability (unless expressly excluded) which promises good title, but once a deed is given, only the express warranties in the deed are effective.

Provision should be made in the contract for the apportionment of charges on the property, water rates, taxes, insurances, etc., as of the date of closing, so that the new owner is charged only for the period that begins when he acquires title. There should be mention made of any tenancies that may exist. The seller should undertake to give the buyer possession on the date of closing.

It is important to note that there are dangers for both parties in allowing the buyer to occupy the premises before a deed is delivered.

Ordinarily, if the property burns down or is destroyed by some other cause before the title is transferred, the buyer can cancel the deal and get his money back. But if he is occupying the premises, he must go through with the deal; the seller isn't responsible for the loss.

If the buyer takes possession before the closing and for some reason the deal doesn't go through, the owner may have trouble removing him from the premises. Eviction proceedings against a tenant are relatively simple; eviction of a prospective purchaser is a lengthy and expensive process.

One last point: A contract for the sale of real property should be recorded in order to fix the purchaser's rights to the property.

Preparation for Closing. Between the signing of the contract, and the delivery of the deed and payment of the purchase price, your attorney is busy examining and dealing with the facts turned up by the title report and various tax and city department searches. He may demand that the price be adjusted downward, for example, if the investigation shows the property to be smaller than represented, or discloses onerous restrictions or covenants that reduce its value. He may find it necessary to have certain liens of record (tax liens, mechanic's liens, etc.) and judgments discharged or violations removed. He will obtain in advance, from the seller or his attorney, a proposed statement of the apportioned taxes, etc.

The Closing. At the time appointed for the delivery of the deed, all interested parties assemble: the buyer, the seller, and their attorneys. If a mortgage loan has been arranged, a representative of the lending institution should attend, too. If title is to be insured, a representative of the title company will probably attend, as well.

The documents are carefully examined; all adjustments are brought up to date; insurance policies are assigned to the new owner; other formalities are completed. Documents disposing of defects in the title are presented and examined by the lawyer of the title insurer since, after the closing, it will be responsible for any defects. The purchase price is paid.

Payment of the purchase price will most likely be made by certified or bank cashier's check. It's preferable that the check be made payable not to the seller, but to the purchaser or his attorney, and endorsed to the seller. If, for any reason, the closing should fail or be postponed, the check can then be deposited to the buyer's account, or in the attorney's special account. When delivered to the seller, the check should be endorsed by him. This creates a record of proper payment.

A deed can be delivered in escrow: It is held by a third party until a condition is performed at which time it takes effect. Once a deed is transferred, the new owner should record the conveyance so that the world is on notice should an unscrupulous vendor try to sell the real estate again.

CONCURRENT ESTATES

Several people can own property together. A *tenancy in common* is the simplest form: Each tenant owns an individual share of the entire estate which he can dispose of as he chooses. A *joint tenancy* is created, say, if Tom, Dick, and Harry acquire their interests at the same time, from the same source, for the same duration and have equal rights to possession. This tenancy is distinguished by the *right of survivorship*—the survivor takes the whole estate because a decedent's interest can't be devised. (But each tenant can convey his share by deed while alive. If this occurs, the new owner becomes a tenant in common with the original joint tenants.) These two types of tenancies apply to personal and real property. Real property conveyed to a husband and wife creates a **tenancy by the entirety.** This only pertains to spouses. At the death of one spouse, the other becomes sole owner of the property; while both are alive, both must agree to any disposition of the property.

CO-OPERATIVES AND CONDOMINIUMS

Co-operative Apartments. "Co-ops" combine apartment occupancy with the advantages of home ownership—most significantly, certain tax benefits, since co-op owners can take deductions for property taxes and financing charges. In addition, the owner actually *owns* the apartment, and so can use it to borrow against, or to sell when its value has increased, as is likely. There's no landlord to make a profit on the apartment, and each tenant has a security of tenancy unavailable to those that rent.

A corporation (or perhaps a trust) set up for the purpose holds title to the land and buildings. Each apartment owner acquires shares in the corporation, based on the value of his unit. The right to live in the apartment is set down in a lease between the corporation (or trust) and the tenant, called the co-operator. While the tenant owns his apartment, he must pay a monthly charge—the maintenance cost—that represents his pro rata share of the building's expenses, taxes, insurance, etc. A board of directors manages the corporation, and its members are elected by the shareholders, just as in any corporation. The board sets the monthly charges, and enforces the leases against shareholders who fail to live up to the agreement. Eviction is a possible penalty. Often, approval by the board is needed before a shareholder can sell his shares—and hence his apartment—to someone.

Landlords frequently desire to change a regular rental building into a co-op. Tenants can't be forced to join. What generally happens is that a certain percentage of the tenants (say, 30 per cent) must agree to the switch. Then, those who don't want to buy their apartments remain as rental tenants, but their apartments, once vacated, are sold rather than re-let.

Condominiums. These are like co-ops in that residents in a multi-unit building each own their apartment and have an interest in the common facilities. But condominium units generally can get a mortgage independent of the other units, while the whole of a co-operative building is covered by one mortgage. The condominium plan allows owners more flexibility in refinancing and in selling their property, while under a co-operative plan there is more danger that other apartment owners will be affected if one owner in the building defaults.

Condominium arrangements require a *declaration* that describes the land, buildings and facilities, as well as each owner's rights and duties to them. This document sets down how the condominium will be managed, how costs are apportioned, and how property can be used or disposed of. *Bylaws* are also required to regulate the running of the condominium. Basically, the condominium is run as if it were a corporation, with the builders providing the original plan and the owners having a voice in the management.

CHAPTER TEN

MORTGAGES

What are the various types of mortgages? What are the rights of the borrower, the lender and the buyer? What is a foreclosure? These questions, and others, are dealt with in this chapter.

DEFINITION OF MORTGAGE

A mortgage is a right in real property given as security for a loan. The loan transaction itself is usually stated in a bond which records the borrower's obligation to repay a sum of money at a certain time, or in installments over a certain period of time. Remember: The mortgage is merely a security device; the *note* is the evidence of the debt.

As collateral for the loan and to secure payment of the bond, the lender is given a right to get his money out of the property if the loan is not repaid (or if any installments of interest or principal are not met) by the borrower. The basis of the mortgage is an already existing debt and so the mortgage only lasts for the life of that debt. The mortgage itself must be in writing and should be recorded. Whoever "owns" the debt, "owns" the mortgage.

Mortgage Language. The one who pledges his land as security for a loan is the *mortgagor*.

The lender who receives the mortgage on the property is the *mortgagee*.

The amount of the loan is the *principal*. The mortgagee's compensation for the use of his money is *interest*.

Payments of principal are called *amortization*.

The date of final payment of the principal is the *date of maturity* or the *law day*. This date generally cannot be moved up by prepayment of the debt unless the mortgagee permits it.

Failure to meet any payment of principal or interest is *default*.

The act or method by which the mortgagee gets his money out of the mortgaged property, in the event of default, is *foreclosure*. This is usually accomplished by a sale. (The mortgagee can also sue on the debt, and this bars a foreclosure action unless the judgment isn't satisfied.) If the foreclosure sale doesn't yield enough to satisfy the original debt, the mortgagee can get a *deficiency judgment* to make up the difference, if the person liable to pay the debt has been made a party to the action. In a foreclosure action, all parties with an interest subordinate to the mortgagee's must be notified so their interest can be extinguished by the foreclosure sale.

DEVELOPMENT OF MORTGAGE LAW

In its early use, under the common law, a mortgage was an actual transfer of the property, subject to cancellation on payment of the mortgage debt. This gave the mortgagee conditional title to the property. It meant, in effect, "This property belongs to you, Mr. Lender, unless I pay my debt to you on the promised day. If I do pay it, the property reverts to me." In some states, this is still the law of mortgages.

In most states, however, the title stays with the mortgagor (the borrower) but the mortgagee (the lender) has a lien on it, enforceable if the mortgagor fails to pay. In some states, the mortgagee automatically gets title on nonpayment. In others, the mortgagee has to take legal steps to acquire title or possession or the right to sell, on the debtor's failure to pay. Mortgagors can consent to the mortgagee taking possession before the debt has been paid, but such consent cannot be given until after default.

TYPES OF MORTGAGES

All of the various types of mortgages in general use have one feature in common. They represent an interest in property to secure an obligation to pay money. We will deal here with mortgages on real property. (Mortgages on personal property are called "chattel mortgages.") Mortgages on real property vary according to the purposes they are intended to serve.

Purchase Money Mortgage. When the buyer of real property is without the necessary funds to pay the seller the full purchase price, and the seller is willing to wait for the balance with the property itself as security, the buyer gives the seller a purchase money mortgage. Such a mortgage can be given to a third party (usually a bank) if the latter supplies the purchase money. Purchase money mortgages are generally given priority over earlier judgments against the mortgagor.

Building Loan Mortgage. This is used when the owner of land requires money to build on it, or when the owner of an existing building desires to make repairs. This type of mortgage loan usually calls for the money to be provided by the lender as the work progresses.

Collateral-Security Mortgage. For a mortgage to be given, the money advanced need not have anything to do with the property itself—for purchase, repair, etc. The property merely serves as security for the loan, no matter what use may be made of the borrowed funds. And remember that the mortgage can be given to secure a debt of someone other than the mortgagor.

Subsequent Mortgages. After a mortgage has been given, it's possible to get another loan with a second mortgage as security. The number of mortgages will depend on the value of the property, and on the amount of money borrowed on it. The first mortgage debt must be satisfied before the property is available to settle the second mortgage, and so forth.

Equitable Mortgage. Some security interests in real property are unexecuted or defectively drafted although they do form the basis for a loan. Courts often enforce these "mortgages" to be fair to the lender who gave money on the strength of the security. (However, a verbal promise to give a mortgage in the future generally won't be enforced.) Equitable mortgages do not have precedence over an innocent purchaser of the property or those holding subsequent legal mortgages.

Absolute Deed as Mortgage. Sometimes the debtor gives the creditor an absolute deed to the property. Courts may find this to be, in truth, a mortgage if the debtor can give convincing proof. Important factors: the property's value greatly exceeds the loan; retention of possession by the debtor; the existence of an obligation to the creditor. If a mortgage is found to exist, but the property has already been sold, the debtor has recourse against the creditor but not against an innocent purchaser.

Future Advances. A mortgage can secure loans to be made in the future. If advances are obligatory under the agreement, any debts incurred after the mortgage has been signed are effective only after the mortgagee's claim has been satisfied.

Recording the Mortgage. Mortgages and deeds must be recorded in the county where the property is located. Unrecorded conveyances of land and rights in land are not illegal. They are good against the mortgagors or grantors, but they cannot be enforced against people who have no knowledge of them. So if you are the recorded owner of a lot, you can give good title to a purchaser, even if you have previously given a deed to your son who failed to record it.

Who Lends? How Much? While the great majority of mortgage loans are made by lending institutions—banks, insurance companies, building and loan societies, etc.—many are made by individuals as investments. Most lenders have the property inspected and appraised by experts.

In making appraisals, experts take into account these factors: the neighborhood; the prospects for improvement or deterioration; local zoning laws; the value of adjacent properties; the quality of construction of the buildings on the property; the type of house that stands or is to be erected on the land.

The more "special" the property is, the smaller its market and, generally, the smaller will be the amount loaned on it. Let's say the builder had very special tastes and used glass to the point of eccentricity. Since this doesn't conform to the general taste, its value, in the eyes of the mortgagee, will be lower than a less costly but more conventional house.

Conduct of Mortgagor. The mortgagor, living in peace and quiet, making his regular payments to the bank, sometimes forgets that he is duty bound to guard the mortgagee's interest in the property. He must do nothing to impair the property's value as security.

Of course, if the mortgagor improves the property, thereby increasing its value, the mortgagee will be delighted. But an improvement in the eyes of the owner may not be one in the opinion of the mortgagee. The latter should be kept informed of all alterations, and his written consent obtained for any important change or improvement.

For his own sake, the mortgagor should keep accurate records of all payments of principal and interest. When the debt has been fully paid, he should get from the mortgagee a "satisfaction of mortgage," a document that should be filed with the county clerk to remove the lien record. (Without it, the mortgagor may be required to pay twice.) Some recording officers insist upon seeing the original mortgage as well as the "satisfaction piece."

If the mortgagor can transfer his interest in the land to a third party (the transferee), the land remains the primary source to pay the debt and the mortgagor becomes liable to the transferee for the latter's loss. The mortgagor will be discharged if the mortgagee and the transferee modify the original obligation. If the transferee *assumes* the mortgage, then he, and not the mortgagor, is primarily liable for the debt.

Termination. The mortgage will end when there has been a full payment of the underlying debt. Generally if, after the debt matures, the amount due is offered to the mortgagee, who refuses it, the lien ends but the debt does not. A mortgage also ends if the two interests in the land merge—for example, if the owner of the land inherits the mortgage.

Defenses. If the obligation secured by the mortgage is invalid, the mortgage is, too. But if a mortgage is conveyed by the mortgagor, the buyer will not be able to use the original mortgagor's defenses against the mortgagee. A mortgage generally may be invalidated if it was gotten through fraud, duress or mistake, if the mortgagor was a minor, or if the underlying debt includes interest at a usurious rate. (This last reason doesn't apply to purchase money mortgages.)

Involuntary Transfer of Real Property. In our chapter on debtors and creditors, we will see how property can be sold by execution (enforcement of a judgment). Such a sale passes the title to the purchaser at the sheriff's sale. Similarly, property can be sold for unpaid taxes and to recover money unpaid on a mortgage loan.

Up until the sale is completed, the former owner (or other party who would be adversely affected) usually has the right to redeem the property. This right to redeem is called "equity of redemption."

FROM AUTHOR TO READER

The foregoing material on real property will be most beneficial to you if it has conveyed the fact that the subject is complex, technical and strewn with pitfalls for the unwary. Every paragraph, indeed every sentence, in this chapter has been the subject of many learned volumes. A book of this size can give you only an intimation of what the problems are.

Even lawyers who specialize in real estate practice often find it necessary to do research in the law applicable to particular situations. It would be foolhardy for the layman to go into any phase of a real estate transaction without professional counsel. This applies to many subjects in this book. It is given stress here because so many of us become involved in real estate transactions, and because newly acquired information may tempt some people to proceed by themselves.

CHAPTER ELEVEN

LANDLORD AND TENANT

When can a tenant be evicted? What happens when a tenant remains in possession after a lease has expired? Under what circumstances can a tenant refuse to pay the rent? These and other questions regarding the rights and obligations of the large segment of the population who do not own, but rent, the residential or commercial real estate they occupy are answered in this chapter.

WHAT IS A TENANCY?

In discussing the landlord-tenant relationship, it is necessary to distinguish between a "tenancy" and a mere "license" to be on someone else's property. This "license," or permission, differs from a tenancy in one important respect. In granting a license to use property, the landlord doesn't give up his possession (in the sense of occupancy), use, or control. In a tenancy, or a lease, temporary *possession* and *control* are given to the tenant.

An example of a license arrangement is permission given by a landlord to a vegetable vendor to set up a roadside stand on his land. Another is the renting of space in a public garage.

On the other hand, the hiring of a complete two-car garage would be a tenancy if the key were given to the renter, and if he had control of the property within the terms of the lease.

The discussion that follows has to do only with the arrangements in which the tenant does have control, and where the relationship is that of landlord and tenant.

Rights of Landlord and Tenant. It must be understood that in their agreement a landlord and tenant may include provisions modifying the rights and obligations we are about to discuss. For example, it is commonly the duty and the obligation of the tenant to keep the property in good order. But this obligation may be transferred to the landlord in the lease agreement. The landlord may desire to do necessary repairs in order to protect his interests more adequately.

If the agreement is silent on the subject of repairs, it is the tenant's obligation to make those repairs that are necessary to keep up the property. But he isn't required to make repairs of a substantial structural character.

However, if there is a provision in the lease requiring the tenant to put the property in first-class repair and keep it so, he is bound by this obligation. If the landlord is required by the lease to make all repairs, the tenant must notify him when such repairs become necessary. If, after notification by the tenant, the landlord fails to make those repairs, the tenant can generally make them himself, and charge the landlord for their reasonable cost. But the repairs must be minor in character. If the needed repairs are major ones, the tenant may sue the landlord on the theory that failure to make the repairs has reduced the rental value of the property. Or, some states allow the tenant to surrender the leasehold if the premises become uninhabitable. The obligation to pay rent then ends.

LEASES

The right given by the landlord to the tenant for the use of the landlord's property is called a lease. The landlord is then called a *lessor,* and the tenant a *lessee.*

The term "lease" is commonly used when referring to the written or oral contract between the parties. A technically more accurate meaning for the word "lease" is the right given by the contract, rather than the contract itself.

In our discussion of the Statute of Frauds, we've seen that in most states a lease of property for more than a year must be in writing, and signed. Leases for less than a year generally needn't be in writing to be enforceable.

A lease is an estate in property—it is a piece of ownership carved out of the landlord's rights and measured in time (usually years). He relinquishes this right to you for that period, although he retains the right to recover the property when the lease term is over.

Term of the Lease. It is usual for the term of the tenancy to be fixed for a specified period of years or months in the lease arrangement. Since the termination date is fixed, no notice is required. It sometimes happens, however, that nothing is said about the term. The owner of a cottage might say, for example, "The rent is one hundred and fifty dollars a month. You may move in at the end of the month." This is called a "tenancy at will." If the landlord wishes to end it, he must give the tenant thirty days' notice in writing. If the tenant wishes to end it, he need only move out. A tenant can't assign such a lease.

When the lease is for a year or years (that is, for a set period of time) and the tenant stays on after the lease expires (becoming a *holdover* tenant), the landlord, in some states, may choose to treat the tenancy as continued for another period on the same terms, or he can bring an action to remove the tenant. In New York, the landlord can't hold the tenant to the whole term but can treat him only as a tenant from month to month.

The treatment of holdovers differs in the various states. In some, a holdover tenancy can be ended by notice of either the landlord or the tenant to the other at any time; in other states, the tenancy can be terminated only at the end of the period; in still others, only by notice at the end of the term.

The statutory provisions regarding holdovers, like those applying to any other phase of the landlord-tenant relationship, are rigidly interpreted. Therefore, strict attention should be given to the letter of the law.

Exceptions to the various holdover rules are allowed when the tenant fails to vacate the premises when the lease terminates because of some special circumstances. If, for example, a holdover tenant is unable to move out because of illness, or because he is negotiating with the landlord over the terms of a new lease, he generally isn't considered liable for another full term's rent.

Renewal Clauses. Many leases contain automatic renewal clauses providing that, unless the landlord or the tenant gives due notice to the contrary, the lease will be renewed for a further period. The state of New York, recognizing that tenants often become liable for another term without desiring it, has made such provisions ineffective. Unless the tenant is warned in writing of the existence of such a clause in his lease, at a specified time before renewal so he can give notice, it is without effect. An option to renew can be exercised by the tenant's assignee but not by a sublessee.

Mutual Consent. The term of a lease can be ended by mutual consent before the originally agreed-upon date. For example, a tenant has a lease for one year. At the end of six months, he decides he would like to move elsewhere and takes up the matter with his landlord. The latter has another tenant waiting and is agreeable to ending the tenancy. The tenant turns the keys over to him, and the landlord enters the property to make it ready for the new tenant.

In such a case there has been a surrender and acceptance which terminates the lease. The tenant has surrendered the premises to the landlord, who has accepted them. Generally speaking, it is prudent in such a case for the parties to release each other in writing.

Suppose the landlord doesn't agree to end the term. He says, "You are liable to me for a full year, and I will not release you." Nevertheless, the tenant moves out. In that case, the tenant remains liable to the landlord and is obliged to pay the rent as each installment becomes due. The landlord is usually not obliged to find another tenant to occupy the property for the balance of the term. However, some courts have required landlords to use reasonable efforts to mitigate damages. If another is found, the obligation of the first tenant ends as soon as the property is occupied by the new tenant.

Assignment and Subletting. A tenant can assign to others all or part of his property right in the landlord's property, without reversion, only when the lease agreement is silent on the matter, or if it specifically grants the tenant the right to assign. The effect of an assignment is to transfer to another the rights and obligations of the original tenant.

But this does not discharge the tenant from his personal responsibility to the landlord for paying the rent and satisfying other covenants. This can only be done with the consent of the landlord.

The one to whom the tenant assigns his lease is called an assignee. If the assignee fails to pay the rent, the original tenant is ultimately responsible. In that case, the original tenant has the right to recover the payment he has made from his assignee, who has the principal obligation to meet all the basic covenants.

A sublease only transfers a part of the sublessor's estate, which will revert to him at the expiration of the term. The sublessee is not liable to the landlord on the covenants in the original lease can limit the sublessee's rights.) on the covenants in the sublease. (But the original lease can limit the sublessee's rights.) A sublease should be in writing. A covenant barring only assignments of the lease doesn't

bar subleases, and vice versa.

Most leases for small terms contain restrictions against assigning or subleasing without the landlord's consent. In such cases, the landlord's consent must be obtained, and he may refuse it no matter what the circumstances. But a covenant against assignment doesn't prevent an assignment by operation of law— for example, if the tenant dies or goes bankrupt.

Wherever negotiation is possible, it is advisable for the tenant to be protected by a clause permitting him to assign or sublet. The landlord generally wishes to have some control over the tenants who occupy his premises. Therefore, he may insist that the lease contain a description of the kinds of tenants or types of businesses for which the premises can be sublet or assigned.

Landlord's Consent. Usually a landlord finds most acceptable a provision that the premises will not be assigned or sublet without his consent, but that he will not "unreasonably" refuse his consent. This wording has often been interpreted in the courts to mean that a landlord cannot arbitrarily forbid a subtenancy or assignment to a tenant who is financially responsible and whose business will in no way be harmful to his property.

Often a tenant will wish to make provision for a possible change in the form of his business organization. He may desire to reorganize as a corporation. Since the corporation will be another entity, he may find that he requires the landlord's consent for it to do business in the same space. This should be considered when leases are entered into for business purposes, and suitable provision is made in the lease.

Implied Covenants. The word "covenant" means "agreement" or "obligation." In the chapter on sales, we showed that there is an implied assurance on the part of the seller that the merchandise he is selling is fit for the use for which it is intended. There is no such implication or promise included in a lease transaction, as yet.

Consider this. A landlord had available the second floor of an office building. A prospective tenant was interested in it for use as a private trade school. The parties entered into a lease for a period of two years.

Before the month was up, the new tenant found that the space would not be approved as a school by the Board of Education. He offered this fact as a defense when he was sued for the rent by the landlord.

This is not a good defense, since the landlord isn't responsible for the fact that his space doesn't meet the requirements of the Board of Education. There was no written or implied covenant on his part that the premises could be used in that manner.

Minor exceptions do exist. Sometimes there are implied covenants of fitness for use in leases in buildings not yet completed. And if you rent a house for a short term (the summer, for instance) there's an implied covenant of habitability and a warranty that the building is structurally sound. Of course, the landlord is liable if he has disguised a trap or maintained a nuisance. (Putting these types of covenants in all leases is an idea that seems to be catching on gradually, however.)

There is an implied covenant in all leases that the tenant will be given possession of the premises, that no one else is there or has a right to the property. Similarly, all leases contain an implied *covenant of quiet enjoyment* which means that the landlord promises that he, or someone with superior title, won't evict the tenant. (This covenant isn't breached if the property is condemned by the government.) Breaches of these covenants are breaches of the lease, and are considered by the courts as an ouster or eviction.

For this reason, when the landlord maintains a nuisance, or molests or disturbs the tenant unduly and to a substantial degree, the latter may move and the landlord may be responsible for damages.

Some concepts are evolving, especially in New York, based on these covenants. A *partial actual eviction* arises if, for example, a tenant loses part of the space he rents—he may withhold all the rent if the loss is the landlord's fault; the rent is apportioned if a superior force is the cause. *Constructive eviction* occurs if the landlord's behavior deprives the tenant of his enjoyment of the property to such a degree as to equal an eviction. The tenant must move from the premises and can then sue the landlord for a breach of the covenant of quiet enjoyment.

Payment of Rent. As a rule the chief obligation of the tenant to the landlord is the payment of rent. This obligation is based on the use of the property and so applies if the tenant has actual possession of what he's rented. When nothing is said about when the rent is due, it has been held to be due at the end of a particular period: if the tenancy is by the month, at the end of the month; if by the year, at the end of the year. This, however, is rare, since the time for paying rent is generally fixed by agreement to be the beginning of a period.

There is, however, no liability for rent until its payment falls due. If a tenant under a year's lease just "ups and leaves" at the end of three months, his obligation for each month's rent comes into being at the beginning of each month. If he refuses to pay, the landlord can obtain a series of monthly judgments against him as the rent falls due.

The obligation to pay rent is so basic that even if the landlord is not providing basic services to his tenants, those tenants can't withhold their rent. But they can pay the rent to a court, to be held in escrow until the repairs are made or services given.

If the tenant fails to pay his rent, the landlord generally can't take back the premises on his own, even though he has a right to possession. Preservation of the peace requires that the landlord use legal process to enforce his right to actual possession.

Summary Proceedings. The various states have provided what are known as "summary proceedings" to provide a quick way for landlords to dispossess tenants for failure to pay rent or for staying on after the lease has terminated. These were enacted to avoid the time-consuming procedures of the common-law ejectment action. Procedures (which differ in the various states) should be followed rigorously.

The landlord has a right to begin such summary proceedings and to evict a tenant who fails to pay the rent installment on the day it falls due. But if it is due on the first of the month, and the landlord accepts it on the fifteenth or even later, he no longer has the right to maintain an eviction proceeding. If he continues to accept the rent each month on the fifteenth, he may be said to have waived his right to receive it on the first. He may reinstate this right by demanding payment on the first.

Even where the landlord starts eviction proceedings for nonpayment of rent, it is the common practice of the courts to permit the tenant to pay the rent and end the proceeding. In such cases, the tenant is required to pay court costs.

Services to Tenants. Most apartment leases require the landlord to furnish services like heat, running water, etc. Failure to supply these may constitute an "eviction," and the tenant could move out of the premises and refuse to pay the rent.

But the failure to provide heat or hot water for a day or two is a minor breach and wouldn't be considered sufficient cause for declaring the apartment untenantable. The withholding of rent, under such circumstances, is generally not approved by the law.

As long as the tenant continues to occupy the premises, his obligation to pay rent exists. In most communities, there are statutes that obligate landlords to provide heat, to keep their fire escapes unobstructed, and, in general, to maintain their buildings in good repair. Usually, the most practical solution to a problem of this kind is a complaint to the local health or housing authorities.

Tenancy Subject to Prior Rights. Since tenancy is only the temporary control of a property, the tenant (or lessee) must respect the recorded rights of others in it. Assume that your landlord's property is subject to a mortgage at the time you take a lease on a part of the property. If the landlord defaults in his mortgage payments, you may be forced to vacate if the mortgagee decides to foreclose.

But if your lease was in existence before the property was mortgaged, the reverse is true. That is, the mortgage is subject to the lease, and you cannot be evicted in a foreclosure. Similarly, if the landlord should decide to sell the property, the purchaser's title is subject to your rights as a tenant.

Jones has a one-year lease, beginning in January, on an apartment operated by the "No-Name Realty Company." In March, the company sells the house. On hearing of the sale, Jones feels that, since he made no agreement with the new owner of the property, he is free to terminate the lease and move elsewhere. Smith, his neighbor, who has the same kind of lease for the same term, is concerned that the new owner may be able to evict him.

Actually, the rights of the tenants, as well as their obligations, have not been altered at all by the change in ownership. Their leases are rights in property which the No-Name Realty Company could not sell to anyone, since they had already been conveyed to Jones and Smith. Their rights are superior to those of the new owner, who acquires the property subject to the leases.

The new owner has also acquired all of the obligations of the landlord to Smith and Jones. And all the obligations Smith and Jones owed to the No-Name Realty Company, they now owe to the new owner.

CHAPTER TWELVE

DEBTORS AND CREDITORS

Whether you owe or are owed money, you should have some knowledge of the legal machinery available for the enforcement and collection of debts. Before the courts will help you, you must prove your claim and get a judgment. The judgment must then be enforced by execution. What property can be attached by the sheriff? What is exempt? What is a lien?

PRE-JUDGMENT REMEDIES

When you have been unable to collect money due you and find that you must seek the assistance of the courts, you should know your rights as a creditor, and the other party's rights as a debtor.

Attachment. Assume that the debtor doesn't dispute your claim, that he unqualifiedly acknowledges that he owes you the money—he simply can't or won't pay you. You have the right to secure payment through attachment on his bank account, on his property, on debts due him, etc. This order, generally to the sheriff, will tie up the property until your claim is settled, insuring that property will be available to pay you after the judgment and giving you priority over subsequent lien holders. Attachment of property can also give you the right to sue a creditor in a court where you might not otherwise be able to.

You should know that courts are often loath to allow prejudgment remedies which tie up a debtor's "necessities of life" or substantial property interests without notice and a hearing so that the debtor has an opportunity to contest the claim. Courts will weigh the creditor's interest, however. So if there's a risk the debtor will abscond or will damage the property the creditor has an interest in (as a seller, for instance), the chance of a prejudgment remedy is increased—as long as the debtor's interests are also protected by speedy action, judicial supervision, and the posting of a bond.

Attachment may be expensive: there are fees to pay and a bond to post, and also the danger that you'll be liable for a wrongful attachment of property.

Garnishment is a collection remedy similar to attachment, but is directed at someone who owes a debt to the principal debtor, or has his property. (See **Garnishment of Salary**, p. 58.) This order serves as a notice to the garnishee that the debtor's property will be looked to to satisfy the creditor's claim, so that the debt should not be paid, or the property returned, to the principal debtor, but held pending the outcome of the creditor's suit.

THE JUDGMENT

In order to enforce the rights you get through attachment or garnishment, you have to obtain a judgment of the court, which perfects your lien on the property.

Proving Your Claim. To secure a judgment you must be prepared to prove the indebtedness. The precise nature of the proof depends on the nature of your claim. Take a claim for merchandise that you sold to the debtor. You must be prepared to show there was a contract—an offer by you and an acceptance by him.

The most common proof is an order in writing, describing the merchandise, stating the price, the terms of payment and delivery. Next you must show delivery. The customary evidence of this is a receipt. (Such routine business papers should be filed as documents; you never know when and how they will be useful.)

In the absence of such papers you will have to prove all of these things—order, agreed price, delivery—by the testimony of witnesses. If you cannot provide such proof, your claim will fail even if the defendant says nothing at the trial. The burden is on you to establish your claim.

If you can prove the delivery and acceptance of the goods but not the agreed-upon price, then by evidence, which may include your own testimony, you must prove the reasonable value of the goods that you delivered and he (the debtor) accepted.

Failure to prove the claim discharges the attachment.

Expensive Informality. Here's where the disadvantage of informal business dealings shows up. Hundreds of transactions are arranged by phone. The customer calls the supplier and gives him an order. The supplier drops the goods off at the customer's place, and sends him a bill when he gets around to it. When an account like this turns sour, the supplier has a headache.

To avoid trouble and misunderstanding, every businessman should establish simple methods of keeping accounts in good order. Orders should be in writing; phone orders should be followed by written confirmations. Receipts should be in writing. Bills should be rendered promptly and duplicate copies kept. Statements should be sent out monthly.

If, after receiving a sequence of monthly statements of a debt, a customer disputes the price, he must explain why he was silent so long. The implication of his silence is that he has agreed to the amount.

After the Judgment. You have proved your claim to the satisfaction of the court which has awarded you a judgment. This is formally entered on the judgment record of the court.

Your attorney will then, if required in your state, send a copy of the judgment to the debtor, and the judgment may have to be entered in other jurisdictions where the debtor has property.

EXECUTION

If the debtor then refuses or neglects to pay you, your lawyer will arrange for an *execution*. This is the term used for the enforcement of a judgment. It requires that the officer designated for the purpose—usually the sheriff or the marshall—satisfy the judgment out of the property of the debtor. The sheriff may go to his place of business, for example, levy on (take possession of) the property described in the writ of execution, and sell it at public sale to satisfy the judgment and meet his own fee. The sale must be by public auction.

Garnishment of Salary. If the judgment-debtor is a wage earner, and the sheriff has been unable to collect the amount due out of his property, his salary may be reached. Most states put a limit on the percentage of earnings that may be attached and on the amount of earnings to which a judgment may be applied. Prejudgment wage garnishment is almost impossible. However, this procedure is more likely after a judgment has been entered, although courts see wages as a necessity of life, and give them special treatment. You should seek to satisfy a claim from almost any other type of assets.

Property Exempt from Attachment. Certain items of property may not be seized to satisfy judgments. State laws have established such exemptions to avoid working undue hardship and distress on debtors, and to prevent them from becoming public charges. In New York, for example, the sheriff may not seize and sell basics such as clothing, certain furniture, food, etc. Generally such statutes are outdated as to what property is considered necessary. Debtors can convert their assets into exempt property to defeat creditors—the assets are then free from their claims—as long as there is no actual fraud.

These exemptions don't apply if the debt was contracted to provide purchase money for any of the exempt items. Nor do they apply if the debt is owed to a domestic servant, laborer, or mechanic as wages. Other special exemptions favor members of the armed forces and veterans.

These examples should be sufficient to illustrate the nature of the exemptions and their purpose to prevent the debtor from being stripped absolutely clean, and hampered unduly in earning a living.

STATUTORY LIENS

Special Rights in Debtor's Property. We have seen how creditors go about enforcing their claims against those who owe them money. Some creditors have special means of enforcing payment, called *liens*, arising from the special circumstances of the transaction or by agreements between the parties.

Suppose a debtor's assets include money in the bank; the building in which he conducts his business; an automobile; a powerboat; merchandise at a railway depot and in a warehouse; machinery and equipment in his plant and other machinery under repair in a machine shop. His equally varied debts include unpaid bills for money owed to a contractor for building renovations; money owed to the garage for storage, service and gasoline for his car; to the operator of the boat basin for service and fuel for his boat; to the warehouse for storage of his merchandise; to the railway for freight held for him at the depot; and to the machinist for repairing his machines.

The garageman, the building contractor, the boat basin operator, the railroad, the warehouse, and the machinist all have liens. Each has the right to hold the debtor's property in his possession until the bill is paid. If it isn't paid within a reasonable time, each has the right (in most states) to sell the property to collect the debt.

Mechanic's Lien. Most "liens," or rights in property, arise from work performed on the property. In the example given above, all of the creditors (lienors) have actual possession of the property, except the building contractor. He has what is known as a "mechanic's lien" against the real estate on which he worked.

The way in which the mechanic's lien may be enforced varies according to the laws of each state. Generally, the claim must be recorded, and notice must be sent to the owner. Often the lien holder is someone who has made no contract with the owner himself but with some general contractor engaged by the owner. This doesn't ordinarily disqualify one who actually works on the property from having a mechanic's lien. The effect of the recording is to give notice to prospective buyers of the property that the claim is in existence and the property is subject to the lien.

Lien Through Possession. All of the other liens depend on possession of the property by the lienor. Should he voluntarily give up possession, the lien is gone. Even if he gets the property back somehow, the lienor has no further right to keep it because he gave up possession before collecting the money owed to him. This doesn't mean, however, that he can't collect his debt like any other creditor; but he has lost his special right in the property, and the special means of collecting his debt.

Artisan's Lien. The language of the New York statute is very plain. It will serve to describe the liens of craftsmen and repairmen on all kinds of movable property. "A person who makes, alters, repairs or in any way enhances the value of an article of personal property at the request or with the consent of the owner, has a lien on such article, while lawfully in possession thereof, for his reasonable charges for the work done and the materials furnished, and may retain possession thereof until such charges are paid."

Hotelkeeper's Lien. An innkeeper may detain the baggage and other property of a guest who fails to pay his bill. This lien also depends on possession. He may detain whatever property the guest brought into the hotel until his charges are paid.

Rights of Lienors. We have already mentioned that the rights of lienors are superior to those of general creditors. What is even more important is the fact that the rights of lienors we have described, in the property in their possession, are superior to other specific rights in it.

To illustrate: Suppose a car in a garage is being held for the payment of a bill for storage. The car has not been fully paid for; it has, in fact, been mortgaged to a bank as security for the purchase price. The mortgage was made when the car was purchased and long before it came into the garageman's possession. It was recorded at the time, so that the bank's rights in the car are, for all legal purposes, known to the world. The bank has the right to repossess the car and sell it to satisfy its claim. Nevertheless, the garageman's bill must be paid first.

If you are a lienor—that is, if you hold property upon which you have worked, or which you made, or which has been stored with you—you must keep it in your possession, or your lien becomes invalid. However, it is usually possible to arrange for a bond to be posted in your favor, in exchange for the property. When the fund out of which your claim can be paid is assured, the property itself can be surrendered.

Arrest. It is rare for a debtor to be jailed for failing to pay someone, but it can occur. Nonpayment of alimony is the most common reason, although nowadays this occurs less frequently as it prevents a party from raising money to meet the obligation. Debtors can also be arrested—by an "execution on their person"—for willful fraud or if there is evidence that they plan to abscond or will try to conceal property to take it out of the reach of creditors.

Devices To Defraud Creditors. Persons heavily in debt, seeing the creditors closing in and the moment approaching when they will lose everything to the sheriff, have been known to do some pretty desperate things to hold on to some part of their property. Such acts, if their purpose is to hinder, delay or deceive creditors, are fraudulent.

When someone who has incurred debts beyond his ability to pay transfers a piece of real estate to his spouse or anyone else, without getting a fair price for it, such a transfer is fraudulent and may be set aside by the court. Even when a fair price is paid, the sale may be set aside if the purpose was to defraud creditors.

In such cases, fraudulent intent must be proved. Ordinarily, when no money is paid for the property, fraudulent intent is presumed. But if the debtor sells property to an innocent party—one who knows nothing, and has no reason to know or to inquire about the seller's motives for the sale—the latter is protected and his right to keep the property he bought and paid for will not be disturbed.

Preferential Settlements. Other people in difficulties, seeing that the more importunate creditors will get all their property with the more considerate creditors getting nothing, have tried to pay some of their debts selectively, giving certain creditors preference over the others. Such preferences are illegal under the bankruptcy laws if the debtor is insolvent at the time the preferential payments are made. (See definition of insolvency in the glossary.) It's not a preference, however, to apply property to secure a new loan or to make a gift (if it's really a gift).

Settlement by Assignment. Still other debtors, desiring to protect all creditors equally, have taken advantage of a measure permitted by law—the transfer of all of their property (referred to as assets) to a person (known as an assignee or trustee) for the benefit of all their creditors, who must receive notice of the plan. The job of the assignee is to convert the assets into money with which to pay the claims of the creditors. Creditors can no longer levy on the property, as legal title belongs to the assignee. The debtor can't retain any benefits in the transferred property, or the plan will be seen as a fraudulent transfer.

If not enough money is realized to pay the creditors in full—and this is usually the case —there will be a distribution in proportion to the amount of each claim. If the sum realized totals 40 per cent of the total debt, each creditor is paid 40 per cent of the amount owed him less the expenses of the assignee. But the debtor generally is still liable for the full amount of his debts.

Preferred Creditors. Certain claims are given priority. Thus, wages of unpaid employees come first and are paid in full if enough money is realized from the sale of the assets. Other preferred claimants include the government for unpaid taxes.

Next come *secured creditors*, people who never extended credit to the debtor, in the strict sense of the word. Instead of relying on the debtor or his business, they demanded some form of security. So a creditor who loaned money on the security of a mortgage on property or, like a pawnbroker, on the pledge of some article of value, is a secured creditor. Secured creditors are entitled to the full amount of their claims.

All the rest are *general creditors* and take a proportionate share of what is left.

Assignments for the benefit of creditors are provided for by state law and must be accomplished carefully, in strict observance of the statute. For this, the assistance of an attorney is indispensable. An assignment is more flexible and speedier than bankruptcy and may raise more money for creditors. But discontented creditors can often force a debtor to declare bankruptcy once he has chosen the assignment route.

A composition—where the creditors agree to accept an immediate payment of less than the amount due—discharges the debtor for the rest of the money owing to the parties to the contract. This procedure, too, may raise more money for the creditors than bankruptcy.

Before discussing bankruptcy, it will be worthwhile to say a word about two special types of creditors. As we have seen above, *secured creditors* have special interests in the debtor's assets which arise from a security agreement. This document must contain certain information and must be filed for it to be effective. In order not to jeopardize your favored status as a secured creditor, you should always work with a lawyer in this area, as the law is very complicated. A *judicial lien creditor* has certain rights because he has obtained a judgment against a debtor. Once he gets the judgment, the creditor should record it as soon as possible. Priority among creditors is established by the order of filing liens (for realty) or by the order of levy (for personalty). It's not at all a simple process—this area of the law is extremely complex and has strict requirements (which differ widely in the various states) that must be followed as to procedure and timing. If you make even a slight error, you can lose the security for your debt—epecially if there are several other creditors and a limited amount of property. Again, to proceed in this area without legal assistance is foolhardy.

BANKRUPTCY

Almost anyone can become a voluntary bankrupt. Creditors can also commence an action for involuntary bankruptcy if the debtor is insolvent and has committed an act of bankruptcy. These actions—like fraudulent conveyances, preferences, and assignments for the benefit of creditors—may be legal, but they involve an admission of insolvency or willingness to be adjudged bankrupt. Bankruptcy is a matter over which the federal district courts have exclusive jurisdiction, and the complex law governing the process is the federal bankruptcy statute.

Bankruptcy Proceedings. These are very formal and technical. Attorneys must follow the rules set down in order to garner the benefits of bankruptcy. The procedure involves, first, a proceeding to have the debtor declared (adjudicated) a bankrupt. Years ago this had criminal connotations. Today it means only that the debtor is insolvent—that is, he lacks sufficient property to pay off his debts. You should be aware, however, that there is a certain stigma attached to bankruptcy, since, in effect, a bankrupt leaves his creditors holding the bag for his mistakes.

The district court acts through a referee who has the powers of a judge to decide all matters that come up in the proceeding. The court will generally appoint a receiver to gather the property of the bankrupt, termed the "bankrupt estate." The assets of the estate include all the debtor's property owned at the date bankruptcy is filed, as well as property transferred to defraud creditors. Assets not yet earned, wages, for example, aren't included. The creditors act through a trustee who ultimately takes over the bankrupt estate from the receiver and settles with the creditors under the supervision of the referee. The trustee can void the liens of many prior creditors, as well as some conveyances (transfers of property), in order to amass the bankrupt estate. The proceeding results in a discharge of the bankrupt debtor from all of his debts that can be discharged by law. (Certain debts are not affected by discharge. If not enough money is realized from liquidation of the assets, the bankrupt will still have to pay them when he is able. These include federal, state or local taxes; debts arising because of fraud; alimony,

maintenance and support of a wife and children; damages for certain other torts; recent wage claims; the costs of the proceedings; etc.)

REORGANIZATIONS

Sometimes the liquidation of a business in bankruptcy proceedings is unsound and wasteful. If the company's difficulty is obviously temporary, or if relief from its obligations for a period of time would permit re-establishment on a sound basis, the law provides another method of settlement. (Comparable plans exist for wage earners, too.)

This calls for an arrangement between debtor and creditors, made with court approval, which would give the business a chance to survive. Such arrangements, or reorganizations, are widely used in the case of distressed companies that have built up a substantial business and employ many people, and which can pay part of the debt immediately. The balance may then be paid over a period of time, on terms agreed to by the creditors and approved by the court, to permit the company to continue in business.

CHAPTER THIRTEEN

PATENTS, COPYRIGHTS, TRADEMARKS, TRADE NAMES

We are an inventive people. Patent applications flow into Washington by the tens of thousands each year. But not all of the applicants are granted patents. More significantly, not all the patents that are issued pass the final test of validity.

In this chapter, we will deal with the procedures to secure and protect rights in inventions, trademarks, trade names, and the exclusive right to publish and sell literary and artistic works. The method is, basically, to give the creator monopoly in the use of his creation, at least for a while. It is felt that this best serves the public by encouraging the invention and dissemination of new products and ideas or by clarifying the manufacturing history of a product.

WHO GRANTS PATENTS?

None of the fifty states can issue a patent to an inventor. That function has been reserved by the Constitution to the federal government. It is carried out by the U. S. Patent Office, one of the bureaus of the Department of Commerce. The Patent Office keeps records of all patents, compares applications claimed to be new with those on file, and rejects the applications or issues the patents.

To encourage invention and new ideas, the government gives a monopoly for seventeen years—less for a design patent. (Generally, there's no right of renewal.) For this period, the creator is entitled to use his invention exclusively, free from interference, in any way he likes. But this uninterrupted exploitation of the invention may be open to attack and interference.

Test Through Litigation. You might think that the issuance of a patent after the detailed searches, claims, examinations, etc., would settle the matter. The fact is that no patent has passed the acid test until it has been the subject of a lawsuit. The courts have declared invalid a great many patents that the Patent Office, after due examination of the applications and acceptance of the fees paid by the patentees, has issued.

Some of the reasons the courts have set so many patents aside are: The invention is not really new or useful; the patent holder was not the original inventor; the invention was in use before the inventor made his application, and the application was made more than a year after the first use or sale of the patented device; the invention had been described in a printed publication before the date asserted by the inventor as the day he made his invention.

Sometimes the patent is perfectly valid, yet does not, by itself, give the inventor the right to manufacture the article. An example is the invention of a new method of manufacturing something which someone else has the exclusive right to produce. About the only thing the inventor can do is to negotiate with the one who has the right to manufacture the article, offering him the improved method.

Is Your Invention Patentable? For a patent to be issued to you by the U. S. Patent Office, your application must show that you have invented or discovered an *art, machine, manufacture,* or *composition of matter*—or any *improvement* of any one of these already in existence. It must be both *new* and *useful.*

Your invention must not have been known or used in this country *before* the date affirmed by you as the time you made your invention or discovery. And, regardless of the date of your invention or discovery, it must not have been patented or described in any printed publication (here or abroad) and not have been in use or on sale in the United States for more than one year prior to the date of application.

Note how important the dates are. These seeming technicalities can make the difference between the grant and refusal of a patent. Therefore, it is urgent for an inventor to keep accurate records, and to make disclosures (usually to or through his patent attorney) of a kind that would enable him to prove, later, the exact date when he conceived his invention, when he made the application, etc.

Is It Necessary To Obtain a Patent? You are under no obligation to appy for a patent. You may, if you wish, maintain complete secrecy regarding your new device, formula, process, etc. If you believe that your secret can be preserved, you can make use of your invention without a patent. This has been done successfully in the past; but if someone discovers your secret, you probably have no legal protection against his infringement, since you could have safeguarded your invention. Few inventions are of a nature to sustain such risks.

Rights in Patents. When inventors collaborate in developing something patentable, both their names appear on the patent and they are called "joint patentees." The patent rights then belong to each separately, in the sense that each has the right to make licensing arrangements with manufacturers.

When more than one person has patent

rights, there is no monopoly. The licensing situation may then become so confused that the value of the patent, as far as realizing profits from it are concerned, may be destroyed. Joint inventors should be under contract with one another to avoid such confusion.

If an employee was hired for the express purpose of making inventions relating to certain subject matters, and does so in the course of employment, the invention "belongs" to the employer and he can have the patent assigned to him.

Assignment of Rights. An inventor can assign all or part of his interest in an invention at any time—before or after he has made the invention, before or after he has applied for a patent, before or after the patent has been granted. Often the inventor is a technician or engineer working for a firm that has engaged him to develop inventions. The firm pays him for his work and provides all the materials, equipment and facilities. In return, it requires an assignment of the resulting patents.

In all cases, the patent must be applied for in the name of the actual inventor. The assignment, if any, will be registered by the U. S. Patent Office if the information is supplied.

It is important that the terms of the assignment be specified in a written agreement between the inventor and the assignee. It is also important, in order to protect the rights of the assignee, that the assignment be recorded with the Patent Office.

License. When a patentee (or his assignee) grants someone else permission to use some of his rights, he does so by a license agreement. Such a document should be drawn with extreme care—although oral licenses are valid, too.

Are the license rights to be exclusive? Are they to be worldwide? Are they to be limited to a certain geographic area? To a certain trade or business? For the duration of the patent or for a shorter time? What happens in the case of infringement? These and other problems that can be anticipated, arising out of the nature of the specific patent and the needs of the parties, should be clearly answered in the agreement.

Generally, the licensee can't transfer the license to someone else. And, if royalties due to the inventor aren't paid, the license isn't affected—the inventor must sue for the money due him.

Patent Violations. If a valid patent has been infringed, the patent holder can get an injunction against further interference, or damages —whichever is needed to protect the property interest. Damages are generally limited to fair royalties for the use of the patented invention.

Patent Counsel. Our treatment of patents is necessarily limited. But from the material presented, it should be clear that this is a highly technical subject. While it is possible for an inventor to secure a patent by himself, it's unwise for him to do so. If he has a worthwhile invention, he should protect his rights in it by getting the help of a competent patent lawyer as soon as he can.

COPYRIGHT

Like our patent laws, the copyright laws are federal. They are managed by the United States Government through the Copyright Office of the Library of Congress. A new copyright law—the first major revision in over sixty-five years—went into effect on January 1, 1978. All works will receive copyright protection from the moment of creation, rather than from the time of publication. The copyright—the *exclusive* ownership of a work and the right to print, publish, display, perform or present it to the public—lasts for the life of the creator plus fifty years. Copyrights already in existence, under the old law, if renewed, will be extended to last for a total term of seventy-five years.

What May Be Copyrighted? In general, all writings and artistic works can be copyrighted. Included in this category are works fixed in tangible forms (as opposed to ideas) such as books of all kinds—fiction, nonfiction, anthologies, encyclopedias, dictionaries, directories,

etc.—periodicals, newspapers, lectures, sermons, addresses prepared for oral delivery, dramatic and musical compositions, maps, works of art, models or designs for works of art, certain reproductions of works of art, drawings or models of a technical or scientific character, photographs, movies and screenplays, etc. As a result of the new copyright law, protection exists in two new areas: the use of copyrighted material in jukeboxes and on cable television is now regulated.

One cannot copyright a work that has been copyrighted previously, or a work that belongs to the public. But it is possible to copyright a collection that includes previously copyrighted works, with the permission of the copyright owner; and it is also possible to copyright a collection that includes works in the *public domain.*

A notice of copyright must appear on published copies of copyrighted works. However, on the whole, formal requirements are fewer than before and there is some leniency in enforcement. Depositing copies of books and such with the Library of Congress, and registration, are no longer necessary to keep one's copyright—although failure to do so may incur a fine, or the loss of certain benefits. The registration fee has been raised to $10, but a number of essays or poems, for example, under certain circumstances may be registered in a single registration.

Who Is Entitled to Copyright? The copyright in most cases is owned by the author, and may be assigned to the publisher or proprietor of the work. The circumstances of each case dictate who should get the copyright. Copyrights and the right to copyright are transferable, and may pass by will or according to the laws of intestacy.

You needn't be a citizen to get a copyright, as long as you reside in the United States. Nonresidents can get copyright protection if they live in a country that offers similar privileges to U.S. citizens.

If a work was made for hire, the employer is regarded as the "author." However, the employee must have prepared the work in the course of his or her employment, and the parties must have agreed, in writing, that the employer is to be the "author." Authors will be able to copyright their contributions to a collective work, which can be copyrighted as a whole by the publisher.

If an author has assigned his copyright, the new law allows him or his family to reclaim the copyright, or renegotiate the contract, after thirty-five years.

Infringement. If the copyright owner has complied with the law, he may bring legal action against anyone who violates his exclusive rights. Infringement can be stopped by an injunction, and the infringer can be made to pay damages as well as to turn over all his profits to the copyright owner. In addition, willful infringement of a copyright is a misdemeanor, and those found guilty are subject to fine and imprisonment.

The new law recognizes that "fair use" can be made of certain copyrighted items. For instance, libraries can photocopy certain material if they follow the proper guidelines. And photocopied material can be used in schools if it isn't done extensively so as to substitute for the purchase of complete works. There will surely be further developments in this area as the new law is tested.

Public Domain. Works that have failed to meet the statutory formalities required for their protection, or whose copyrights have expired, are said to be in the "public domain." This means that anyone is free to print, publish, sell or use them without interfering with anyone's rights. If you wish to present a copyrighted play, you must make arrangements with the owner of the copyright. You are free, however, to produce any of Shakespeare's plays, for example, or any other play whose copyright has expired. These are in the public domain.

How Copyright Is Obtained. Of first importance, in the case of published materials, is the notice of copyright. This consists of the symbol, ©, or the word "copyright" followed by

the name of the owner and the year in which the work was published.

Within three months of the date of publication, two copies of the printed work, with the imprinted notice described above, and a copyright application should be sent by mail to the Register of Copyrights, Washington, D.C. As we have seen, this deposit, and the registration of the copyright, don't affect the copyright, but should be done to preserve all your rights. The new copyright law has changed a number of the formalities and a good many of the benefits relating to copyright protection. For this reason, it is advisable to avail oneself of competent legal counsel. Questions about the new law can also be addressed directly to the Copyright Office.

TRADEMARKS

The purpose of a trademark is to identify or distinguish merchandise so that it can be recognized as being sold, produced or manufactured by a particular person or firm. The longer it has been used, the stronger is the right of the person using it. Unlike patented inventions, a trademark needn't be new or original—but it can't be in use as a trademark already.

A trademark may be registered with the United States Patent Office if it is a distinctive design, combination of letters, words or figures. Generally, a person's name won't be registered as a trademark unless it is incorporated in a distinctive design or written in a distinctive manner. The picture of a living person can't be registered without his written consent. The Patent Office will refuse to register an immoral or scandalous design. And no mark will be accepted if it uses the flag of the United States, of a foreign country, or any similar emblem.

Other considerations must be weighed in choosing a trademark. A coined word ("Kodak") is best; a common descriptive term ("Gold Medal") is a weak mark. A descriptive term often leads to litigation because competitors feel they should be able to use it, too. In using the trademark in advertising, it's best to use the name of the product as an adjective preceding the generic term for the product to keep the trade name from passing into the language as a common noun. Don't make a verb out of the name, or use it with your company's name as a possessive. Also, set off the trademark from the rest of the advertising copy and note in the ad that the name is a trademark. In this way, you are protected against the chance that the trademark will become descriptive of the type of product rather than of a specific brand.

Need for Registration. It's entirely possible to use a trademark without registering it. Under the common law, the use of your trademark or trade name by someone else is unfair competition, and you can probably stop it by legal proceedings.

However, registration has the effect of giving notice to the world that this mark is yours. After registration, no one can offer the excuse that he never heard of your mark. And after using the mark in commerce for five years, registration will strengthen your position should the use of the mark be challenged.

Classifications. A trademark is registered as belonging within a certain category of merchandise. It is possible for a different manufacturer to use the same mark on merchandise in another class so different that there is no likelihood of confusing or deceiving the public. For example, if your product is bicycles, there is no likelihood of public confusion or deception in the use and registry of your trademark by a manufacturer of cosmetics. In some cases, however, a name may be so distinctive that its use in connection with a product in an entirely different class might be considered unfair competition. This is especially true if the second product is shown to be of inferior quality, which would reflect badly on the first product.

This field, too, is highly technical, for there are several methods of registration and classification. If you have a trademark with

any sort of purchaser recognition, it is advisabe to see an attorney who specializes in this area in order to protect the good will that this trademark has created. Remember: If you proceed improperly in this area, and don't keep the proper records and a careful eye on the competition, you might lose the right to use your trademark exclusively.

TRADE NAMES

Often people say "trade name" when they mean "trademark." "Trade name" is specifically applied to a business rather than to a product.

For business reasons, an individual may adopt or use a name, not his own, for his firm. If Horne, a dealer in prefabricated barns, wants to be known as the Eastern States Prefabricated Barn Company, he must file a certificate in the state where he conducts his business, giving both his trade name and address, and his own name and address. This makes it possible for people dealing with the Eastern States Prefabricated Barn Company to ascertain, if they wish, that Horme is the man behind the trade name.

The county clerk, or any other official in charge of registering trade names, will generally refuse to accept one that is identical with another name already on file, or so similar to it as to cause confusion. State law governing unfair competition generally allows the first user of a trade name to enjoin its subsequent use by another if confusion or economic injury is likely to result.

CORPORATE NAMES

Individual corporate names are important so that the public knows exactly whom it is dealing with. Each state maintains its own index of corporate names. Clerks in the Secretary of State's office will examine the index to establish whether the proposed new name will conflict with any existing corporate name. It is important to remember, however, that the grant of permission to use a certain name in one state is no guarantee that it will not conflict with a name registered in another state.

POINTERS

Before selecting a name for your firm or product, have a search made. Searching services are available to your attorney at moderate cost. They cover the fifty states. A search of this kind will assure you that your name will not conflict with another, Furthermore, the fact that you made the search will serve as evidence of your good faith, if any conflict should arise.

UNFAIR COMPETITION

It isn't illegal to compete. There is nothing in the law to prevent one person or firm from entering into the same business as someone else who is already established, and trying to take his trade away. (In a way, this is what federal antitrust laws set out to accomplish.) Competition can be damaging to the man who was first on the scene; but there is nothing he can do but actively *compete* to keep his business.

However, the *methods* used in such competition *are* the concern of the law. If a manufacturer tries to confuse the consumer into believing that his firm is actually his competitor's, by making his name sound or appear to be the same, or by using a mark, design or package that would lead a not-too-careful buyer to believe that the merchandise sold is the same as the other manufacturer's—that is unfair competition. So is spreading false tales about a competitor that are just short of slander, or, in some cases, hiring away key employees in order to get secret business information about a competitor. Courts will not only stop such conduct by injunctions, but will often award damages. Most of the laws in this area are state statutes designed to raise the standards of business morality. The aim is to attack improper methods; so if one can get another's customers or trade secrets by fair means, that's perfectly acceptable to the states.

Sometimes companies, in an effort to halt the loss of certain secrets by the hiring away of knowledgeable employees, will bind the employees to refrain from competing with the employer. Such convenants are legal as long as they don't restrict the employees too much. For example, they can't bar competition in too large a geographic area, for too long a time.

Federal Trade Commission. Sometimes the methods used in competition are damaging not only to a competitor, but to a whole industry or to the public. In such cases, the Federal Trade Commission may act to stop the unlawful practice.

Among the practices watched by the Commission are: false or misleading advertising, misbranding, failure to indicate that a product is of foreign manufacture, price discrimination, price fixing, illegal restraint of trade or competition. Some of these problems are also monitored by state consumer groups.

The Commission acts on complaints from consumers and businesses, and does a certain amount of investigation and "police work" on its own. When a complaint is entered, the Commission notifies the accused of the nature of the charge and schedules a hearing at which the accused firm can answer the complaint and defend its practice.

If the decision goes against it, the accused may have recourse to an appeals procedure calling upon the Commission to review its decision. A finding in favor of the defendant can also be reviewed.

If the final decision is that the firm's practice is illegal, an order halting the practice is entered. Federal statutes also provide for stiff penalties for practices that hinder competition. If, before the hearing takes place, the firm voluntarily agrees to stop the criticized practice, the proceeding might be dropped.

CHAPTER FOURTEEN

WILLS: THE INHERITANCE OF PROPERTY

Sooner or later all property in a state passes through its courts. This is because the law regulates the distribution of everybody's property after his death. One of our most valuable rights is the right to make a will and to control the disposition of our worldly goods after death. But whether we make a will or not, the inheritance of our property is strictly regulated by law. In this chapter, we discuss wills—why and how they should be made.

The Right To Make a Will. One of our most important rights is the power to dispose of our property after we die. Every adult of sound mind can make a will disposing of any kind of property. In many states, minors can make wills disposing only of personal property.

In every case, the law of the state should be followed to the letter. But if a move to a different state is foreseen, comply with the stricter guidelines. Each state has its own definition of what a valid will is, and its own special procedure for executing it.

Since wills become effective after death, many people mistakenly believe they should wait until death is imminent before making their wills. Others superstitiously fear that arrangements to take effect after death will bring them prematurely to the attention of the Grim Reaper. And others have the mistaken notion that the act of making a "Last Will and Testament" has such finality that they can't change their minds.

All are in error. A will should be made early in life or, at any rate, while one is not under the stress of a critical illness. Making a will has never been a cause of death. And a will is not final unless it is the last one made. The person making a will can change it simply by making a new one or by adding a codicil to the will he already has. He can do this as often as he wishes.

Informal Wills. Another error is the idea that any expression of wishes or a letter of instruction can serve as a will. It can't. To be valid, a document must fill the minimum requirements of state law. A letter may prove to be a good will, but it would have to be an unusual letter indeed to comply with state law.

Oral wills are recognized only in the most extreme circumstances—these are described in the laws of each state. In New York, only a soldier, sailor or merchant seaman in actual service can make such a will. Even so, the oral will must be proved by at least two witnesses.

The same people—soldiers, sailors and merchant seaman in actual service—are permitted to make handwritten wills. These need not be witnessed. If, after making such a will, the soldier or sailor is discharged from service, such a will remains effective for only a year after his discharge.

Is a Will Essential? Not if you are satisfied with the way your property will be distributed without a will. The laws of each state provide for dividing up the property of those who die and leave no will. In these statutes, the legislatures had in mind the average family, with average relationships, obligations and loyalties.

But what family is average in every respect? If you want to favor one relative over another for reasons of your own, or if you want to leave some of your property to a friend or relative who would get nothing under state law, you must make a will. And it must be a valid will.

The only way you can assure yourself that your will, when executed, will accomplish what you desire is to have it drawn by a competent person. This means you must have the advice and assistance of a lawyer—not a notary, not an accountant, not a bank clerk, not a stationer who sells you a printed form, but a practicing lawyer in whom you can confide.

You should have a full and uninhibited discussion with him concerning your property, your insurance and your plans for your family. This may save considerable hardship, bitterness and expense for those you love. And it may make the difference between the success or failure of the plans you want realized.

Important Terms. A man who makes a will is called a *testator;* a woman, a *testatrix.*

One who dies without making a will is said to have died *intestate.*

A man charged with carrying out the terms of a will is called an *executor;* a woman is called an *executrix.*

A man appointed by the court to manage the distribution of the property of one who dies intestate is called an *administrator;* a woman is an *administratrix.*

The document by which the court authorizes the administrator or administratrix to act is called *letters of administration.*

A *trust* is a right in property (real or personal) held by one person for the benefit of another. A person appointed by the testator to carry out the terms of a trust is called a *trustee.* Trusts may be *revocable* or *irrevocable* depending on whether the creator has kept a power to end the trust. There are different tax consequences for the two types of trusts.

Property entrusted to a person to be held and managed by him for the benefit of another, is said to be given *in trust.*

A *testamentary trust* is created by will; an *inter vivos trust* is created before death.

The one for whose benefit trust property is held or managed is called the *beneficiary.*

A transfer of property in a will is called a *legacy.*

One who receives such a transfer is called a *legatee.*

A transfer by will of real property is called a *devise.*

A transfer by will of personal property is called a *bequest.* Thus, there can be *devises in trust* and *bequests in trust.*

The entire property left by a testator or intestate is called his *estate.* The property left after all specific legacies have been made is called the *residuary estate.*

A *codicil* is an addition or amendment to a will.

The administrator or executor of a man's estate is also called his *personal representative.*

A devise or bequest that cannot be carried out by the executor is said to **lapse.**

Proving that a will is real and complies with state law is called *probate.* A will is *offered for probate* in *probate proceedings* before the *surrogate,* who presides over the *surrogate's court.* This court is especially designated by law to deal with the property of *decedents*—people who have died.

The terms *heirs, heirs at law* and *next of kin* have various meanings depending on how they are used. They have often been used carelessly and this has given rise to a great deal of litigation. Most states define these terms in the law that fixes the distribution of the property of an intestate.

In general, *heir* means one who has the right to inherit any property of a decedent.

Heirs at law are those who would receive the property by law if the decedent died intestate. Those who receive an intestate's property are also called *distributees.*

No one can be an "heir" of a living person. He can be an *apparent heir.*

A beneficiary isn't obliged to accept what someone leaves him—he can *disclaim* a bequest in whole or in part as long as he hasn't already accepted it or its benefits. All he has to do is send a written and irrevocable refusal of the interest to the decedent's representative within nine months of the creation of the interest. This device can be beneficial both to the estate of the decedent and to the beneficiary.

Provisions of the Will. The first part of your will is like thousands of others. It is the conventional declaration of what the document is:

I, JONATHAN FRANCIS JONES, *being of sound and disposing mind and memory, do make, publish and declare this to be my* LAST WILL AND TESTAMENT.

Then you give instructions for the payment of your debts. If you have any special wishes as to funeral arrangements, you state them here to help facilitate matters—certain localities require formalities to be met before cremation is allowed, for instance. (Instructions of this sort should also be left with someone you trust in case the will is not consulted until after your burial.)

1. I direct that all my just debts and funeral expenses be paid by my executor hereinafter named.

You then get down to the business of giving away your worldly goods. In the case of specific legacies, it is advisable to provide that their share of estate taxes, as well as any shipping costs, be borne by the residuary estate so that the beneficiaries aren't required to pay to receive their legacies.

2. I give, bequeath and devise to my trusted friend and secretary, Gerald Jackson, my property at Lake Hopatcong, and all of its contents and furnishings.

3. I give and bequeath to my chauffeur, Stanley Smith, my Cadillac automobile.

Now we come to the family and we try to deal with each child according to the special problems raised by his age, personality, or financial position. Or, perhaps you consider one the black sheep and want to cut him off. In most states it is possible to disinherit children for any reason, or for no reason. But even when disinheriting a child, you should mention him in the will. Otherwise, there might be a presumption that he was accidentally overlooked. To cover the case of the black sheep, language like this can be used:

4. I have in mind, but have deliberately made no provision for, my son Bertram, for reasons which I deem good and sufficient.

Some testators prefer a token gift:

To my son Bertram I give and bequeath the sum of ten dollars ($10).

To take care of one who is already well fixed:

5. I have in mind but have made no provision in this, my Will, for my beloved daughter Florence, since she has been well provided for by her uncle Oscar.

Children born after the death of the testator (posthumous children) are usually treated like the other filial heirs, or are given the share they would have received had the parent died intestate. Adopted children are generally treated like nonadopted children.

To make provision for a minor child, you may wish to set up a testamentary trust for him during his minority, the principal of which will pass to him when he reaches a mature age:

6. I give and bequeath to my trustee hereinafter named (or to his successor) the sum of $250,000, in trust, for the following uses and purposes: to invest the same in bonds of the United States, in mortgages on improved real estate within the states of New York and California and in the common stocks of corporations regularly paying dividends, giving my said trustee full authority to vary the said investments at his discretion, and to apply the income from the said trust fund to the support, maintenance, education and general welfare of my son ROBERT, *until he shall have attained the age of 25 years, at which time I direct the principal of said fund to be paid over and transferred to him to be his absolutely and forever.*

A variation of this paragraph can be used to establish what is known as a "spendthrift trust," by which it is possible to pay the principal to Robert in installments, increasing as he grows older, rather than in one lump sum. You can also provide that this income can neither be assigned by Robert nor attached by his creditors.

A father often desires to establish a trust with the bulk of his estate, if it is a substantial one, giving his widow all the income from it during her lifetime, with the principal going, at her death, to the surviving children or to "issue then surviving." However, new tax laws make this type of ploy less attractive if too many generations are involved. Here the words used are important. Often the Latin terms *"per stirpes"* and *"per capita"* appear. It will be of some interest to know how these terms are applied.

Suppose the testator is survived by three children, each of whom is married and has children of his own. At the time the principal of the estate is distributed, two are dead. The surviving son has two sons of his own. The testator's dead children had two and three children, respectively. If the estate is to be paid over to *"my issue then surviving* PER CAPITA" (by head), the trustee or executor must actually count heads. There would be eight in our example, each entitled to an equal share. If the estate is to be paid over to *"my descendants (or issue)* PER STIRPES," it would be divided first into three shares, one for each child of the testator. Then the share of each deceased child would be divided into as many parts as he had children.

Usually the bulk of an estate goes to the residuary legatee, who gets the balance after all special gifts are taken care of. This can be an outright gift or it can be a testamentary trust.

7. All the rest, residue and remainder of my estate, real, personal or mixed, of which I shall die seized or possessed or of which I shall have the right to dispose by will, I give, devise and bequeath to my wife, GEORGIANNA, *to be hers absolutely and forever.*

Infinite variations are possible to suit every family situation, and every size and kind of estate. Inheritance tax considerations play an important part in determining which estate plan is best for you. Even if space were available to discuss more of them here, it might be a *disservice* to readers if it tempted them to copy the examples in the belief that they could thereby dispense with necessary legal advice.

After the legacies are made and the trusts set up, it is necessary to appoint people to carry them out. In addition to executors and trustees, it may be advisable to name a guardian for young children who might be orphaned. The clause naming the executors, trustees and guardians, if any, is of critical importance. It varies according to the job assigned, the kind of property in the estate, etc.

If the estate is not to be settled in a short time, it is advisable to make provisions for successors to the people you name. If the estate is to be managed for many years, it may be well to consider naming a bank or trust company.

The identity of the executor or trustee is important. More crucial, however, is the nature of the powers you authorize him to assume. Here is the simplest form.

8. I nominate and appoint my wife, GEORGIANNA SMITH, *to be executrix of this, my Will, and I direct that she be permitted to serve without giving bond or other security.*

In paragraph 6, above, we've indicated the powers of the trustee of the trust fund created for son ROBERT. "Powers clauses" in wills frequently come up for interpretation by the courts, and the tendency is to adhere strictly to the instructions of the decedent. Therefore, the language used must be chosen with care to enable the managers of the estate to do what the testator wants done—no more, no less. State laws do grant certain basic powers to personal representatives, and these needn't be repeated in the document unless you foresee moving to another state.

The final clause is the concluding *testimonium*. This is not required by law but, with suitable modifications, is invariably used by lawyers.

IN WITNESS WHEREOF, *I have hereunto set my hand and seal this 17th day of March, 1978.*

Signature of testator

Following is the all-important *attestation*

clause that precedes the signatures of the witnesses.

Signed, sealed, published and declared by the said testator as and for his Last Will and Testament, in the presence of us and each of us, who in his presence and in the presence of each other, at his request, have hereunto subscribed our names as witnesses thereof, the date and year first above mentioned.

Then come the signatures and the residence addresses of the witnesses. This should be notarized.

WHAT TO HAVE IN MIND WHEN DRAWING A WILL

1. **Allow for the Unexpected.** When the head of a family prepares to draw his will, he has a tendency to believe that, as the eldest, he will die first; that, in due course, his wife will die next; and that she will be survived by all their children. We know from experience that this pattern does not always hold true.

The wife may predecease the husband. An accident may occur in which husband and wife are both killed. One of the children may die before the father. Obviously, when an estate plan is formulated so that it depends on the testator's own idea of the order people will die, it is just as weak as his prediction.

The safe thing to do is to provide alternative arrangements to meet possible variations from the normal order of life expectancy. It is not practical to try to anticipate every contingency, but it is good practice to make some provision for the distribution of the principal part of the estate if the chief beneficiary dies before the testator. Consequently, in a well-thought-out will, there is usually a provision which begins "In the event that my beloved wife should predecease me . . ." and names successor beneficiaries.

2. **Discuss Your Family Situation.** You should make provisions for anything that is out of the ordinary in your family history. Did you have a prior marriage? Have you any children by that marriage? Do you have any stepchildren or adopted children? Do you have any illegitimate children?

If you answer "yes" to any of these questions, your lawyer will avoid the use of general terms that might have the effect of including or excluding members of your family inadvertently. In most states adopted children are given the same treatment as natural children. The same is true, in some states, of illegitimate children. But where such relatives exist, they should not be grouped together under the term "children," unless language is used which specifically defines what you mean by that term.

3. **Debts Owing to the Testator.** Occasionally, we see in a will a provision forgiving some indebtedness owed to a testator. But in the absence of such a release, it is the duty of the executor to take all steps necessary to collect all debts due the estate.

4. **Prior Gifts Made by the Testator.** Sometimes the testator, before his death, makes a gift of a portion of his estate to the one who would inherit it. Sometimes substantial gifts are made before death which are not intended to take the place of a legacy. (The value of gifts made within three years of death is brought into the decedent's estate and taxed.)

Whenever the drawer of a will has made a substantial gift to any of his beneficiaries, it is good practice to make a clear statement in his will indicating whether or not the prior gift is to make any difference in the legacies he has established. (Gifts made while the testator is alive no longer have the tax advantages for his estate that existed before 1977.)

5. **Order of Abatement.** Suppose you have overestimated the value of your estate, or your investments have substantially decreased in value before your death, leaving your estate smaller than you anticipated when making your will. Generous specific bequests could substantially decrease the residuary estate, which often goes to the chief beneficiary. To take care of such a possibility, you may, in a separate clause in your will, give preference or priority to particular bequests.

For example, you can say that if, after calculation of the value of your estate, your executor finds that your wife and children would receive less than $100,000 if all legacies were to be paid in full, then all other legacies should be "abated" proportionately, or even eliminated, to assure a minimum of $100,000 in the order of abatement.

This subject should be given very serious consideration, since it has become almost a convention that the bulk of the estate passes to the residuary legatee. By this we mean that the principal beneficiary gets everything left after specific gifts have been disposed of.

6. **Taxes.** If the estate is to be subject to death or estate taxes by the federal or state government, the testator should indicate whether he wishes each of the beneficiaries to pay the taxes proportionately, or if he desires any of the legacies to be paid free of taxes. This is another matter completely under the control of the testator. Generally, the estate pays all such taxes.

7. **Property Should Be Identified.** Real and personal property, especially if left to different legatees, should be adequately described so as to be clearly identified. The testator should also consider whether or not he wishes to give substitute gifts in the event that any specific property he has at the time he is drawing the will should be sold or otherwise disposed of.

8. **Nature of the Estate.** Is the testator a businessman? Does he desire his business to be continued after his death? Does he wish his business to be liquidated? Does the testator have investments or securities that he desires his executor or his family to keep intact? Does he wish his executor to hold, exchange, mortgage, sell or lease any real property? These questions have to do with the powers and instructions given to the executors who are named in the will.

9. **What About Minor Children?** Is it desirable to name a guardian of their persons and property? Normally, custody and guardianship of minor children will be left to the surviving parent. But suppose there is no surviving parent. Is any property to be left in trust?

It is possible to suspend the transfer of absolute title to property, but only for a limited time. The usual formula is "a life in being upon the death of the testator, plus 21 years." By this we mean that property, real or personal, can be held in trust during the life of a son and, after his death, during the life of his as-yet-unborn daughter, until the infant reaches the age of twenty-one years.

By the twenty-first birthday of the daughter, the trust must end and absolute title must go to *someone*. The reason for this rule is that the law does not favor the suspension of the absolute right to dispose of property for too long a period.

In establishing a trust, consideration should be given to its practicality. Some testators, believing their wives and children to be incapable of managing money, take precautions against their having the bulk of it to spend. But when outright ownership of property is suspended, only the income from it is generally available for the use of the beneficiaries.

Obviously, the principal must be pretty large if the income or interest is to be depended on for the support and maintenance of a family. Furthermore, management of trusts must be paid for out of income or principal. Trustees are entitled to commissions set by state law, which, however, can be waived.

Assume that the testator desires to establish a testamentary trust, who will be the trustee? Does he wish to name a co-trustee, or substitute trustees, in case those named by him should fail to act or fail to complete their jobs? Some consideration should be given to the appointment of a financial institution, especially if the trust is to last a long time.

What powers are the trustees to have? Unless they are given *discretionary* power to make investments, they will usually be restricted by law to a list of securities that the state considers to be safe and conservative, but on which the return is less than it might be.

Are the trustees to have the right to "invade" the principal? Testators often give this right to trustees so they can use funds from the principal whenever the interest or income is insufficient for the support or education of children, in the event of serious illness, etc.

Table 4—AGE REQUIREMENTS—FOR PURPOSE OF EXECUTING WILLS

State	Real Property	Personal Property	State	Real Property	Personal Property
Alabama	21	18	Montana	18	18
Alaska	18	18	Nebraska	21	18
Arizona	18	18	Nevada	18	18
Arkansas	18	18	New Hampshire	18	18
California	18	18	New Jersey	18	18
Colorado	18	18	New Mexico	18	18
Connecticut	18	18	New York	18	18
Delaware	18	18	North Carolina	18	18
District of Columbia	18	18	North Dakota	18	18
Florida	18	18	Ohio	18	18
Georgia	14	14	Oklahoma	18	18
Hawaii	20	20	Oregon	18	18
Idaho	18	18	Pennsylvania	18	18
Illinois	18	18	Puerto Rico	14	14
Indiana	18	18	Rhode Island	18	18
Iowa	18*	18*	South Carolina	18	18
Kansas	21	21	South Dakota	18	18
Kentucky	18	18	Tennessee	18	18
Louisiana	16	16	Texas	18	18
Maine	18	18	Utah	18	18
Maryland	18	18	Vermont	18*	18*
Massachusetts	18	18	Virginia	18*	18
Michigan	18	18	Washington	18	18
Minnesota	18	18	West Virginia	18	18
Mississippi	18	18	Wisconsin	18*	18*
Missouri	18	18	Wyoming	19*	19*

*In these states, the pertinent statute does not mention an age, but speaks of "adulthood," or "at majority."

When the trust is terminated, who is to get the principal? Some person or organization should be named, or the state might get your property.

10. **Possibility of Contest.** Does the testator anticipate that the will will be contested? This should be the subject of a detailed discussion with the attorney, who can then take precautionary steps in drawing the will as well as prepare for other contingencies.

11. **Prior Wills.** Has the testator made any prior wills? The mere making of a new will is sufficient to revoke any previously made one unless no inconsistency arises. It is a common practice, nevertheless, to include a statement in a new will revoking any previously signed. This avoids litigation.

If you want to revoke an old will without making a new one, it is best to discuss the matter with an attorney. Generally, this can be done by destroying the old will; but the safest thing to do, if no new will is to be drawn, is to execute a document of revocation that must be as formal as the will itself.

12. **Mutual and Contractual Wills.** It is necessary to determine whether or not the testator is under obligation to leave his property in a certain way. It is perfectly legal to make a contract to bequeath or devise property. The contract is made during the lifetime of the testator, and is carried out by his executor or administrator. Under certain circumstances, people contract to make mutual wills, each leaving his property to the other, and contracting at the same time not to change the will. This effectively limits the customary freedom on the part of the testator to make, revoke or modify his will or any provision contained in it. If no valid contract exists, a testator could revoke his will without liability.

Changes in wills are sometimes made by codicils, but more often a completely new will is drawn. Codicils, or provisions in a will that breach the terms of a contract, usually result in litigation. So it is obvious that any obligation of this nature should be discussed fully with your attorney.

CHAPTER FIFTEEN

WILLS: INTESTACY AND OTHER INHERITANCE PROBLEMS

This chapter deals with many questions: Why do some legacies fail? What happens when they do fail? What is testamentary capacity? What is the effect of undue influence? Who can be cut off? What happens when no will is made?

WHEN LEGACIES FAIL

Ademption. In sample clause number 2 (page 71), J. F. Jones left his property at Lake Hopatcong to his secretary, Gerald Jackson. Suppose that before his death Jones sells the property—it is no longer part of his estate.

The legacy is then said to have *adeemed*. It fails. Jackson is not entitled to the money realized in the sale and, if there is no other provision for him in the will, he gets nothing.

Suppose Jackson dies before the testator, Jones, who makes no change in his will. In this case, the property either goes into the residuary estate or passes like intestate property, depending on state law. The legacy is said to have "lapsed." In some states, if the legatee who dies before the testator is his child, parent, brother or sister, the legacy is not allowed to lapse, and the share intended for the dead beneficiary goes to *his* heirs.

Suppose that, after making the will, Jones and Jackson have a disagreement. Jones fires Jackson and hires a new secretary. He makes no change in his will before he dies. Does the legacy fail because Jackson is no longer secretary? Does it go to the new secretary?

The answer to both these questions is "No." The language used by Jones as testator only identified Jackson. It placed no condition on his receiving the legacy.

To illustrate *ademption* further, let's take sample number 3, the bequest of the Cadillac automobile to the chauffeur, Stanley Smith. If the testator, before his death, sold the Cadillac and bought a new car, chances are that Smith would get the new car. Ademption is based on a *substantial* change in the character of the property.

Legacies also fail when they are invalid or against public policy, as explained later in this chapter.

Testamentary Capacity. The testator must be of sound mind. This doesn't necessarily mean that he must be in the best of mental health. The courts have held it to mean that he must have the capacity to understand what he is doing. It is possible for persons very weak in body and mind to make a valid will. The law seeks to protect the right of a person to dispose of his own property. It is only when there is proof that mind and memory were so far gone that the testator could not remember what property he owned, and could not fully comprehend the meaning of his act, that the court will refuse to admit the will for probate.

Undue Influence. It is necessary that a testator express his free will. Undue influence is very much like fraud in that it is used to obtain the consent of the testator by some sort of force or duress. Mere persuasion is not undue influence unless the testator is shown to have been feeble-minded, in which case the persuasion might be seen as coercion.

THE LAWS OF INTESTACY

When No Will Is Found. If a person dies **intestate,** that is, if he leaves no will disposing of his property, his estate will be distributed according to a formula set down in the laws of the state in which he resided at the time of his death.

In what state a decedent established residency may become a point of dispute if, during his lifetime, he maintained residences in more than one state. If his *domicile* is shown to have been in New York, for example, that state's laws of intestacy will apply.

Domicile is an important word. Its legal sense is *permanent* address. A person may spend little time there, but if he intends it to be his home and demonstrates that by his acts and declarations, it is his domicile. Sometimes several states claim to be a decedent's domicile in order to be entitled to the death taxes on his estate.

Intestacy Laws of New York. We are concerned here only with the distribution of the estate of a man who dies intestate. Since it is impractical to reproduce the intestacy laws of the fifty states, we will look into those of New York as an example of what such measures seek to accomplish.

New York is excellent for that purpose. Because of the great concentration of wealth and population in that state, its intestacy laws are highly developed and are regarded as a good model.

Whether the decedent is male or female, if he or she dies without a valid will, the estate will be distributed as follows:

1. If the decedent leaves a husband or wife, and children: the surviving spouse will get $2,000 and one third of the rest of the property, and the balance will go in equal portions to the children. Should any of the children have died before the decedent, their share will go to those who have the right to inherit from them.

If the decedent leaves a spouse and had one child: the spouse gets $2,000 plus one half the rest of the property, and the child, or his heirs, gets the balance.

If the decedent leaves only children, they share the property *per stirpes.*

2. If the decedent was childless, or had children who died leaving no descendants, but is survived by a spouse and both parents: the spouse gets $25,000 and one half the rest of the estate, and the parents divide what's left. (One surviving parent gets the full parental amount.) If only parents survive, they get the whole estate.

3. If the decedent leaves a spouse, but no parents or issue, he or she takes the whole estate.

4. If the decedent leaves brothers and sisters (or their children, if they predecease the decedent), but no spouse, parents, or issue, the whole estate goes to the brothers and sisters, or their issue *per stirpes.*

For example, John Doe dies a bachelor with no children and his parents are both dead. He had two brothers and one sister. The brothers are alive but the sister died before John, leaving three children. The estate is first divided into three shares—two for the living brothers, one for the dead sister. The sister's one-third share is then divided into three shares, one for each of her children.

The intestacy laws (which differ from state to state) go into further details—such as the rights of illegitimate children and their parents, relatives of the half-blood (half-brothers or half-sisters, etc.) and nearer or more remote relatives.

So, in effect, the state supplies a will if the decedent has failed to take care of this important task himself during his lifetime.

Should You Make a Will? Provisions like those above appear in the laws of all the states. They are arbitrary, but their purpose is to assure a *fair* distribution of the decedent's property according to our customs. They were designed for the average case and the average family.

If the intestacy laws of your state distribute

your property exactly as you wish, perhaps you can do without a will. If, on the other hand, you wish to have your property distributed in another way; if you wish to name the one who will manage your estate through liquidation and distribution; if you want your business or other property to be continued for a designated period as it was before your death—in any of these cases, you will require a will to accomplish your purposes.

Sometimes it is advisable to make a will even if the intestacy laws seem adequate to carry out your wishes. EXAMPLE: During his lifetime, John Homer thought about making a will. Instead of having a professional talk with a lawyer, he asked a law student friend, "What would happen to my property if I die without a will?" The friend, knowing that John had a wife and a young child, gave him the answer you will find in the list above. Since there was no one else he wanted to provide for, John decided this was good enough; he would not make a will. He died soon after and the bulk of his estate was a rather large house—too big for his widow and child to live in and maintain after his death. It became necessary to sell it. This was a complex and expensive procedure. Because the minor child had a substantial interest in the house, a special guardian had to be appointed by the court to safeguard his interests in the transaction. The court's approval had to be obtained and special steps had to be taken so that good title could be transferred to the buyer—all at substantial expense.

Administration and Execution. If you draw your will with the assistance of your attorney, he will inform you of your right to appoint your executor, and may make certain suggestions. If your estate will include a going business, you will want to appoint someone whose business judgment you can rely on in regard to the business's management or liquidation. If you leave no will, letters of administration will ordinarily be granted to your nearest surviving relative.

You can provide in your will that your executor shall have certain discretionary powers over your estate, your investments, the disposition of trust moneys, etc. But if you leave no will, the administrator will have only those powers specified in the law.

You may have confidence in your executor and provide that he be allowed to act without furnishing a bond. In the case of an administrator, a bond is usually compulsory. This entails a certain expense and involves the bonding company in the administration of the estate.

Comparative Expenses. Except for the proving, or "probate," of the will—which, unless it is contested, is a simple proceeding, incurring no great expense—the cost of administering the estate of one who dies intestate is about the same as the execution of a will. Administration can be more expensive if it's necessary to dispose of the claims of many relatives, and to investigate whether certain of them are alive or dead, etc.

Administrators and executors are entitled to commissions for their work. Commissions are fixed by state law and are paid out of the estate as one of its expenses. The rate depends entirely on the work entailed in settling the estate, on the size of the estate, the nature of the property, the problems of liquidation and distribution, etc.

Administrators and executors are entitled to have legal help. Counsel fees are allowable as an expense, but must be approved by the court. If property in the estate must be preserved, sold, stored, etc., any of these functions may involve some expenses that must be paid out of the estate.

If there are minor children whose interests must be protected, the court will appoint a special guardian for that purpose. The guardian will also be compensated out of the estate.

Taxes are payable by the estate, and it is the responsibility of the administrator or executor to file the returns and have the taxes assessed and paid. It generally makes no difference in the computation of taxes whether or not a will has been made. However—and this is very important—the making of a will as part of an estate plan can result in considerable savings in both state and federal death taxes, because some tax savings have to be elected by the testator.

The Advantages of Leaving a Will. It should be clear from the preceding that it is advantageous to leave a will.

Those whose property is limited to what the law would entitle the surviving spouse to receive, leaving nothing for others to share in, may be of the opinion that a will would serve no purpose. But it is possible, in these days of plane and car crashes, that husband and wife may die in the same accident. In that case, the property would be distributed as though it belonged to the last to die. Let's see what that might lead to.

Suppose husband and wife have no children, but both have parents. Husband has property worth ten thousand dollars and has been advised that, according to the laws of his state, his wife would receive all at his death. They both die in an automobile accident, with the wife surviving the husband by a few hours.

Under such circumstances, the wife, having been the survivor, would normally be entitled to receive all of the husband's property; then, on her death, her parents would receive all, his parents nothing. A will could remedy a situation like that.

WHAT A WILL CANNOT ACCOMPLISH

Cutting Off Husband or Wife. Only a few states permit a husband or wife to disinherit the other by will. Some permit this with respect to personal property only, giving the husband or wife rights in any real property, whether or not mentioned in the will.

In most states, an amount approximately equal to the intestate share (that is, the amount that would go to the surviving spouse if no will had been left) is regarded as a minimum. If the willed amount falls below this, the surviving spouse can "elect" to disregard the will and take the minimum provided by law. A decedent can provide that the minimum be put in trust, with all the income going to the

spouse. If that minimum is met, no election against the will is usually possible.

Failure to exercise the right of election within a certain fixed period of time is regarded as a waiver; thereafter, the terms of the will must be followed. But if the surviving spouse chooses to elect against a will, he or she cannot take advantage of any favorable provisions in the document.

Most states provide, however, that a divorce during the decedent's lifetime terminates the right of the surviving former spouse to take the minimum provided by law instead of abiding by the terms of the will. Some states go further and permit disinheriting the spouse who has abandoned the other, and annul the right of election.

If there has been a separation instead of a divorce, generally it is only the party guilty of misconduct who is barred from the right to inherit, no matter what the terms of the will may be. The one who obtained the decree of separation for the misconduct or abandonment, cruelty or nonsupport by the other may still inherit.

Jointly Owned Property. Often real estate is held by a husband and wife jointly. All of it then automatically belongs to the survivor. The will cannot change this. Upon the death of a joint owner, the property goes to the other, no matter how it may be devised in the decedent's will. The same applies to any property, including bank accounts, held jointly.

Estate taxation of jointly held property is a complex affair. For pre-1977 joint tenancies, the surviving spouse must show how much he contributed in acquiring the property in order to lessen the taxes on the deceased spouse's estate. For joint tenancies created after 1977, a couple can elect to treat the creation of it as a taxable gift in order to get an even distribution of the property's value between their two estates. This new rule doesn't apply to joint bank accounts.

Cutting Off All Relatives. A man may become embittered at all of his family and relatives. Sometimes he is affected by conscience or extreme piety. Whatever the reason, he may decide to leave his family nothing and give all to some favorite charity.

In some states, such a will is enforceable. In others, the amount that can be left to charity is restricted. New York, for example, does not permit more than one half a decedent's estate to be left to charity if there are a spouse, issue or parents who contest the bequest and who would profit from a successful contest.

Leaving Money to Corporations. Corporations cannot be legatees unless their charters specifically give them authority to receive gifts by will.

Conditions Against Public Policy. The public policy of a state is determined by what is regarded as being beneficial or harmful to it. For example, the state favors the institution of marriage. If a father's legacy to his daughter carries the condition that she should never marry, the condition is not enforceable as being against public policy.

However, the condition in a will that the testator's wife not remarry is valid.

Life Insurance. Generally, unless the beneficiary of the policy is the estate of the insured, the proceeds of the policy aren't included in the decedent's estate. The beneficiary receives the proceeds directly from the insurance company. Neither the executor nor the administrator has any responsibility in connection with the funds. However, if the insured retained any powers over the policy (called incidents of ownership), the proceeds of the policy will be included in his estate.

Transferring an insurance policy from the insured is a common element of estate planning. But such a move is not advisable in all cases. The insured should have a life expectancy that is shorter than the new owner's.

THE DRAWING OF THE WILL

Statutes. The manner in which a will must be drawn is set forth by statute in every state. It cannot be repeated too often that this is a highly formal document and should be drawn only with the assistance of a lawyer.

As we have seen in the previous chapter, some states permit informal wills in the handwriting of the testator, but most do not. In states where they are permitted, these wills (called holographic wills) need not always be witnessed, but invariably they must be signed, at the end, by the testator. The one thing to remember about them is that they should be avoided.

Wills Must Be in Writing and Signed. The document must be written, usually typewritten, and signed at the bottom by the testator. Without the signature at the bottom, it's most likely that the will will be declared invalid, and refused probate.

If the signature appears elsewhere than at the bottom, the probate court may admit all that appears above the signature as a valid will, if it can be read as such. There should be no erasures or corrections—they are usually presumed to have been made after the execution of the will.

Signing in Presence of Witnesses. The actual signing of the will should take place in the presence of witnesses. An alternative is allowed in New York and elsewhere—the testator can simply acknowledge, in the presence of witnesses, that the signature at the bottom of the will is his.

It should be remembered that the will must one day be admitted to probate and that the witnesses will then be called on. They must be in a position to testify that the will was signed by the testator in their presence, or that the testator acknowledged to them in their presence and, often, in the presence of each other, that the signature was his. Therefore, it's best for the witnesses to be people who were acquainted with the testator and who are easily traceable.

The Declaration. It's not enough to say to the witnesses, "Will you witness my signature on this document?" There must be an understanding on the part of the testator and the witnesses that what he is signing is his last will and testament.

It is enough if the testator, in the presence of the witnesses, is asked by one of them or by his attorney who is present, "Is this your will?" But it is better to say simply, "This is my last will and testament. I have read it and ask you to witness my signature and to sign your names as witnesses." It isn't necessary for the provisions of the will to be made known to the witnesses, or for any part of it to be read aloud in their presence.

The Witnesses. Most states require two witnesses to a will. However, a number of states require three; so it is a good practice, whenever possible, to have more witnesses than the law calls for, because the assistance of witnesses is required in order to probate the will. For this reason, it is also good practice to select people who are younger than the testator, and in good health.

The witnesses should never be people who are to receive anything under the will. No one who benefits under its terms is permitted to do anything to enforce it. If the testimony of someone mentioned in the will is needed in order to establish its validity in probate or in a contest, he cannot give such testimony without forfeiting his legacy.

Witnesses are required to write their residence addresses next to their names in some states. This is a good practice everywhere.

CHAPTER SIXTEEN

CIVIL WRONGS

It is a principle of law that every wrong has a remedy. In the following two chapters we will deal with the general characteristics of civil wrongs and their remedies through awards of damages. Negligence is the most frequent cause of action in civil cases, so we will devote this chapter to it, concentrating on automobile accident cases because they are the most numerous.

TORTS AND CRIMES

A civil wrong is an injury done by one person to the body, the property or the reputation of another. This private wrong is called a *tort*. For a tort, a wrongdoer is answerable in a civil court in a suit for damages. When the injury or wrong affects the community, it is a crime punishable by the state. A civil wrong to an individual may at the same time be a wrong against the state. For example, one guilty of the crime of assault has not only inflicted injury upon his victim, but has also broken the peace. Therefore, the state may punish him.

The distinction between a tort and a crime may perhaps best be shown by the different ways in which the two actions against the wrongdoer are handled. In a tort or civil wrong, the case is brought by the injured party against the one who has injured him. The case reads: "Jones against Smith."

Where the offense is against the community, the charge is brought by the district attorney, and reads, for example; "People of the State of New York against Smith."

The result in a civil action usually will be a judgment for money damages payable by the wrongdoer to the injured party. The result in a criminal action will be a fine payable to the state, or imprisonment. It will be in the nature of a penalty rather than compensation.

The conduct of the two trials also differs. In order to prove the defendant guilty of the crime with which he has been charged, the district attorney must prove guilt beyond a reasonable doubt. But in a civil case the rule is greatly relaxed. It is enough for the plaintiff's lawyer to show that the weight of the evidence is against the defendant in order to establish a claim for damages against him.

PARTICULAR CIVIL WRONGS

Negligence. The most common tort, the one that occupies most of the time of our courts, is negligence. It takes in a tremendous field—automobile accidents, personal injuries, property damage, and all cases in which someone causes damage or injury by failing to meet his responsibilities to others.

Negligence may be defined as a failure to use the care necessary to safeguard others from damage or injury. To establish a proper claim for negligence, there must be: (a) a legal duty to use care; (b) a breach of that duty; (c) injury or damage **proximately** resulting from the failure to use care. ("Proximately" means that the damage or injury has resulted from the negligence.)

During an explosion in a warehouse a passerby was quite seriously injured. It appears that he wouldn't have been injured if someone close to him hadn't pushed him slightly just before the explosion. The injured man sued the man who jostled him, holding him responsible. The court denied judgment on the grounds that the injury was not the proximate result of the defendant's action—he had moved the plaintiff in an effort to protect him from the blast.

The test for negligence as the proximate cause of an injury is whether or not the injury could or should have been foreseen by the person committing the act. Here is the opinion of a legal authority on the matter:

"The breach of duty upon which an action is brought must be not only the cause, but the proximate cause of the damage to the plaintiff. . . . The proximate cause of an event must be understood to be that which in a natural and continuous sequence, unbroken by any new cause, produces the event, and without which that event would not have occurred."

Degree of Care. We have seen that one of the essential elements in negligence is the obligation to use care. But how much care? The degree depends on the circumstances. The greatest degree of care is required from those who operate public conveyances—airlines, railroads, steamships, bus lines, etc. Operators of such conveyances are practically insurers of the safety of their passengers. The law is specific about this liability. When a passenger is injured in an accident on a public conveyance, ordinarily all that he has to show is that he was a passenger and that he suffered the injury in transit. From these facts alone, the negligence of the transportation company will be presumed. The injured party need not prove it. It is up to the transportation company to prove that it was not responsible.

A high degree of care is also demanded from people who invite others on their premises. People who maintain places of public resort—restaurants, amusement parks, theaters, etc.—are responsible for the safety of their patrons. They should warn all comers of any dangers on the premises that they know about. And they are responsible for dangers that they should know about if they exercised reasonable care by inspecting the condition of their premises and fixtures. For example, a restaurant would be responsible for damages suffered when a loose chandelier fell, even if the management did not know of the defective condition.

Who Are Invited Persons? Generally speaking, if his presence on the premises brings some benefit to the one who invites him there, a person is an invitee. A man who pays admission to a theater is bringing some benefit to the theater owner to him, in the case of an accident, is less than if he were a paying cusone, without paying admission, gains access to it, he is not an invitee. The responsibility of the theater owner to him, in the case of an accident, is less than if he were a paying customer.

Duty to Trespassers. The obligation to maintain property in a safe condition doesn't extend to people who have no right to be on the property. (But there are special obligations if you know that people, especially children, use your property even without permission.) Normally, a trespasser—one who enters the property of another without permission—can't hold the owner responsible for any injury he sustains because of the unsafe condition of a path, etc. For a trespasser to recover damages, he must show that the owner willfully and intentionally caused him harm. Owners have been held liable—that is, made to pay damages—when it was shown that they deliberately set traps to injure trespassers, or used more force than was necessary to remove the trespasser from the property.

Duty to Licensees. We have seen that while a high degree of care is owed to invitees, practically no care is owed to trespassers. There is another class of persons who are neither invitees nor trespassers. They are permitted to enter property by virtue of the owner's express or implied consent. They are called "licensees." In this category are social guests, bill collectors, deliverymen, etc. Policemen and firemen who enter property in the course of their duty have sometimes been held by the courts to be invitees, sometimes licensees.

A property owner's duty to licensees is to warn them of known latent dangers that subject them to a risk of harm, and to refrain from conduct dangerous to them. Otherwise, the licensee takes the property as he finds it, which means, basically, he must look out for himself.

CONTRIBUTORY NEGLIGENCE

It must be remembered that not every injury gives rise to a claim for damages. Everyone must act reasonably to ensure his own safety. If a man should break a leg while getting off a bus, he has a claim if he can show that the injury was caused because the bus lurched while he was descending, or because he was pushed due to overcrowding, etc. But, even though the bus driver was negligent in failing to come to a full stop before opening the door, the passenger won't be able to establish a claim for damages if, knowing that the bus was still in motion, he voluntarily executed a fancy jump to the pavement. That "contributory negligence" will prevent his collecting damages from the bus company in many states, if it was a substantial factor in bring about the result. Some states now apportion damages among parties according to how much each contributed to the injury, but deny recovery to a plaintiff who was the prime contributor to the injury. This concept is called "comparative negligence."

In states where the doctrine of contributory negligence is still followed, a claimant must show he's free of contributory negligence in order to recover for someone else's negligence. But even if the claimant was contributorily negligent, he might still recover if the defendant knew of the claimant's predicament and could have avoided injuring him by exercising reasonable care.

AUTOMOBILE ACCIDENTS

In many places throughout the country, because of court congestion, a claimant often has to wait years before his case comes to trial. Negligence claims are largely responsible for this backlog. Automobile accidents are a common basis for negligence suits, and we will talk about them separately because they present some special problems.

The principles governing such cases are the same as in other types of negligence actions. The driver of a motor vehicle is required to exercise the same degree of care as a reasonably prudent man would in any circumstances where he might conceivably cause injury to others or their property. Breach of this obligation to use care must be proved if the operator or owner of a car is to be held responsible. In addition, the negligence of the driver must be established as the proximate cause of the injury.

Suppose that, on a dark night, a car without lights collides with another car coming in the opposite direction on the wrong side of the road. Both drivers were negligent. Probably neither will be allowed to recover damages against the other, unless a court finds that one driver's fault was greater than the other's.

What To Do After an Accident. One thing is distinctive about all auto accidents. They happen fast, usually with startling suddenness. Recollections of what happened, and how, are often confused. Even people who know what should be done to protect their own interests, or those of others, are often so upset that they forget the most elementary steps.

It may be someone's need for emergency medical care that drives other considerations out of one's mind. At the risk of appearing callous, it should be remembered that it's best to leave medical attention to experts if that's at all possible. The truth is that, in his agitation, a person may take steps that are as wrong for the victim's physical well-being as they are neglectful of his legal rights. Consequently, in the case of an injury, call the police first.

Getting Witnesses. In regard to the legal rights of the parties involved in an accident, the first consideration is the evidence. To form the basis of a claim for damages, the facts you use must be supported by evidence. The best evidence is that of eyewitnesses. They should be contacted before they leave the scene.

Another reason for calling the police immediately is that their reports will contain data that can serve as evidence in a negligence claim. For example, they will take note of the exact position of the vehicles involved, which is often a good indication of what happened and who was at fault.

The names of the parties, their addresses, license and registration numbers will also appear in the police report. But the police will not always take the names of witnesses. This should be done by the people involved. You should also note the location of the accident, the direction in which the cars were traveling, the time of day, the weather, the light conditions, and the condition of the road surface.

Note the year, make, model, and condition of the cars. Find out if the owners were driving; if not, find out if the cars were being driven with the owners' permission.

If you suspect one of the drivers is under the influence of alcohol, mention this to the police or to one of the witnesses.

Manufacturer's Liability. In dealing with the liability of a manufacturer, let's bear in mind the principle of proximate cause and the relationship of the injury to the obligation to use care on the part of the one who caused it. From this it might be deduced that the manufacturer of a product would be responsible for negligence only to the person to whom he sold it, if the product proved harmful or defective.

This is no longer true. The rule now is that manufacturers of packaged goods, bottled drinks, canned goods, etc., which reach the consumer in the same state in which they left the factory, are responsible to the purchaser and to those who might reasonably use the purchased item.

This principle has been often extended to include goods not sold in sealed packages. An automobile manufacturer was held responsible for injuries due to defective materials in a car purchased from a dealer by the injured person. The maker of a scaffold was required to pay damages for an injury suffered by a worker, even though he had made the scaffold on the order of a contractor. True, he built it for the contractor, but he knew what it was used for, and he owed the workmen the duty to build it with care, even though he had no direct dealings with them. And there are even cases allowing recovery to passengers and bystanders injured by defective automobiles. (An interesting point regarding auto accidents: There may be a mitigation of what the manufacturer must pay if the plaintiff didn't use an available seatbelt.)

Damages. Once a court has determined that a wrong has been committed, and that the plaintiff has the right to recover damages, the problem arises of fixing the sum the defendant will have to pay. There is no set way of determining in advance how much will be allowed—usually a jury decides the amount. If an injury results in disability or death, damages will generally be greater for a man of higher earning capacity than for someone from a low-income group. Of course the loss of a husband or father hits a poor family as hard as a wealthy family. Nevertheless, it is money rather than emotion that the jury has to deal with, and the income of the deceased or incapacitated is an important factor. In fixing damages the jury will consider: pain and suffering, medical expenses, loss of earnings, loss of profit (for a businessman), loss of society (companionship) of husband or wife. Of course, juries can be affected by other factors, too. Their sympathy for the plaintiff may increase the damage award. For example, an incapacitating or disfiguring injury to a young person will probably engender a higher award than the same injury to an older, less active person.

Insurance. The insurance policies available to car owners are not uniform. They vary according to the risks they cover; some policies cover more risks than others. The good insurance broker is in a position to furnish insurance coverage for all foreseeable risks, or for as many as his client wants protection against. He will explain all of them.

Car owners often develop sales resistance in the presence of insurance brokers. To get by with the lowest possible premium, they order the "minimum." It in only when they have an accident that they read a policy with the attention it calls for.

There are situations in which a broker doesn't appear at all (as when a car is purchased "on time," and the insurance policy is included as part of the deal). It's always wise to examine such policies carefully to see that they provide the amount and kind of protection the car owner wants.

Why You Should Examine Your Policy. Here's an example: Bill bought a car and had it financed by a local bank. Bill wanted his insurance to be included in the loan so he could pay the premiums in installments. The bank accommodated him, adding the insurance premiums to the price of the car, and divided the whole amount into eighteen monthly payments.

However, the clerk neglected to tell Bill that the policy was for one year, and not for the whole term of the loan as Bill thought. For the last six months, he was uninsured.

During those six months, he had a minor accident—and major troubles. The trouble wasn't the small repair bill he had to pay out of his own pocket. The trouble was with the threatened loss of his driver's license. He had to furnish proof of financial responsibility in accordance with the laws of his state.

This wasn't hard to get from his insurance company once he purchased a new policy. But he had to pay a higher premium because insurance companies often classify as special risks all drivers who have to furnish such statements to the Bureau of Motor Vehicles.

TYPES OF INSURANCE COVERAGE

Liability. Since we have just been discussing negligence, the first risk we will deal with is your liability or responsibility for damage or injury to others as a result of your negligence. This is divided into personal injury and property damage.

If you are insured, the company that has issued the policy to you stands in your place to answer the charge of the complainant. If you weren't negligent, they don't have to pay. If you were, they do.

It's important to remember that the insurance company stands in your place only to the extent of the amount of insurance that you've purchased. If, for example, your liability coverage is $10,000 and an accident for which you are responsible causes the death of a young man with good earning capacity, the chances are that his widow will obtain a judgment for a great deal more than $10,000. You will be required to pay all of the judgment in excess of the $10,000 out of your own pocket.

An important responsibility of the insurance company to you is to defend you and bear all of the expenses of litigation. You, in turn, are required to assist them, and to do nothing to injure or impair the defense of the action. One of the things you are required to do is to send them prompt notice of the accident. You should do this whether or not you consider yourself responsible for the accident. You should do it even if the other party acknowledges that the negligence was his, unless you wish to pay repair costs yourself.

If you are sued for $100,000 and have, for example, a $10,000 liability policy, you obviously have a considerable interest in the defense of the action against you. In such a situation it is wise to retain your own counsel in spite of the fact that the insurance company is required to defend you.

Damage to Your Own Car. Quite apart from your responsibility to others is the risk of loss to yourself, whether or not you are negligent, for damage caused by collision, fire, theft, etc. Most collision policies are written with a so-called "deductible" clause so that accidents of a minor character aren't covered. A $50 deductible clause insures the owner for damages in excess of $50 in each accident. Since most accidents on the road or in traffic result in dented fenders which can be repaired for less than that, many car owners assume the risk themselves. Others buy insurance with a smaller deductible amount, or none at all.

Miscellaneous. Many policies contain insurance for emergency towing, medical expenses for injuries to the driver or other occupants of the car, etc. If these aren't contained in a policy offered to a car owner, he can have them included simply by ordering them from a broker.

No-fault Insurance. Many states (over twenty at press time) require a special type of insurance for automobiles—no-fault insurance. The concept is complicated, and the states' plans vary greatly as to specifics. But some points are common to all plans. Recovery in automobile accidents isn't based on who caused the accident. No-fault insurance is distinguished by "first party coverage," which means that an injured party is recompensed by his own insurer. And the recovery procedure is fast and efficient (a boon to the injured, who have expenses that must be met). State law usually specifies what is recoverable for what types of injuries and by whom. Some states allow recovery only for personal, not property, damage.

Generally, tort liability is superseded by the no-fault coverage. However, most plans retain conventional tort liability for serious injuries, or if medical expenses exceed the specified ceilings. Pain and suffering and mental anguish aren't recoverable, except for serious injuries. However, as a trade-off, the injured party is assured of payment regardless of fault.

States that have this system require that all resident drivers have no-fault insurance. If they don't, they are penalized. Penalties range from criminal liability to simply the end of the immunity to tort liability. Generally, motorcycles, buses, trucks, and farm vehicles needn't have no-fault insurance. And there's no recovery for those driving while intoxicated or drugged, those engaged in crimes, those whose injury was intentional, and those taking part in drag races, etc. Pedestrians are covered, usually, and collect from the motorist's insurer.

Coverage generally includes medical expenses, rehabilitation expenses, loss of income, and replacement costs (for example, hiring a housekeeper if a wife and mother is injured). Often the recovery is reduced by amounts paid by collateral sources—Medicare, Social Security, workmen's compensation, etc.

General Liability Insurance. Special policies exist to cover almost every type of liability for torts. To cover negligence, for example, there are policies tailored for restaurant owners, innkeepers, storekeepers, theater owners, etc. Publishers may be insured against liability for libel and slander; doctors and hospitals, against malpractice claims; employers, against workmen's compensation claims.

All these policies have one thing in common. They obligate the insurance company to stand in the place of the one who is insured. The insurance company must defend the action and pay the damages the insured would otherwise have had to pay—with this exception: if the amount of damages awarded to the plaintiff exceeds the amount of the insurance, the insured person must pay the difference.

Large firms maintain a special staff to see that they are adequately covered with insurance in each new development of their business. Too often small businessmen neglect this aspect of their operations. Then, because they are small, an unforeseen accident for which they have no coverage can be a disaster. Home owners are exposed to liability claims of deliverymen, repairmen, domestic servants, and even canvassers, against which they should seek coverage in their insurance.

Settling Negligence Claims. The fact that you rate yourself pretty high in your trade, business, or profession doesn't mean that you're qualified to negotiate a settlement involving your legal rights. When you suffer loss or injury as a result of someone's negligence—when, in other words, you are a claimant—remember this old adage: "The man who is his own lawyer has a fool for a client."

Since, in most cases, the one who is guilty of negligence is covered by insurance, the person you will have to deal with to settle your claim will be an insurance adjuster. Claims adjusters are specialists. They are highly trained, and their skill—their value to their employers—is measured, naturally, by how little money they have to spend in order to get your signature on a release.

This is not to say that the insurance companies are out to cheat claimants. However, it's obvious that if the maximum amount were paid on every claim, the insurance business wouldn't be very profitable.

How To Deal With the Insurance Adjuster. One of the first rules a claimant should observe is to take his time. Don't act in haste. In most states you have at least three years in which to press your claim. Often the full effects of an injury aren't known until weeks, sometimes months, after an accident. What appears to be a simple bruise, for which you are glad to accept a small payment from the insurance adjuster, may turn out to be a serious bone injury.

The adjuster, in doing his job, may call you "just to find out how you are feeling," and to express the regrets and solicitude of the company. Your natural inclination is to say, "I'm getting on all right, thank you," or, "It doesn't hurt much." This will appear in the adjuster's notes and may be used against you later.

Observations will also appear in his notebook on what you were doing, your general appearance, etc. His knock on the door may have gotten you out of a sickbed, but the fact that you weren't in bed when he spoke with you goes into his notes. His objective—what he is paid to do—is to dispose of the claim as cheaply and as quickly as possible. Your signature on the release ends the matter.

If you have retained a lawyer to represent you, he will advise you to refer all inquiries to him. He will counsel you to refrain from any discussion of the matter with anyone else.

UNETHICAL PRACTICES

Many evils have resulted from the great number of negligence claims. The unscrupulous professional adjuster is matched by the unscrupulous negligence practitioner. Investi-

gations by bar associations have disclosed unethical methods used by, or on behalf of, some lawyers. These practices are unethical in the sense that they violate the standards set up by and for the legal profession.

Members of hospital staffs and others in a position to be near an accident victim soon after he's been injured, have been known to "steer" cases to certain lawyers. This practice is unethical, not necessarily because it is damaging to the claimant, but because lawyers are highly restricted in the steps they can take to obtain clients.

Another practice that has been criticized is the contingent fee. This is a practice whereby the lawyer receives for his services a part of the sum recovered by the claimant. Contingent fees of 50 per cent of the amount of a judgment aren't unusual. This arrangement is defended on the grounds that claimants are rarely prepared to pay their lawyers a normal retainer fee in advance. There are also certain disbursements that the lawyer has to make.

Often two or three lawyers are involved in a claim. After the first lawyer has presented the case, he may find it advisable to obtain the assistance of another attorney. The second lawyer will probably specialize in claims against insurance companies, or at least will have experience and success in dealing with insurance cases.

Here the purpose is to obtain a favorable settlement without going to court. This practice is justified by the fact that often, especially in large cities, where the court calendars are so crowded, it may be years before your action comes up for trial. This would be hard on the accident victim, who may be without income and in need of a settlement.

Again, if the case is a complicated one, the attorney may feel that the client's interest will be best served if he retains special trial counsel when the case comes up.

Insurance companies, which have to defend so many actions in negligence, usually retain very competent lawyers whose experience in negligence matters is more extensive than that of the general practitioner. Your attorney will retain an expert to cope with such a situation if, in his judgment, that is advisable.

WORKMEN'S COMPENSATION LAWS

Years ago, workers were said to assume the risks of their employment. An injury to a worker in the course of his employment wasn't necessarily followed by compensation from his employer. Moreover, under the so-called "fellow servant" rule, it was possible for the employer to disclaim negligence, on the ground that the injury was caused by the negligence of another employee.

The Workmen's Compensation Laws have put an end to this. In most states, all that an employee need show is that he was injured in the course of his employment, that he didn't intentionally bring about his injury, and that he wasn't intoxicated at the time he suffered it. There is also recovery if the worker dies. In either case, the question of fault is irrelevant.

An award under these laws is the employee's sole remedy unless the injury was intentionally caused by another, or if the employer doesn't have the required compensation coverage.

In most states, the law provides that compensation be guaranteed by compulsory insurance, unless the employer can qualify as a self-insurer. Awards are made on the basis of the extent of the injury, the disability it has caused, and the wages the worker was earning at the time of the accident. The amount is generally fixed by a government agency. Any agreement by employees to waive their rights to compensation are void.

Here, too, the claimant should be represented by a lawyer, since the amount of the award will largely depend on the facts presented to the hearing examiners. At such hearings, the insurance companies are always represented by counsel whose objective is, naturally, to reduce the amount of the award. The tendency is for the agency or board that hears the case to assist the claimant who is not represented by counsel. Labor unions are also generally able to help their members in presenting claims. Nevertheless, there are always facts in such cases that can only be discovered by the careful study a lawyer can give to a situation. So hiring one's own lawyer is always advisable.

It should also be remembered that, in many cases, the claimant's lawyer is not paid by the claimant, but by the employer's insurance company. His fee is fixed by neither the claimant, the insurance company that pays him, nor the employer, but by the state agency hearing the case. The size of the fee is generally dependent on the amount of work the attorney puts in and the result he produces.

CHAPTER SEVENTEEN

CIVIL WRONGS: OTHER THAN NEGLIGENCE

In this chapter we continue our discussion of torts and deal with libel, slander, false imprisonment, assault and battery, fraud, and malicious prosecution.

LIABILITY FOR THE TORTS OF OTHERS

Employer-Employee. Within limitations, you can hold an employer responsible for the acts of his employees. Generally, at the time the civil wrong was committed, the wrongdoer must have been in the employ of the liable party, and the wrong done must have been committed in the performance of his duties.

For example, if an assault and battery were committed by a railroad guard on his tour of duty, the railroad company would be responsible for damages. In the same way, if someone is libeled by a columnist or reporter, the newspaper which published the libel might be held responsible for damages.

But here is a case where a company was not responsible for damage claims incurred by one of its employees. A salesman, driving his own car, on a business mission for his firm, gave a girl a lift. He was on his way from one business call to another. Due to his negligent driving, there was an accident in which the girl passenger was severely injured. The company wasn't liable, because, for reasons of his own, the driver had decided to make a side trip where he had no duties to fulfill for his employer. The accident had occurred through the negligence of the corporation's employee, but not in the course of business for the corporation.

Husband and Wife, Parent and Child. Ordinarily, a man is not responsible for the actions of his wife or of his child unless they are acting for him as his agent or under his instructions. In such cases, the same rules apply as with employers and employees. Parents, however, do have a duty to control the conduct of their children.

Other's Use of Car. Many states make a car owner who lends his vehicle to another responsible for the driver's negligent conduct. But an owner may not be liable if the driver has disobeyed specific instructions. (For example, "Don't go to New York City" rather than "Drive carefully.")

LIBEL AND SLANDER

Defamation is the tort that arises when a false statement is made about a living person, if the words adversely affect his reputation. The words must relate to an individual rather than to a group in general. When the defamatory words are spoken, the tort is called **slander.** When the words are written or printed, it is called **libel.** Libel is considered more serious than slander because the writing or printing is more permanent, is likely to be more widely circulated, and is more deliberate than words that are spoken.

Publication. One of the essential elements of defamation is publication. This does not necessarily mean that a large number of people must hear the words or see them in print. Communication to a single third party is sufficient to constitute publication. Every repetition of the defamatory material is a new publication. But mass publication in a magazine, for instance, gives rise to only one cause of action. If a statement is defamatory, it is no defense to say that the words were quoted from another publication.

Defamatory Statements. The following classes of statements have been held to be actionable:

1. Statements that imply that a person has been guilty of the commission of a crime.
2. Statements that have a tendency to injure a person in his profession, trade or calling.
3. Statements that would hold a person up to public scorn, ridicule or contempt, or that would impair his enjoyment of the society of the community.

In some cases it is necessary, if legal action is taken, to show that the defamatory words actually caused damages. In other cases, the words themselves, without proof of damages, give the victim the right to maintain a lawsuit.

When Statements Are Libelous "Per Se." This occurs if the defamation is complete on its face, without a knowledge of additional facts. For example, if a person holds public office, and the words falsely state that he is unfit, he need not show special damages to bring suit. Statements that falsely say or imply that a man is dishonest or incompetent in the conduct of his profession, trade or business may also be the subject of a suit.

Similarly, if one calls another a thief, a traitor, a forger, a murderer, or an ex-convict —these words, if false, are actionable without showing any special damage. The same is true of words that accuse a woman (but not a man) of being unchaste (or simply imply it). Anyone falsely accused of having venereal disease or leprosy can bring an action without proving damages, because such words, if believed, could deprive him of the society of his friends. Only these types of falsehoods, if spoken, are actionable without additional proof of harm. As to libel, however, any false statement, complete on its face, is actionable without a showing of damages.

In all other cases of defamation, it is necessary to show that the aggrieved person has actually suffered from the dissemination of the words. The publication must be of a kind that would tend to hurt the reputation of the target. If the people to whom the words were addressed did not understand the sense of the allegation, there is no publication.

Defenses to Defamation Claims. The best defense is the truth of the statement. A person cannot recover damages if a statement is shown to be true, no matter how damaging it is to him. (If a statement is only partially true, collectible damages are mitigated.)

Another defense is *privilege*. This means that the statement was communicated to someone who had a special interest in the subject matter and whose relationship to the one making the statement was confidential. So statements relating to judicial or legislative proceedings can't be the basis for a defamation action. And, generally, there is no defamation if one makes a statement to another when both parties have a common interest or duty in regard to the subject. So when evidence against a school principal was collected and sent to members of the board of education in connection with charges brought against her, the communication was held to be privileged. But a commercial report on the financial status of a firm is not privileged. If such a report is damaging to a firm and is untrue, it is libelous.

Under the Constitution, a public official can't recover for falsehoods relating to official conduct, unless there is proof that the statement was made with, at least, reckless disregard for the truth. Public figures—private citizens involved in news events, etc.—are similarly treated, although a tougher standard may be forthcoming.

When Reputation Is Bad. Ordinarily, it is defamatory to publish a statement that implies that a woman is unchaste. But if such a statement is made about someone who has previously been involved in public scandals or has been named as corespondent in a successful divorce action, the result may be a verdict awarding the plaintiff token damages. This is a recognition that the statement was defamatory, but damages are denied because when the reputation is bad or nonexistent prior to the publication, there is no real injury for which compensation can be made.

Damages. The jury is usually left with the task of fixing a money award to compensate the injured party for the loss suffered as a result of the defamation. Jurors are allowed to take into account any loss to the plaintiff's earning power as well as the general damage to his good name and reputation. If there has been actual malice (that is, a determined effort to harm the plaintiff) the court will allow *punitive damages*. By this we mean that the amount of the verdict will include not only compensation for the injured party but also punishment for the wrongdoer.

If the defamatory statement is retracted in a manner equivalent to the original publication, or if the defamer can prove grounds for his erroneous belief, damages might be mitigated. Remember: The fact that you were merely repeating another's defamatory words, by itself, won't end your responsibility to pay damages.

If a statement is defamatory *per se,* an action can be maintained without pleading or proving that any damages have been suffered at all. The assumption is that the words are so injurious that some harm must have been inflicted. The jury estimates the monetary value of that harm. In other cases, recovery is allowed only if *special damages* are shown—and these must consist of some financial loss. Without proof of them, a jury can't estimate what loss the defamed party suffered. However, once special damages are proven, claims for embarrassment, mental distress, and general harm to reputation—*general damages*—may be made.

FALSE IMPRISONMENT

After looking over a display of watches in a jewelry department, a shopper was approached by a store detective. One of the watches was missing, he informed her, and she would have to submit to a search. She found herself surrounded and detained by employees of the store, although no one laid a hand on her. While this was going on, the missing watch was found elsewhere. The shopper sued for false imprisonment and recovered damages.

Any intentional and unjustified restraint on a person's liberty, whether by actual force or verbal threats, is a false imprisonment. The place where it occurs doesn't matter: it need not be a locked room or an actual jail as long as boundaries are fixed by the defendants. Merely blocking one exit is not sufficient if other known paths are open. One isn't required to use unreasonable efforts to make an escape, though. The restraint need not be malicious. A person may be liable for false arrest if he instigates the confinement of another, as when he causes another to be arrested wrongfully.

To justifiably arrest and detain a person requires a warrant, legally drawn and issued by an officer invested with the right to do so. A law officer who makes an arrest without a warrant, or with a defective warrant, or who, with a legal warrant, arrests the wrong person, may be sued for false imprisonment. However, he can make an arrest without a warrant if a crime is committed or attempted in his presence, and in a few other strictly defined circumstances. A private person may make an arrest without a warrant if a crime is committed in his presence, but he risks liability for false arrest.

MALICIOUS PROSECUTION

A person renders himself liable to suit for malicious prosecution if he brings a criminal action against another without "probable cause"—that is, without reasonable grounds for such action—or if he starts a civil action that has no other object than to damage and harass the defendant. The action must terminate in favor of the defendant if he is to collect for any damages he suffered.

The X Insurance Company accused Jones

of embezzling company funds. A warrant was issued for Jones's arrest, and he was summoned to appear in court. But the magistrate dismissed the case. Jones then brought an action for malicious prosecution and obtained a judgment for damages.

It developed that the accusation was made by the company on suspicion alone and wasn't justified by the facts. There were no reasonable grounds of a kind that would lead a prudent man to believe Jones guilty. The absence of such grounds is enough to indicate malice. An acquittal on the charge alone does not establish a lack of probable cause, however.

Examples of civil actions giving rise to recovery include wrongfully brought lunacy or attachment proceedings, if the victim can prove actual damages brought about by the wrongdoing.

FRAUD AND DECEIT

The scene is a used-car lot. A customer is inspecting a rather respectable-looking automobile. However, its appearance proves to be the only respectable thing about it.

It has had a stormy past. Major collisions have twisted the frame. The engine works, but three of the six cyclinders have half their rated compression. The brakes need relining. The front end will stand up—but not for long. Last but not least, the odometer has been doctored to show a total mileage of 32,000 miles. In fact, the last owner, a traveling salesman, drove it 90,000 miles himself.

With the customer is the salesman and a third man, his friend, who just seems to be hanging around.

The salesman speaks: "Here's a car that's an outstanding buy. This make and model always has a good resale value. It's got all the features you find in new cars—hydraulic brakes, automatic transmission, radio, heater, directional signals. The rubber is fine and the battery is practically new. You won't have to buy another one for two years. This is a real buy."

Though the customer does not seem to be

sold, there's something about the way he looks at the car which denotes the beginning of a sentimental attachment. The salesman turns to his idle friend. "Bill," he says, "what do you think of this job?"

Bill pitches right in. He says, "I happen to know the last owner. Never had an accident. Guy never drove much—the mileage shows it —a real Sunday driver. Nothing wrong with the engine either; she's got plenty of pep."

Customer buys car; car collapses; customer gets lawyer and goes to court. What happens?

Investigation shows that the salesman knew all about the car's past. His friend Bill knew nothing about it at all, and had never met the former owner. The customer was awarded a judgment for damages by the court for the fraud of both the salesman and his friend.

Let's analyze why. In his statement the salesman told no lies. Examine his words and you'll find he made no misrepresentations of fact beyond asserting that the car was a good buy. Exaggerations of this kind are expected of salesmen. Puffing or enthusiasm for the product expressed in words is normal and not generally regarded as fraud.

The question may arise whether or not his silence about the defects he was aware of was fraudulent. This is a close question; the general rule is that a seller is not required to volunteer all the information he has about a piece of property, especially when a reasonable inspection and inquiry by the buyer would reveal the defects, unless it's clear that the buyer is acting under a misapprehension. (However, sometimes a duty to disclose basic facts about title or safety has been found.)

More importantly, the salesman had profited knowingly from the false statements of his friend Bill. Bill is definitely guilty of fraud. He showed a disregard for truth when he voiced, as facts, statements whose truth or falsity he could not know. (Its a different story if he only offered an opinion.) Since his statements turned out to be false, and the customer had relied on them to be true, Bill committed fraud. Moreover, his assertion that he knew the former owner was a lie; and this he knew to be a lie.

Here are the elements of fraud:

(a) There must be a misrepresentation of a material fact by words or conduct;

(b) There must be knowledge on the part of the one who makes the statement that it is false. Or, as in the case of Bill, there must be a disregard for the truth in making positive statements when their truth or falsity is unknown to him;

(c) The statement must have been intended to influence the one who was deceived;

(d) The deceived party must have heard and been misled by the statement.

(e) There must have been a reliance on the statement, in good faith, by the one who complains, and his loss (of money or other property) must be traceable to such reliance.

All these elements must be present for the plaintiff to make out a case in fraud that would entitle him to damages. When the fraud is unintentional, as when the person making the statement believed it to be true, or did not know it to be false, there may be reason to cancel the transaction. The absence of guilty knowledge and intent will preclude the collection of damages.

There are cases where deception is due to negligence rather than fraud in the strict sense. For example, Bruno sued the directors of a corporation for fraud because he had been induced to buy its shares by a circular containing false statements. It turned out that the directors did not know the statements were false; they believed them to be true. However, investigation, such as prudent men would make, would have disclosed to them that the circular was erroneous. In failing to make the investigation, they were negligent, and they could be sued for negligence. But because they had no guilty knowledge or intent to defraud, they were not required to pay damages for fraud.

POINTERS:

Buy With Care! One of the hoariest legal maxims is still expressed in its original Latin: *"Caveat emptor."* This means: "Let the buyer beware."

A person entering a business transaction, such as making a purchase, has the duty to inform himself about what he buys by examination and inquiry. He can't just go ahead blindly and then put the responsibility on the seller for not volunteering information he should have secured for himself.

If you do have a cause of action against, say, a merchant who sold you inferior merchandise, it's often easier to bring an action for deceit rather than one for breach of contract. A lawyer can best advise you how to proceed.

Get Specific Information. Expressions of value and quality are regarded as opinions, not statements of fact. "This is good steel" is an opinion, But "This is sixteen-gauge steel" is a statement of fact. "This car is a good buy" is an opinion, but "This car has only been driven sixteen thousand miles" is a statement of fact. If a statement of fact is not true, it may be actionable. An erroneous opinion is not actionable.

Watch Your Statements. We are often called upon to make some kind of recommendation. In a harmless recommendation, you may say, "I'd like to see you hire John. He's a nice guy and I'd be pleased to see him get ahead." But if you say, "I know John to be an honest man. He's had ten years of experience as an accountant," that may have troublesome consequences. If the facts you've asserted aren't true, and someone who has relied upon your statements gets hurt, you might be held responsible for damages.

ASSAULT AND BATTERY

An assault does not involve physical contact. It consists of some intentional and overt action that reasonably puts someone in fear of physical attack. A threatening act is required; words alone do not amount to an assault. One who waves a weapon in a threatening manner is committing an assault. Similarly, pointing an *unloaded* pistol and threatening to shoot has been held to be an assault, if the victim believes the gun to be loaded.

Battery, on the other hand, involves some harmful or offensive touching of the victim, or of something closely associated with him. Punching a man or grabbing a package he's holding are two types of battery. The battery must be intended by the actor. One can be guilty of assault and battery for one completed action.

Excusable Use of Force. A person who uses force in self-defense is not guilty of assault or battery, provided he uses only as much force as is needed to defend himself. (Defense here does not include retaliation.) One generally isn't required to retreat first unless deadly force is used. If a victim uses more force than is necessary for his protection, he becomes the aggressor, and may himself be guilty of assault and battery. The degree of force required in self-defense depends on the circumstances. Even killing another has sometimes been held justifiable because of the nature of the attack, and because less drastic means wouldn't suffice. A person is also justified in using reasonable force to defend a third party if help appears to be needed.

The same is generally true of actions in defense of property. However, a request to leave or desist from the intrusion should always precede action. A man can then forcibly eject a trespasser from his home, or can use reasonable force to regain property taken from him. Court decisions have also held that the use of force to compel the physical removal of a discharged employee is not an assault and battery. But only as much force as is necessary to eject the trespasser may be used. The bodily security of the trespasser overrides the privilege to use force. For example, a railroad company went beyond its rights to so frighten a boy who was stealing a ride that he fell off the train and sustained severe injuries. And the owner of property has no right to set up dangerous devices like spring guns or traps for the purpose of injuring trespassers. One can't cause serious bodily harm for a mere trespass.

However, if life, and not just property, is threatened, greater force can be used.

SOME OTHER TORTS

Privacy. There does exist, to some extent, a right to be left alone. Almost all states protect a person's right to the value of his name and features for trade or advertising purposes. Some states allow recovery for noncommercial invasions of privacy beyond the limits of decency—a vague but flexible standard. However, if one is part of a public event, or if one's name is on public record, there probably won't be a recovery for an intrusion into private affairs that relate to the public matters. However, an action to halt the unauthorized commercial use of one's name or likeness will probaby be more successful.

Nuisance. A person can't make an unreasonable use of his property so as to interfere with or injure another. So if Bill's home repair work makes so much noise that his neighbor, Kurt, can't use his property in peace, Kurt can get an injunction against, or collect damages from, Bill. However, the interference must be a substantial one—it must persist over a period of time and must do more than simply affect someone's special sensibilities. If the nuisance affects the public at large, an injunction is the usual remedy, although, in such cases, the social utility of the nuisance is often considered. For example, a smoky factory might not be closed if that would mean economic harm to an area.

A private nuisance, which affects a limited number of people, can give rise to an action based on negligence, intentional harm, or **strict liability.** A person is strictly liable for using his property in an abnormal or very hazardous manner, when the potential for harm cannot be eliminated by the use of reasonable care. To recover, a person must only show that another's hazardous activity interfered with his own normal use of his property. There won't be any recovery, however, if the harm that occurs is not a foreseeable result of the abnormal use of the property, or if it arises from an intervening force.

Prima Facie Tort. Any intentional infliction of harm which does not fall into the category of an established tort is known as a prima facie tort and may be actionable. In these cases, a plaintiff must prove his financial injury, and that the actor's sole motive was to inflict harm. This type of action can't be used to escape the requirements of the statute of limitations relating to other, established torts.

CHAPTER EIGHTEEN

DOMESTIC RELATIONS: ENGAGEMENT AND MARRIAGE

Marriage as a social institution has the blessing of the community. It is useful to bear this in mind in any discussion of domestic relations. Because the state approves of it, the policies and principles behind the laws affecting marriage encourage, foster, and protect the institution. That's why it is easier to get into wedlock than to get out. Additional protection to marriage is given in laws relating to property, desertion, abandonment, maintenance, support, community property, etc.

Some people get dizzy when they look down from great heights; lawyers get dizzy by trying to keep track of the domestic-relations laws of the fifty states. Since the basic laws of every state except Louisiana have been taken from the same source—the common law of England—you would expect them to resemble each other except in minor details. While this is true of practically every branch of law, marriage and divorce are exceptions. It is possible, for example, to have no wife in one state, be a law-abiding married man in another, and be a bigamist in a third—all at the same time.

WHAT MARRIAGE IS

A broad definition, accepted practically everywhere, is: The union of a man and a woman for life by civil contract, with the consent of both parties, in which they assume a status granted by the state. Each state has its own requirements regarding licenses, medical examinations, age of consent, and the details of the ceremony. Some states require that a certain time pass after the issuance of the license before the marriage takes place. Others require that the marriage take place within a certain period after the license is issued, or it becomes invalid.

Engagement. When a man proposes marriage to a woman and is accepted, the arrangement between them is sometimes recognized by the law as a binding contract. Just as in a business contract, the parties have the right to change their minds and, by mutual consent, terminate the contract—call the whole thing off.

This is sensible because during the engagement, the couple gets to know each other and to become acquainted with each other's family, friends and background. If they find the engagement to be a mistake, they can break it without much trouble. But if the decision is all on one side, the other party will feel rejected and may suffer material damage.

Breach of Promise. A business has the right to sue for breach of contract and recover damages, but a spurned fiancée can't always sue for breach of promise. This type of action has been outlawed in many states. But other remedies may exist. In New York, for example, certain tort actions are possible.

The reason for disallowing breach-of-promise suits can be found in examples of "heart balm" suits. Lurid courtship details and originals or facsimiles of love letters were usually offered in evidence in court. The states which have outlawed these suits have done so to stop this type of conduct, especially since the suits were often used to bilk lonely, wealthy people out of large sums. But the greater evil lay in the cases that never came to trial. These were settled out of court for large sums in order to forestall any press coverage.

What Happens to Gifts? When an engagement is broken, the parties usually have some property settlement to make. Wedding gifts might have been received from family and friends. The couple might have exchanged expensive presents, and the woman was probably given an engagement ring.

The wedding gifts should go back to the donors because, if the marriage doesn't take place, the basis for the gift is gone. The engagement ring should be returned for the same reason—regardless of who breaks the engagement, although in some cases retention may be allowed if the man severed the engagement. Other gifts, however, such as jewelry and other items exchanged by the parties, which might have been given had no engagement been entered into, may be kept by the donees. These rules relating to gifts are pretty generally followed throughout the United States, whether or not suits for breach of promise are allowed or not, but variations will arise according to individual circumstances.

Contracts Before Marriage. People who have special money or property problems may arrange their affairs by contract before marriage. Such contracts will generally be binding unless they conflict with what is known as public policy. In the case of marriage, the public policy is to encourage and preserve the institution, and not to modify the relationship and obligations of husband and wife. So if, before marriage, the parties agree not to live together, or to abstain from sexual relations, or if the terms excuse the husband from his duty to support his wife, the agreement won't ordinarily be enforced by the courts—these terms materially alter the traditional relationship of husband and wife. (But traditional thought about support obligations is changing, and special situations may arise where the wife is the wealthier party.)

Similarly, *any* pact providing for a later divorce, or separation, or alimony payments in the event of separation, isn't likely to be sustained in a court of law. The type of agreement the courts *will* enforce is one that has to do purely with property. Marriage usually creates rights in favor of husbands and wives in the property of the other, and these rights can be modified or disclaimed, and the property divided as the parties agree, so long as the contract is fairly entered into and doesn't promote divorce.

Premarital contracts are becoming more common and are used to set down and clarify what each party expects of the other in the relationship. For example, a husband and wife who both plan to continue working might specify housekeeping and child-rearing arrangements in the contract so that the wife isn't obliged to leave work to raise the family. These terms aren't legally enforceable, but they force the couple to confront certain problems before entering marriage.

Inheritance Rights. Generally, a spouse has an interest in the property of his deceased spouse. Unless the couple has been legally divorced, a husband, for example, can't cut off his wife in his will. A husband generally has an equal right to share in his wife's estate. Most states fix a minimum the spouse will receive out of the property of the decedent. If less is provided for in the decedent's will, the survivor has the right to disregard it and to take the legal minimum. Remember: This can be modified by an antenuptial agreement (premarital contract). So if a husband-to-be has obligations to his family, his fiancée may agree to take a smaller share of his estate. Or, a wealthy widow may wish that her children inherit her late husband's money, so she has her second husband agree to accept a smaller inheritance than the statutory minimum.

Common-law Marriage. This is a union without formality of any kind—no license, no ceremony, no justice of the peace. All that is required is that the man and woman live together and hold themselves out to the world as husband and wife.

Cohabitation can become a common-law marriage by the simple, even unspoken, consent of the parties or through the introduction to others as marital partners. "This is my husband" or, "I'd like you to meet my wife," said in public over a period of time may be enough to establish such relationships.

Fourteen states and the District of Columbia recognize common-law marriages. Other states recognize them if performed before certain dates (which vary), or if established in states that do recognize these marriages. If you are interested where your state stands on this matter, consult Table 6.

Who May Not Marry? Most states bar marriage when either party is under age (the minimum varies), has been adjudged a lunatic, or already has a spouse. Most states prohibit the marriage of people closely akin (between first cousins, for example). States can't bar marriage on racial grounds. When illegal marriages take place, they are usually voidable. This means that they are recognized until attacked in the courts.

Nature of the Marital Relationship. The laws relating to husband and wife have undergone profound changes in recent decades. Once, marriage was considered as the merging of two people into one, whose identity, for all practical purposes, was the husband's. Now the law recognizes the individual rights and identities of the parties. A married woman today has virtually the same rights as her husband.

Some vestiges do remain of the view that the wife's identity merges with her husband's. Such laws are open to challenge, however. Today, the thoughts and inclinations of the couple are often more controlling than any specific law in the matter of the woman's position in the marriage.

When a Spouse May Sue. Generally, a husband's remedy for his wife's failure to fulfill her marital obligations is dissolution of the marriage. But he can sue others for damages if, through their negligent or willful acts, they deprive him of the companionship of his wife. This is the reason husband and wife usually join together in a suit for personal injuries to the wife. A wife has similar claims to her husband's companionship and support.

Legal Responsibility for a Spouse. A husband isn't responsible for the acts of his wife, and vice versa. If, for example, one party commits a tort, the other cannot be required to pay damages, unless the act was done in the capacity of an agent.

Can Spouses Bring Civil Actions Against Each Other? Many states don't permit actions for civil wrongs by husbands or wives against the other. The reason is to protect marital harmony, and to forestall any possibility of collusion between the parties. So if a wife is injured while a passenger in a car negligently driven by her husband, she probably can't sue him even if he's heavily insured against such accidents. New York, for example, will allow such suits but permits insurance companies to bar such claims.

Under New York law, a man can be guilty of the crime of larceny if he steals from his wife. Long ago this would have been impossible because, after marriage, the wife's property became the husband's. Now, wives have independent property rights, and states have removed the common-law bars to such actions in most cases.

Support of the Wife. A husband is obliged to support his wife. This is an essential part of the marriage relationship and can't be altered by contract. It applies even if the wife is independently wealthy or is in no need of her husband's support. There is growing approval of the idea that support obligations are reciprocal, so that a woman might be obliged to support a man if she were the major wage earner.

This obligation frequently has to be translated into dollars. It's not an easy job and, in a suit for support, it is foolhardy to try to say in advance just how much the court will allow.

Chief among the determining factors are the financial situation of the husband, and the manner in which the parties are accustomed to live. Support can mean food, clothing and shelter; it can also mean penthouses, servants and luxuries.

When a judge has to fix the amount, he often takes into account the behavior of the parties. If the conduct of the wife is subject to criticism, this can influence his decision.

The same flexibility applies to the term "necessaries." This word is important in connection with the husband's responsibility to merchants and others who provide necessaries to his wife. Here, the wife is regarded as the agent of her husband in providing her with the necessities of life, and a merchant can sue the husband for their price.

However, the wife doesn't have an unlimited right to the use of his credit. The merchant who sells expensive clothes to a woman and charges it to the husband sometimes takes a chance. If she is already well provided with necessities according to the husband's income, the merchant may not be able to collect.

How a Husband Can Disclaim a Wife's Debts. He can't just stop paying after he has honored a series of the merchant's bills. His previous payments of bills for his wife's purchases approved her authority to act as his agent. If he wants to stop wild buying on her part, he must notify all the merchants his wife has dealt with.

You will frequently see newspaper notices reading: "My wife, Myrtle, having left my bed and board, I am no longer responsible for her debts." This gives public notice that Myrtle is no longer authorized to use her husband's credit. But to be safe in such a situation, the husband should give additional notice, in writing, to those who were accustomed to dealing with her.

Property Rights. Husband and wife have rights in each other's property. These vary from state to state. A number of states have passed community property laws under which the property acquired, after the marriage, by

husband and wife is considered to belong to them equally. This is an extreme advance from the earlier view that everything belonged to the husband, nothing to the wife. For income-tax purposes, husbands and wives are permitted to file joint returns even when one has no income, and the marital deductions reflect this sense of co-ownership in the estate and gift tax area. These provisions are intended to give couples in non-community-property states parity with couples in states with such laws.

Dower and Curtesy. Under the common law, the wife had what was called the right of "dower." This gave her an interest, for her life, in one third of the real property owned by the husband at the time of his death. The corresponding right of the surviving husband in the property of his wife was called "curtesy." Property subject to these rights can only be conveyed free and clear if both spouses join in the deed. However, most states have replaced these common-law rights with statutes defining property interests, although the common law still holds, in most cases, in regard to property owned before the enactment of the statutes.

Substitute for Dower and Curtesy. In New York, for example, dower and curtesy have been replaced by a provision in the law governing inheritance. (See chapter on inheritance and intestacy.) This gives to the survivor the right to a share of all the property (real or personal) of the deceased. State laws on this matter vary widely; but they exist in some form throughout the United States.

These rights don't apply to a divorced couple. And, generally, if the parties weren't living together at the time of the death of one spouse, for a reason considered to be the fault of the survivor, claims of a right in some part of the deceased's property can be resisted.

Nonsupport: The Criminal Aspect. We have seen that the obligation of a husband to support his wife is recognized in the civil courts, and that a husband may become responsible to third parties who supply necessaries to his wife. In many states, nonsupport is a crime punishable by imprisonment, especially if the wife would otherwise be a public charge.

Family Courts. The idea of special courts to deal with domestic relations has caught on. Most of these courts proceed on the theory that a husband who neglects his wife is a disorderly person—remiss in his duty, not just to his family, but to the community. Family courts can compel a defendant to appear, and punish him if he doesn't. They have, generally, the power to compel the regular payment of support under penalty of jail, in most cases.

The courts today do more than attempt merely to keep the wife from becoming a public charge. They now try to deal with the cases before them as family problems, with all their ramifications. Counseling and rehabilitation programs are common. Alimony awards now take the circumstances of the couple into consideration, and don't merely provide enough support to keep the wife off welfare.

ADOPTION OF CHILDREN

Adoption is purely statutory. That means it was unknown under the common law, and exists in the various states only in accordance with special legislation. The laws of the fifty states differ in many respects, but there are basic similarities that allow us to give a general explanation of the subject.

Who May Adopt? One must be an adult to become an adoptive parent (unless an underage person adopts a spouse's child). In some states it's required that the adoptive parent be at least ten or fifteen years older than the adopted child. Generally, married couples are preferred by the courts, but it has become increasingly possible for an otherwise qualified unmarried adult to adopt a child. In adoption proceedings, the state, through its courts, acts in a paternal capacity as guardian of the children of the state. The first consideration is always the welfare of the adoptive child, rather than the desires of the proposed adopters.

Consent Is Required. Consent is required from the natural parents, often from the child, and, in some cases, from authorized institutions which have custody of the child. There are exceptions. Consent isn't required from the parents if they are mentally incompetent, if they have abandoned the child, or if a court has removed the child from their custody because of cruelty or neglect. However, notice of the action must be given to the parents so they can try to prove that they are fit parents or that they unknowingly gave up the child. In the case of an illegitimate child, the consent of the father isn't usually required, although notice of the action is generally given so that he can observe that the best interests of the child are being considered. The mother's consent must be obtained. The consent of the child may be dispensed with if he is under the age fixed by law in the state. These ages appear in Table 5. The consent of parents isn't required if the adoptee is not a minor.

Procedure. A petition must be made to the court and a judicial hearing is held in which the court examines the qualifications of the prospective parents, and either grants or denies their petition. A general practice is to provide for a probationary or trial period before and after the judicial hearing. During this period, the child lives with the adopting parents. Some states provide for the test period by making the judicial order of adoption interlocutory (or tentative), the order becoming final after a specified probationary period.

Change in Legal Status. The legal rights and the legal status of the child, the natural parents, and the adopting parents are very much involved in adoption proceedings. State statutes define how these rights and obligations are affected. Generally, the adopted child is treated as if he were the natural child of the adopting parents. One item of importance is the question of inheritance, especially whether or not the child loses his right to inherit from his natural parents. See Table 5 for the rule in the various states.

Generally, when the adoption is made final, a new birth certificate is issued and all papers relating to the action are sealed. Recently, however, there's been a tendency to grant people who have been adopted access to those papers.

ILLEGITIMACY

Laws in this area vary throughout the United States. Generally, a child is legitimate if his parents marry after his birth. Divorce, or the annulment of a marriage, doesn't affect a child's legitimacy. Support for an illegitimate child can be ordered from the father in a filiation proceeding—but this doesn't make the child legitimate. And the father generally isn't relieved of his obligation of support if the mother marries another man, unless the child is adopted by the new husband. An illegitimate child usually inherits from his mother and her family as if he were legitimate. Obstacles in state law that bar inheritance from the father's side are probably no longer valid in light of a recent Supreme Court decision. There is a growing tendency to give illegitimate children parity in this and other areas. Nevertheless, the problem of proving paternity must first be dealt with, and unless there is an admission of paternity, this will involve an often protracted court proceeding.

Table 5—ADOPTION

State	Infant's consent required if over age of	Probationary period	*Inherits from Adopting Parents	*Inherits from Natural Parents
Alabama	14	6 months	X	X
Alaska	(adult)		X	
Arizona	12	6 months	X	
Arkansas	14	6 months	X	X
California	12		X	
Colorado	12	6 months	X	
Connecticut	14	D	X	
Delaware	14	1 year	X	
District of Columbia	14	6 months	X	
Florida	12		X	
Georgia	14		X	
Hawaii	10	E	X	
Idaho	12		X	
Illinois	14	6 months	X	
Indiana	14	C	X	X
Iowa	14	6 months	X	
Kansas	14		X	
Kentucky	12	3 months	X	
Louisiana		1 year	X	X
Maine	14	1 year	X	X
Maryland	10	A	X	
Massachusetts	12	1 year (B)	X	
Michigan	10	1 year	X	
Minnesota	14	6 months	X	
Mississippi	14	6 months	X	X
Missouri	14	9 months	X	
Montana	12	6 months	X	X
Nebraska	14	6 months	X	
Nevada	14	6 months	X	
New Hampshire	12	6 months	X	
New Jersey	10	1 year	X	
New Mexico	10	6 months	X	
New York	14	6 months	X	
North Carolina	12	1 year	X	
North Dakota	10	6 months	X	
Ohio	12	6 months	X	
Oklahoma	12	6 months	X	
Oregon	14	6 months	X	
Pennsylvania	12	6 months	X	
Puerto Rico	10		X	X
Rhode Island	14	6 months	X	X
South Carolina		F	X	
South Dakota	12	6 months	X	X
Tennessee	14	1 year	X	
Texas	12	6 months	X	X
Utah	12	6 months	X	
Vermont	14	6 months	X	X
Virginia	14	6 months	X	
Washington	14	6 months	X	
West Virginia	12	6 months	X	
Wisconsin	14	6 months	X	
Wyoming	14	6 months	X	

In most states where inheritance by the adopted child from the natural parents is not provided, a child legally adopted by the husband or wife of the natural parent may inherit from the natural parents.

*Applies only in the absence of a will or some other testamentary disposition.

FOOTNOTES

(A) The period must not exceed one year.

(B) The period applies only if the child is under the age of 14.

(C) The probationary period is in the discretion of the court.

(D) The period must be at least 12, but not more than 13 months.

(E) The period must not exceed 6 months.

(F) The probationary period ends at the conclusion of court action.

X—means YES.

Table 6—MARRIAGE

	Common Law Marriages § Permitted	Age at Which Marriage Is Permitted for		Age at Which Marriage Is Permitted Without Consent of Parents for	
		Man	Woman	Man	Woman
Alabama	X	17	14	19	18
Alaska		18	*16	18	18
Arizona		18	*16	18	18
Arkansas		17	†16	18	18
California		*18	*16	18	18
Colorado	X	*16	*16	18	18
Connecticut		*16	*16	18	18
Delaware		18	16	18	18
District of Columbia	X	16	16	18	18
Florida	X	†18	†16	18	18
Georgia	X	†16	†16	16	16
Hawaii		*16	*16	18	18
Idaho	X	*16	*16	18	18
Illinois		16	16	18	18
Indiana		17	*17	18	18
Iowa	X	16	14	18	18
Kansas	X	14	*16	18	18
Kentucky		18	18	18	18
Louisiana		*18	*16	18	18
Maine		*16	*16	18	18
Maryland		†16	†16	18	18
Massachusetts		14	12	18	18
Michigan		18	16	18	18
Minnesota		*18	*18	18	18
Mississippi	X	17	15	17	15
Missouri		*15	*15	18	18
Montana	X	*18	*16	18	18
Nebraska		18	16	18	18
Nevada		18	*16	18	18
New Hampshire		*18	*18	18	18
New Jersey		*18	*16	18	18
New Mexico		*16	*16	18	18
New York		16	*16	18	18
North Carolina		†16	†16	18	18
North Dakota		†16	*16	18	18
Ohio	X	18	†16	18	18
Oklahoma	X	*16	*16	18	18
Oregon		17	17	17	17
Pennsylvania	X	*16	*16	18	18
Puerto Rico		18	16	21	21
Rhode Island	X	*18	*16	18	18
South Carolina	X	16	14	18	18
South Dakota		18	18	18	18
Tennessee		*16	14	18	18
Texas	X	*14	*14	18	18
Utah		16	14	21	18
Vermont		*16	*16	18	18
Virginia		16	†16	18	18
Washington		17	*17	18	18
West Virginia		18	†16	18	18
Wisconsin		16	16	18	18
Wyoming		18	16	18	18

X –Yes

* Marriages under this age permitted by special permission of the court.

† Marriages under this age permitted if parties are parents, or expecting a child.

§ Common law marriages which were valid where and when contracted are recognized everywhere.

DOMESTIC RELATIONS: ANNULMENT, SEPARATION, DIVORCE

When an ailing marriage is brought before the court by a complaining husband or wife, one of four things can happen: (1) ANNULMENT, a cancellation of the marriage; (2) DIVORCE, a dissolution of the marriage; (3) SEPARATION, legally living apart while the marriage relationship continues (sometimes called partial divorce); and (4) STATUS QUO, the parties are left in their unhappy situation.

ANNULMENT

Annulment is a proceeding to declare the marriage void. The grounds for annulment differ in the various states. What they have in common is the fact that they must have been in existence at the time the marriage took place.

The basis and the theory of most annulment actions is that the consent of one of the parties was obtained by concealment or fraud. Lack of physical capacity is a ground for annulment in many states, but not if developed through some illness or accident after the marriage. Another ground is the inability of either party to consent to marry because he or she was underage or insane at the time. A marriage will also be declared void if it involves bigamy or incest, defined differently in different states.

Generally, there is some recognition that the marriage did exist. So, for example, children born before the annulment are the legitimate offspring of both parents. The court granting the annulment can generally pass on who owns the couple's property. An annulment usually revokes each party's will, and ends the right of election and any intestate rights.

Annulment for Fraud. Mary met George at a summer resort. He was well dressed, drove an expensive car, gave her to understand that he was a well-paid executive, and said he was a bachelor. They had a "whirlwind" courtship.

When they began to discuss marriage, Mary, a serious woman, thought they ought to agree on such matters as how big a family they wanted, the kind of marriage ceremony they'd have, and the sort of home they could afford to establish. George agreed to have at least three children. He consented to a church wedding after the civil ceremony, and promised that they would live in an apartment only until they found a suitable house to buy. After a short engagement, they were married by a justice of the peace and went off on their honeymoon. On the way back, George made some confessions.

He really was only a low-income junior clerk. The car? Borrowed. The summer resort? Her engagement ring? The installment plan. Why the lies? In the beginning, he told her, it was to get her attention. Later he was afraid to tell the truth for fear he would lose her. This was all a shock to Mary, but she decided to make the best of it.

When they got home, Mary explained the situation to her parents, and prevailed on her father to find a place in his business for George. For six months they lived in a furnished apartment, the rent paid by Mary's father. Mary kept pressing for a church wedding, but George continued to put her off. Also, during this time George, over Mary's objection, used contraceptives. Then one day Mary found out that George had been married before; that when they met, George was waiting for his divorce to become final. One hour after she heard this, she had him confirm it and went home to her parents' house.

In Mary's annulment case against George, she alleged that the following fraudulent statements had been used to procure her consent to the marriage: George lied to her about (1) his means; (2) his being a bachelor; (3) his wanting children, when he never intended to have any; (4) a church wedding he never intended to go through with; and (5) living in a apartment.

Let's take a look at Mary's allegations in light of the following rules.

Fraud Must Be Material. The courts are not too quick to consider misrepresentation as to wealth sufficient grounds for voiding a marriage. It doesn't go down well that consent to marriage can be obtained by such bait. The fraud must be one that goes to the heart of the relationship and one that, in the judgment of the court, influenced the consent to the marriage.

Deception as to a prior marriage is usually held to be material. So is deception in respect to having children. And where it can be shown that one party is devout and wouldn't have consented without the promise of a religious ceremony, such a fraud can be the ground for an annulment.

Fraud Must Be Acted Upon or It's Waived. If, after discovering a material deception, a person continues to live with the husband or wife, the right to an annulment on that ground is waived. (And if an under-age spouse continues to cohabit after reaching his or her majority, an annulment is barred.)

Mary continued to live with George after he confessed his deception as to his position and means. Therefore she had already waived that as a ground for an annulment.

But his deceptions as to children and the religious ceremony couldn't be discovered until a reasonable time had passed. Those grounds were still good—they weren't waived by their living together. She acted immediately on the discovery of his fraud regarding his previous marriage—and, in most jurisdictions, she would be granted an annulment on that ground alone.

The business about living in an apartment isn't really fraudulent, but simply a broken promise. In any regard, such a promise is not seen as sufficiently important to be the basis for an annulment.

SEPARATION

Husband and wife cannot, on their own, enter into a valid agreement that annuls or dissolves their marriage, but they can make a separation agreement. Such agreements are generally given full recognition by the courts, provided there is no fraud, and no attempt is made by one party to take undue advantage of the other.

Normally it is possible to accomplish in an agreement everything the court can establish in a decree. This would include provision for the parties to live apart without interference with each other, a settlement dividing the property of the couple, arrangements for the support of the wife and of any children, etc. Often the waiver of all support for the wife voids a separation agreement, because a husband is always obligated to support his wife as long as the marriage exists. It is advisable for the parties to contract for the duration of the support obligation, as long as the time period is related to the marital relationship—for example, the duty could end on remarriage, divorce, or if one of the parties commits adultery.

Where children are involved, provision for custody, for visits by the parent who doesn't have custody, arrangements for education, or, preferably, a method so that such matters can be worked out in the best interests of the child, can be established in the agreement.

Beware: There can be no direct requirement in the agreement that either spouse obtain a divorce. If the agreement isn't honored, the traditional contract remedies apply. Recission and perhaps a court order of support are common remedies. It should also be remembered that such agreements are contracts, so the support obligation can't be increased or decreased because of changed circumstances. Generally, the wife must sue to enforce the agreement, although, in rare cases, children may sue to enforce it.

The prerequisite to a separation agreement is mutual consent. When this is absent, only the court can, on proper grounds, compel a separation by decree. Free consent is so essential in these agreements that each party should be separately represented by counsel. This prevents any later claim that the wife, for example, was at a disadvantage because she was unaccustomed to transacting business or that a lawyer who had previously acted for her husband in business matters was biased in his favor.

Advantages of Separation Agreements. The separation agreement is a great deal more flexible than the separation decree of a court. To begin with, in order to succeed in a suit for separation, the plaintiff must be able to prove legal grounds—although this has been made easier in recent years. These usually include, among others, mental and physical cruelty. An out-of-court agreement may be made without establishing such grounds. The parties must have separated, but the reasons for the separation may be other than those provided in the law as grounds.

An agreement is also preferable because specific arrangements for support, custody of children, etc., can be made to suit individual circumstances. A judge is, after all, a stranger. The parties themselves are in the best position to know what serves their children's needs and their own interests. Agreements can be terminated by inconsistent behavior—that is, if one party applies for court-ordered support, or if the couple resumes cohabitation with the intent to end the separation.

Separation Is No Permanent Solution. The separation of the parties, whether by agreement or court decree, doesn't dissolve the marriage. Neither party is free to marry again, and even after separation, each owes sexual fidelity to the other. (The adultery of either party will give the other grounds for divorce.) Only those bound by religious laws prohibiting divorce consider separation a permanent solution of their difficulties.

The separation agreement can serve another purpose. It can govern the conditions of the parties' lives to some extent after a divorce, if there should be a divorce action. A husband and wife can't enter into an agreement to obtain a divorce. However, they can, in a separation agreement, make a valid provision that, in the event either party obtains a decree of divorce, the separation be incorporated in the decree. In this way, the terms of their property settlement, provisions for support, agreements regarding children, etc., can be dealt with before a divorce proceeding is begun. And the court then has the power to increase or reduce support if there are changed circumstances—a move which is nearly impossible if the separation agreement hasn't been incorporated in the decree.

GROUNDS FOR COURT ACTION

In recent years it has become easier to dissolve a marriage that isn't working. The trend has been to "no-fault" divorce, where the adversary character of the divorce action is reduced to a minimum—the question of who is at fault is not of primary importance. (Most states have some form of this type of procedure.) And there's also a tendency to bar defenses to divorce actions, except if the grounds are adultery. Where defenses are allowed, they can sometimes be used to prevent a wife from claiming alimony from her husband. When granting a divorce decree, courts effect equitable distributions of property owned by the couple and can order alimony that's based on need and ability to pay. Child support is generally seen as a mutual obligation. Remember, however, that each state has its own laws governing the dissolution of marriages, and the proper procedure must be followed. The basic grounds for no-fault dissolution of a marriage is "the breakdown of the marriage," a term used in the laws of twenty-eight states. Other states look for "incompatability," or for a period of separate living, as evidence that the marriage is dead.

A "conversion" type of divorce is allowed in several states. Under this system, an absolute divorce is granted if a couple lives apart for a certain time pursuant to a judicial decree of separation, or pursuant to a valid separation agreement. To win the divorce, there must be proof of substantial performance of the separation plan. Defenses in this type of divorce are generally confined solely to violations of the separation agreement or judgment.

If the dissolution of a marriage is contested, things become more difficult. Adultery is grounds for divorce throughout the United States; desertion is almost as common. We will discuss some of the more common grounds without regard to whether the specific act or situation is grounds for separation, annulment, or divorce. Consult Tables 7 and 8 for a survey of the laws of the fifty states.

Adultery. Some states make a distinction between an act of adultery and "living in adultery." For the most part, a single act of adultery on the part of one spouse is sufficient to establish the other's right to a divorce.

What is adultery? The act involves voluntary sexual intercourse by a married person with someone other than the husband or wife. In most states it is a crime punishable by fine or imprisonment, but such laws are almost never enforced.

Proof of adultery for the purpose of sustaining a criminal conviction is quite different from the proof required to furnish grounds for divorce. Since sexual intercourse is generally not engaged in before witnesses, divorce courts will accept evidence of opportunity and mutual inclination. If a man and woman register at a hotel as man and wife and occupy the same room for the night, testimony by witnesses as to the registration and as to having seen them enter and leave would be sufficient.

Collusive, Coercive or Forgiven Adultery. Proof of adultery, by itself, will not always result in a decree of divorce. If the complaining party (the plaintiff) has connived in the adultery, or if the act of intercourse was not voluntary, the court will generally not permit it to be used in a divorce action. And if, after learning of the adultery, the complaining party continues to live with the other, the act will be considered to have been forgiven and a divorce will be denied, as long as there is no repetition of the act.

In an action for divorce based on adultery, it is often a good defense, if proved, that the other party committed adultery, too. In such a case, the court will leave the parties as it found them: Neither party will be granted a divorce, although it would seem that a divorce would be doubly justified in such a case.

Collusion and Co-operation. Most of the divorce cases that come before the courts are undefended. The wife makes her complaint and gives her evidence without opposition from the husband. While this appears to be co-operative, it doesn't necessarily imply collusion. Even where the suit for divorce is not opposed, the plaintiff must give testimony, corroborated by others, sufficient to constitute convincing evidence that the facts are as stated in the complaint.

The line between co-operation and collusion is sometimes obscure. It is improper to stage an adulterous situation to win a divorce, but it's okay to co-operate by volunteering information regarding one's infidelities.

Most uncontested divorces are maintained with the full co-operation of both parties. How good are divorces so secured? To answer this, it's necessary to examine the laws of the place where the parties live. If they have gone out of state to obtain the divorce, the laws of both the state of residence and the state granting the divorce must be examined.

Jurisdiction in Divorce Actions. The heart of the matter is the jurisdiction of the court.

Suppose husband and wife live apart and desire to end their marriage. The wife leaves her New York home and travels to Nevada to obtain a divorce there. The husband approves of her action.

Once in Nevada, she establishes her residence and, six weeks later, begins her suit for divorce. She has a complaint and summons served upon her husband in New York, by mail. He retains a lawyer in Nevada and instructs him to put in no defense—to make no opposition to his wife's complaint, but simply to put in an appearance.

This act, the lawyer's appearance on his behalf in Nevada, will prevent him from trying to set aside the Nevada decree at a later date on the ground that the courts of that state had no jurisdiction in the matter. If, however, the husband didn't "appear" in Nevada, the divorce would be valid there but could be attacked in New York, and a charge of bigamy would lie against the wife, if she later remarried.

Desertion. Desertion (sometimes called abandonment) is a common ground for divorce. Usually the desertion must last for at least one year. Like adultery, desertion is also a crime punishable by imprisonment or a fine. As grounds for divorce, however, it has aspects that are not criminal. In some states, refusal to have sexual intercourse has been held to be desertion and therefore qualifies as grounds for a divorce.

The one who packs up and leaves is not necessarily guilty of desertion. If a husband decides to move and his wife refuses to accompany him, although he has offered to take her, she is the one guilty of desertion, unless the place where he has chosen to live is adjudged to be completely unsuitable. If a wife leaves because of cruel treatment or other intolerable conditions imposed by her husband, she is not guilty of desertion.

No court, civil or criminal, can compel a wandering husband or wife to come home. One who deserts his family, however, may be punished for it. He may be compelled to support his wife and children. His leaving may be grounds for divorce or separation decrees and alimony awards. But there is no provision in the law compelling such a person to rejoin his spouse against his will.

Enoch Arden Situations. When a spouse is absent for a long period, and no information as to his whereabouts is available, or when attempts to locate him have failed and there is no reason to believe he is alive, the courts will presume his death and dissolve the marriage. If he should later turn up and claim his rights as a spouse, the divorce remains effective.

Most states have a law of this kind. They vary, however, in such details as the duration of the absence, the necessary proof of efforts to locate the missing one, and the kind of notice that must be given.

In New York, before a marriage is dissolved for this reason, at least five years must have passed since the last time the missing partner was heard from. In addition, a notice that the divorce action is being taken must be published once a week for three successive weeks, in a newspaper most likely to be read by the absent spouse.

Cruelty. In many states cruelty is grounds for divorce or separation. "Cruelty" is defined differently throughout the country, however. Today, the term usually encompasses a broader range of conduct than it did previously.

Formerly, cruelty meant physical maltreatment of an extreme kind. Now the term includes abusive language; humiliating treatment in the presence of others; abusive treatment, not of the spouse, but of friends or relatives. Cruelty can also mean special attentions paid to someone else that humiliate the husband or wife, or it can even mean compelling a wife to do menial work when the husband can well afford a domestic servant.

The definition adapts itself to the people and circumstances of the case. And, as we have already noted, it varies from state to state. Most states, however, do distinguish it from mere incompatability and require that it have some sort of effect on the claimant's health.

Impotence. This is grounds for divorce in more than half the states. In most, it is also grounds for annulment if the condition existed at the beginning of the marriage.

Impotence should not be confused with sterility, which is not usually grounds for divorce. The inability to have children is accorded less importance in the law than the inability to engage in normal sexual intercourse. In a few states, however, sterility is permissible grounds for divorce. In others, it is grounds for annulment, as fraud, if the condition was concealed.

The legal definition of impotence is the lack of physical capacity to perform the sexual act. It doesn't extend to what some medical authorities include in that term: the inability of a husband to provide sexual satisfaction for his wife.

Neither does the law always recognize a condition in a wife analogous to impotence in a man—frigidity. However, if the wife withholds herself from sexual access to her husband, this behavior is seen, in some states, to be the equivalent of desertion. In those states, it may constitute grounds for annulment, separation or divorce.

ALIMONY

With respect to alimony and awards made by courts, the law differs widely from state to state. Furthermore, it differs widely within each state, from court to court and from case to case.

In most states, alimony is flexible and depends on the circumstances of each case. Some states limit alimony to a certain percentage of a husband's income. Others award a lump-sum judgment payable in installments. And some states permit the husband to collect alimony from his wife, but such judgments are rare. Some states allow alimony for a wife only if the husband is proved guilty of misconduct, and deny it to a wife if she committed adultery or engaged in other types of misconduct. All this applies to husband and wife, not to children. A father will be excused from the obligation of supporting his children only when he is physically or mentally incapable of doing so.

Generally the courts will honor an agreement between husband and wife with regard to alimony. Only when the wife is left destitute, or if it can be shown that some unfair advantage was taken of her in order to obtain her consent, will the courts disregard an agreement between the parties. (See discussion of separation agreements.)

Whether the alimony has been allowed by judgment of the court or by agreement, the amount is not fixed for all time. The court, in the role of protector of women and children, will make changes if they are justified by changed circumstances.

If the husband's income increases materially, or if the wife's needs are increased by illness or inability to work, the courts will take the new situation into account and will probably increase the amount of alimony. They will also, on occasion, revise the amount downward on application of the husband, if the original amount was liberal and his income has declined. It is more difficult to change agreed-upon amounts if the alimony is paid under a separation agreement.

Alimony for the wife usually ends on her remarriage. If the husband remarries, his obligation to pay alimony to his first wife continues, as does his support of his children.

Tax Aspects of Alimony. If a husband makes "periodic payments" to his wife, the payments are taxable as income to her, and the husband gets an income-tax deduction for the amounts he pays. Payments are "periodic" if they *are* paid under a decree of divorce, separation or support, or under a separation agreement, and if they *are not* of a definite duration. Remember: The husband bears the income-tax burden of a lump-sum payment. Installment payments of a fixed sum are "periodic" if the sum is to be paid over a period of more than ten years, or if certain occurrences (e.g., remarriage) could vary the amount due.

At most, 10 per cent of the total is taxed as income to the wife, each year. The portion of alimony payments specifically related to the support of minor children is not taxable to the wife.

Temporary Alimony and Counsel Fees. When a wife brings a matrimonial action against her husband, she may make an application to the court for temporary alimony pending the outcome of the action, and for a sum to cover her lawyer's fees. The first is necessary because it usually takes a long time before such actions are resolved, and the wife must be able to sustain herself in the interim. Lawyer's fees are awarded on the theory that they have become one of the "necessaries" of the wife for which the husband is responsible. Often they are awarded only at the close of the action—even if the wife has lost in her claim. Both types of award can also be given if the wife is the defendant in the action.

This is usually the opening skirmish in the divorce battle. It is bitterly fought because the amount fixed by the court for temporary alimony is generally based on a decision as to the amount the husband can afford to pay (reduced by the wife's ability to be self-supporting), and is usually a forecast of what the court will eventually award in its final decree.

Collection of Alimony. Failure to meet temporary or permanent alimony payments gives rise to a cause of action against the defaulting party for contempt of court. Jail is a possibility, but usually as a last resort, since it limits one's ability to raise money to meet the obligation. No counsel fees are awarded when one seeks to collect under a valid separation agreement, unless it has been incorporated in a judgment.

CUSTODY OF CHILDREN

It used to be the rule that custody of the children of a divorced couple would go to the father on the theory that he was better able to take care of them. Today, the trend is to give very young children to the mother and to allow older children to choose with whom they want to live. However, the court's primary concern is with the welfare of the children rather than with the claims of the parents.

Ordinarily, the parties can agree on the matter of custody just as they can on alimony and other property matters. The courts will abide by their expressed wishes, provided they are not contrary to the best interests of the children.

The usual arrangement provides for custody by one parent and visits by the other. However, some divorced couples have arranged to have their children live part of the year with each parent. This is usually practical only where the two parents live nearby so that the child isn't constantly uprooted. The preferable arrangement is a flexible one that allows the parties to get together, or leaves it to a trusted third person, to decide what is best for the children.

Custody decrees by the courts, as well as arrangements and provisions for child support, are always subject to modification where changed circumstances indicate that the original plan is no longer suitable.

If the court should find that both parents, or the available parent, is unfit, it may award custody to other parties, and even go so far as to deny visitation rights if there's a danger that one parent will injure or upset the child, or will abscond with him. Such treatment of a parent happens only in extreme cases. A mother would be denied custody of her child if, for example, she had a drug or drinking problem, was overly promiscuous, or didn't maintain a suitable home for the child. In such cases, a more responsible father, or even grandparents, would be awarded custody. In the last resort, the state would assume responsibility for the child.

ON YOUR OWN

In recent years, simplified separation and divorce procedures have made it possible for people to dissolve their marriages on their own—without the aid of lawyers. "How-to-do-it" books exist, keyed to individual state's laws, and with the aid of the appropriate court clerk you can act for yourself. However, this is practical only if the action is uncontested, and if there are no disagreements over property, child custody, or financial arrangements. Even so, this initial saving of a lawyer's fee may not seem like such a bargain later on. Are you sure you dealt with all the assets and obligations you two earned or incurred? For example, who pays unpaid bills that a financially dependent wife incurred for, say, her dental work? How does your "sensible" plan for child visitation hold up when one parent moves away? In short, expert legal assistance helps you to plan for the future as well as to deal with the past by suggesting complications that you haven't considered, and by offering advice. Remember: At the time of a divorce, both parties are too upset for clear thinking, and an impartial party can view the situation more realistically. Too often, one party dominates a do-it-yourself divorce or separation, or one party doesn't realize just what he or she may be entitled to. This can result in a return to court in an attempt to remedy the original settlement.

COUPLES WHO COHABIT

This is an example of a case in which the law hasn't fully caught up with a not uncommon social practice. When an unmarried, cohabiting couple splits up, property rights are unclear. Generally, property acquired before the relationship began is unaffected. However, household items and any real estate that the two bought together can present problems. The best advice is to keep track of what each of you owned before the relationship began, and what you bought together. Avoid joint purchases if at all possible. But if you do buy things together, have an agreement (preferably written) that clarifies what becomes of the property if you split up. Remember: Things may be rather bitter later on, so be sure that these things are provided for at the beginning of the relationship. Here's one way to settle ownership questions regarding jointly purchased property: One party chooses an item and buys out the other's interest in it, then the other party chooses—and so forth.

Recently, in cases involving unmarried couples who have split up, some courts have awarded the women money and other property just as in a divorce action. Experts say that this will be more common in the future. At present, however, it's best to have at least an oral contract regarding property settlements. There are no statutes covering property distributions in nonmarital relationships, but courts will tend to enforce contracts between unmarried partners. If there's no express contract to be looked to, courts may search for an implied contract, or may reward one party for his or her services (nonsexual) during the relationship. Recovery in such a situation, however, is far from assured.

Special problems arise if there are children, or if property of great value is involved. People who cohabit without marriage should realize that their situation is a special one, and should plan for every possible contingency on their own.

Table 7—MAJOR GROUNDS FOR ANNULMENT

	Fraud	Impotence	Physical Defect Preventing Intercourse	Force or Duress (No Voluntary Consent)	Under Age	Mental Incapacity at Time of Ceremony	Prior Marriage Existing	Prohibited Degree of Relationship (Incest)	Marriage Not Performed by Authorized Official
Alabama	X			X	X	X	X	X	
Alaska	X			X	X	X	X	X	
Arizona	X			X	X	X	X	X	X
Arkansas	X			X	X	X	X	X	X
California	X	X	X	X	X	X	X	X	
Colorado	X	X	X	X	X	X	X	X	
Connecticut	X			X	X	X	X	X	X
Delaware	X	X	X	X	X	X	X	X	
District of Columbia	X	X	X	X	X	X	X	X	
Florida	X			X		X	X	X	X
Georgia	X			X	X	X	X	X	
Hawaii	X	X	X	X	X	X	X	X	
Idaho	X	X	X	X	X	X	X	X	
Illinois	X			X	X	X	X	X	
Indiana	X			X	X	X	X	X	
Iowa	X	X		X	X	X	X	X	
Kansas	X	X	X	X	X	X	X	X	
Kentucky	X	X	X	X	X	X	X	X	
Louisiana	X		X	X			X	X	
Maine	X				X	X	X	X	
Maryland	X			X		X	X	X	
Massachusetts	X			X	X	X	X	X	
Michigan	X			X	X	X	X	X	
Minnesota	X			X	X	X	X	X	X
Mississippi	X	X	X	X	X	X	X	X	
Missouri	X	X		X	X	X	X	X	X
Montana	X	X	X	X	X	X	X	X	
Nebraska	X	X	X	X	X	X	X	X	
Nevada	X			X	X	X	X	X	
New Hampshire					X		X	X	
New Jersey	X	X		X	X	X	X	X	
New Mexico	X			X	X	X	X	X	X
New York	X	X	X	X	X	X	X	X	
North Carolina	X				X	X	X	X	
North Dakota	X	X	X	X	X	X	X	X	X
Ohio	X	X	X	X	X	X	X	X	
Oklahoma					X	X	X	X	
Oregon	X			X	X	X	X	X	
Pennsylvania	X			X	X	X	X	X	
Puerto Rico		X	X		X	X	X	X	
Rhode Island					X		X	X	
South Carolina	X			X	X	X	X	X	
South Dakota	X	X	X	X	X	X	X	X	
Tennessee	X			X	X	X	X	X	
Texas	X		X	X	X	X	X	X	
Utah	X			X	X	X	X	X	X
Vermont	X	X	X	X	X	X	X	X	X
Virginia	X			X	X	X	X	X	
Washington	X	X	X	X	X	X	X	X	
West Virginia	X	X	X	X	X	X	X	X	
Wisconsin	X	X	X	X	X	X	X	X	
Wyoming	X	X	X	X	X	X	X	X	

TABLE 8—GROUNDS FOR DIVORCE AND SEPARATION

KEY: D — Divorce
S — Separation

	1. Incompatibility	2. Irretrievable Breakdown of Marriage or Irreconcilable Differences*	3. Adultery	4. Impotence	5. Physical Defect Preventing Intercourse	6. Desertion	7. Non-Support	8. Mental Cruelty	9. Physical Cruelty	10. Habitual Drunkenness or Drug Addiction	11. Venereal Disease
Alabama	D	D	DS	DS	DS	DS			D	D	
Alaska	D		D	D		D		DS	DS	DS	
Arizona		D									
Arkansas			DS	D	D	D	D	D	D	D	
California		D									
Colorado		D									
Connecticut		D	D					D	D	D	
Delaware	D	D	DS	DS	DS	DS				DS	
District of Columbia			DS			DS		S	S	S	
Florida		D									
Georgia		D	D	D		D		D	D		
Hawaii		D									
Idaho			D			D	D			D	
Illinois			DS	D		DS	S	S	DS	DS	D
Indiana		D		D							
Iowa		D									
Kansas	D		D			D	D	D	D	D	
Kentucky		D								D	
Louisiana			DS			DS	S	DS	DS	DS	
Maine		D	D	D		D	D	D	D	D	
Maryland			D	D		DS		S	S		
Massachusetts		D	DS	DS		DS	DS	DS	DS	DS	S
Michigan		D								D	
Minnesota		D								DS	
Mississippi		D	D	D		D		D	D	D	
Missouri		D								DS	
Montana		D								DS	
Nebraska		D								DS	
Nevada	D									D	
New Hampshire		D	DS	DS		DS	DS	DS	DS	DS	
New Jersey			D			DS		D	D		
New Mexico	D		D	D	D	D				D	
New York			DS			DS	S	S	S	S	
North Carolina			D	D		S		S	S	S	
North Dakota		D	DS			DS	DS	DS	DS	DS	
Ohio			DS	D		D	DS	D	DS	D	
Oklahoma	D		DS	D		DS	DS	D	DS	DS	
Oregon		D								DS	
Pennsylvania			DS	D		D		DS	D		
Puerto Rico	D		DS	DS		DS		DS	DS	DS	
Rhode Island		D	D	D		D	D	D	D	D	
South Carolina			D			D		D	D	D	
South Dakota			DS			DS	DS	DS	DS	DS	S
Tennessee			D	D	D	D	D	D	D	D	
Texas		D	D			D		D	D		
Utah			DS	DS		DS	DS	DS	DS	D	
Vermont			DS			DS	DS	DS	DS		
Virginia			D			DS	DS	S	S	S	
Washington		D							DS		S
West Virginia			DS			DS	DS	DS	DS		
Wisconsin			D			D	D	D	D	D	
Wyoming			DS	DS	DS	DS	DS	DS	DS	DS	

CAUTION

When using this chart, keep in mind that changes frequently take place in statute and case law. Moreover, the "if's" and "but's" are necessarily omitted from a quick check list of this kind. Those seriously concerned are urged, through counsel, to consult the laws of the various states.

12. Insanity	13. Conviction of Felony	14. Life Imprisonment	15. Fraud	16. Living Apart without Cohabitation (in years)**	17. Refusal to Have Sexual Relations	18. Prior Marriage Existing	19. Incestuous Marriage—within Prohibited Degree of Relationship	20. Force or Duress	21. Unexplained Absence for ___ Years	22. Pregnancy of Wife at Time of Marriage
DS	DS	DS		2						
D	D	D								
D	D	D		3	D	D				
DS										
D			D	1½		D			7	
D		D		1				D		
D			D	2					D	
D	D	D		5	D					
	DS	DS				D				
D	D	D								
D	D	D				D				
S	DS	DS		2	S					
D	D	D		3		D	D			
	DS	DS					S			
D				1						
D	D	D				D	D			D
D				1					2	
D	DS	DS		1½						
		D		1					5	
D	DS	DS		1	DS					D
DS	D	D		S		D				
D			DS	2		D				D
D	DS	DS	DS				D			
	D	D	D	D		D	D	D		
	D			2						
	D	D		3		D	D			
				3						
DS	DS	DS		S	DS					
	D	D		3	D	D				D
D	D	D		3	D					
D	D	D		3						
DS	DS	DS		½					7	
	D	D		D	DS					D
DS	DS	DS		2						
D	D	D	D	1	D					
	D	D		D						D

*In granting divorces on this ground, a court will decide if, after considering all the facts presented, there have been acts detrimental to the marriage or whether there is a likelihood of preserving the marriage. Generally, you can get an order of separation on this ground, but divorce is the remedy that's sought most often.

**The statutes of certain states do not specify the number of years without cohabitation accepted as grounds for divorce or separation. The matter is then left to the courts. In these cases, we have simply indicated whether "living apart without cohabitation" furnishes the grounds for divorce (D) or separation (S). Also, in many states, the length of time without cohabitation is shorter if the separation has been voluntary.

CHAPTER TWENTY

CRIMINAL LAW

Criminal law affects everybody. No one, no matter how strictly he observes the law, how righteous his behavior, or how careful his business conduct, can be certain that he will never become involved in a criminal case. He may be unjustly, erroneously, or maliciously accused, or caught in circumstances beyond his control. And the way criminals are convicted and punished for their acts has social repercussions ranging from the safety of potential victims to the treatment of the accused.

The operations of the criminal law and the police fascinate everybody because of the drama of violent interference with people's liberties and property, and because of the suspense that surrounds the accused's trial. But there's more to it than that. The subject is closely connected with a sense of how our society operates, and the way in which a society deals with crime is a good way to tell if it is functioning effectively.

WHAT IS A CRIME?

A crime can be defined as an act or omission forbidden by the law, and punished upon conviction by the following penalties: death, imprisonment, fine, removal from office, disqualification to hold an office of trust, honor or profit, or other penal discipline.

In general, crimes are violations of the law in which the accused is prosecuted by the people and is punished by the state. Lawyers may consider this description oversimplified or even flippant. For hundreds of years, eminent legal authorities have attempted a concise definition, and every textbook on criminal law devotes many pages to it.

The chief difficulty arises from the confusion between torts (the civil wrongs discussed in another chapter) and offenses against the public at large. We have shown that civil wrongs may be crimes, too. Negligence may be criminal as well as civil, and the same is true for assault. There are many other offenses which fall into both categories. The laws of each state define which acts (or omissions to act) are crimes.

The key to the problem is the fact that, even though only one individual or his property may be harmed, the community has declared by law that, in this act, *the public* has been hurt. In a civil suit, it is the wronged party who, as the plaintiff, brings the defendant into court. In a criminal action, it is the state, acting through a public prosecutor (district attorney), which initiates the action. In a civil suit, the object is to compensate the one who has been wronged. In a criminal action, the object is to punish, and, it is hoped, reform, the wrongdoer.

Felonies and Misdemeanors. All crimes are either felonies (sometimes called "infamous crimes") or misdemeanors. Felonies are acts which the state regards as particularly vicious and punishes by incarceration for, generally, at least one year, or, rarely, death. All other crimes are misdemeanors.

Most states have removed certain other illegal acts from the category of crimes, and have called them "minor offenses." An example of this is illegal or overtime parking of an automobile and similar minor traffic violations. However, in many states, major traffic violations are crimes—driving while intoxicated, for example, driving at excessive speeds, leaving the scene of an accident, etc.

Principal and Accessory. Those who directly commit a criminal act are "principals." And those who encourage its commission with full knowledge of the actor's intent, and do something in furtherance of the criminal act (whether or not at the scene of the act), are also principals.

An "accessory" is one who harbors, conceals or aids a criminal *after* the commission of the crime, with the purpose of helping him to avoid arrest, trial, conviction or punishment. An accessory before the fact contributes to the crime by advice, encouragement, or inducement to act, but doesn't aid in the act itself. Such accessories are often treated as principals. Parties who plan an illegal act but do not take part in it can also be found guilty of conspiracy to commit the act. They are responsible for anything that occurs during the crime—even if the occurrence wasn't planned for—as long as it occurs incidentally to the execution of the plan.

START OF CRIMINAL ACTION

Criminal proceedings start with an **information** and **indictment.** The information is a sworn statement presented to a magistrate giving the facts of the crime and identifying the person accused of committing it.

An information is simply an allegation made to a magistrate by a public official that a person is guilty of a designated crime. It serves the purpose of advising the accused person of the charges against him. It must contain facts sufficient to establish the crime.

The magistrate questions the prosecutor and his witnesses, and takes their sworn statements. Then, if he is satisfied that the crime complained of has been committed, and that there is reasonable ground to believe that the defendant has committed it, he may issue a warrant for the defendant's arrest. If the act

complained of is a minor offense, he may simply issue a summons directing the appearance of the defendant before him.

An arrest can be made by a peace officer without a warrant under special circumstances: when a crime is committed or attempted in his presence, or if he has reasonable grounds to believe that a person has committed or will commit a felony.

Arraignment Before Magistrate. Following his arrest, a defendant must be brought, without unreasonable delay, before a magistrate who may hear whatever proofs are offered for or against him, release him on bail pending trial, or hold him for action by a grand jury. If the court isn't in session, the prisoner may be held in custody for safekeeping, but the current trend is to release him on bail as quickly as possible, if such treatment is advisable.

The magistrate conducts a preliminary hearing to decide whether or not there is **probable cause** to hold the defendant—that is, if the evidence seems sufficient to make out a probable case against him. The magistrate may release the defendant if he considers the evidence insufficient. The preliminary hearing may be waived by the accused. The usual practice is to hear only the prosecutor's case and to inquire into its probable sufficiency.

In some states, the defendant may offer evidence through his witnesses at a preliminary hearing. And it is common practice to consider evidence from the accused that might show mistaken identity.

Custody of the Defendant. If there is unreasonable delay in bringing the accused before a magistrate, the hearing may be expedited by a **habeas corpus** proceeding. This is a judge's order to the detention authorities to produce the accused and explain the reason why he is being held. Habeas corpus will be discussed more completely in our section on civil rights.

If the magistrate finds there is probable cause to believe that the accused committed the crime, he can order the prisoner kept in custody. If the charges against him constitute a misdemeanor, the next step will be his court trial. If those charges constitute a felony, he will be held for the grand jury. Release on bail pending the trial, for misdemeanors and felonies, has become more common of late.

Police have been known to make an arrest on suspicion without having sufficient evidence to convict. Under such circumstances, the release of the accused can be accomplished by a habeas corpus proceeding. The state, therefore, is obliged to bring the defendant to trial or secure a grand jury indictment as soon as possible. Today, "speedy trial" laws compel prosecutors to bring defendants to trial within prescribed time periods.

The Grand Jury. An indictment, unlike an information, comes from a grand jury. This is made up of twenty-three jurors who hear the facts as presented by the police and other witnesses. (Some states have smaller grand juries.)

If the state secures an indictment, this constitutes its first act in its case against the accused. The indictment must set forth clearly and concisely the act (or omission) complained of. This must be sufficient, on its face, to enable a court to pronounce judgment, and to allow the accused to prepare his defense to the charge.

A grand jury indictment is necessary in all felony cases. Misdemeanors can be prosecuted on the information, in the magistrates' courts and other courts of lesser jurisdiction than those that try felony cases.

The Constitution of the United States and those of all fifty states have adopted the grand jury system. Its object is to protect the citizen from oppression, unlawful arrest and prosecution by officials acting arbitrarily against him. It had its origin in monarchical times, as a means of appeal to a body of the prisoner's "peers," against the action of the government. The grand jury hears the complaint of the government against the individual. Their finding of an indictment is the necessary preliminary to legal action against an individual in the courts.

The Indictment. This is the formal accusation of the defendant, charging him with the commission of a crime. It's presented by the grand jury to the court that is competent to try the accused for the crime. In its consideration of the matters brought before it by the state, the grand jury receives only legal evidence. It hears witnesses, examines documentary evidence, and it may, if requested by the defendant, hear the defendant himself.

The grand jury may request and receive the advice and assistance of judges, the district attorney and his assistants. It is the duty of the D.A. to serve the grand jury and, on their request, to question witnesses brought before them. He is also required to summon witnesses to appear before the grand jury when requested to do so. At least twelve of the grand jurors must concur before an indictment is found.

Double Jeopardy. A person can't be prosecuted twice for the same offense. The defendant must have been "in jeopardy" in the first place. This means he was charged by a proper and complete accusatory instrument before a competent court, and the trial opened. A trial opens when the jury is sworn in or, in a nonjury case, when the first witness is sworn. The reason why the trial was terminated is immaterial except if the trial was halted because, for example, a juror died or the jury couldn't reach an agreement. A **mistrial** is declared in such a case, and a new trial can be ordered. Convictions set aside by appeals or other court orders generally don't bar new trials.

Under normal circumstances, if a defendant was in jeopardy in any federal or state court, and is freed, prosecution is barred in other courts, unless the acquittal arose from a lack of certain evidence that isn't required in the second court's jurisdiction.

Right to Bail. The Eighth Amendment to the Constitution of the United States provides that "excessive bail shall not be required." This has been applied to federal and state proceedings. Similar provisions also appear in the constitutions of many states.

The general rule is to fix bail in an amount sufficient to ensure the attendance of the defendant in court for the trial of his case. The amount varies with the gravity of the case, the means of the defendant and the probability of his trying to escape the jurisdiction of the court. The freer use of bail has been encouraged in an effort to control crowded jail conditions for those awaiting trial.

Presumption of Innocence. A defendant in a criminal action is presumed to be innocent until the contrary is proven. He is entitled to an acquittal if there remains a reasonable doubt that he is guilty.

In many countries, this isn't the case. There, the fact that the police have arrested you raises the presumption that you are guilty.

The presumption of innocence is one of the oldest principles of our common law and one of the substantial protections against improper verdicts. This presumption exists until a verdict is found against the defendant. Its effect is to place the burden on the government to prove the guilt of the accused. The latter is under no compulsion to prove his innocence. (He does have to prove certain affirmative defenses, however. These include duress and entrapment.)

Furthermore, the government must show the guilt of the defendant "beyond a reasonable doubt." Therefore, the defense lawyer seeks not only to rebut the evidence offered by the prosecution, and to attack its veracity, but to show that reasonable doubt exists.

What Is Reasonable Doubt? Suspicion, suspicious circumstances, surmise and speculation are not sufficient to convict. The state has the burden of removing any reasonable doubt concerning the guilt of the accused. This means that the facts proven at the trial must, by virtue of their probative force, establish the guilt of the accused.

In the case of People v. Friedland, a New York case tried in 1896, the court said: "A reasonable doubt is one that arises from the evidence and its character, or from the absence of satisfactory evidence, and is such a doubt that a reasonable man has a right to entertain after a fair review and consideration of all the evidence."

Since the guilt or innocence of the defendant is for the jury to decide, it is in their minds that the reasonable doubt has effect. Therefore, the judge's charge—his instructions to the jury regarding reasonable doubt—is a crucial part of the case.

If his charge doesn't properly instruct the jury that they must acquit the defendant if a reasonable doubt remains in their minds, or if it doesn't properly explain the meaning of the term, this constitutes "error" which will result in a reversal, on appeal, of a guilty verdict.

Trial by Jury. The Constitution of the United States provides for trial by jury. The constitutions of the various states have all included a similar provision. However, this doesn't always apply to minor crimes. Jury trial is always available in felony cases, but many states permit the right to be waived. If agreeable to the defense and the prosecution, a jury can be dispensed with or reduced in number, except in crimes involving capital punishment. Some states allow less than unanimous verdicts for conviction.

The jury must be an impartial one, however, for the trial to be in conformity with "due process of law." Where juries aren't selected from a cross-section of the population of the jurisdiction, but exclude one major segment or class, the jury may be regarded as improperly selected, and a new trial must be ordered.

Mental States. An important element in most crimes is the defendant's mental state. Let's look at New York's law. A defendant acts *intentionally* if his aim is to engage in the conduct outlawed by statute. It's almost as serious if he acts *knowingly*—without premeditation but aware that his conduct is outlawed. But he can also be guilty if he acts *recklessly*—consciously disregarding a known risk or grossly deviating from normal conduct. Even if the risk isn't perceived, the defendant can be guilty of *criminal negligence*, if he should have been aware of the risk.

A defendant won't be guilty of a crime, however, if he was coerced into committing it, since his will wasn't involved. And a defendant can plead entrapment as a defense, if he can show he was induced to act wrongly by a government agent when he wouldn't otherwise have been disposed to commit the act. Involuntary incapacities—such as insanity—are also defenses to criminal responsibility. And a plea of voluntary intoxication may rebut a charge of intent and reduce it to recklessness.

Intent shouldn't be confused with motive. A person's motive—the aim that stimulates the conduct—in committing a crime might conceivably be a worthy one, but this doesn't change the character of the act. His intent to commit the crime is established by his motive, even if it was a good one.

Crimes of Children. A child who is so young as not to be able to distinguish between right and wrong, or to understand the nature and the consequences of a particular act, is not responsible for it. Generally, a child under the age of seven is *conclusively* presumed to be incapable of committing a crime. And children between the ages of seven and fourteen to sixteen, who commit serious offenses, are treated as juvenile delinquents. Courts basically offer guidance to the child, and perhaps some form of monitoring, rather than punish him. The state has to show that the child knew the nature and consequences of his act when he committed it. Recently, due to a disconcerting rise in juvenile crimes, there have been moves to treat and punish children (teenagers, at least) who commit serious offenses as adults.

Confessions. A confession of guilt made before or during a criminal proceeding may be used against a defendant, provided it wasn't secured by fear or threats, or by a promise that he wouldn't be prosecuted. And it's only usable if the defendant has been told his constitutional rights before he made it. These rights include the right to have a retained or appointed lawyer present during any questioning by the police, the right to remain silent, and the right to be informed that any statement he makes can be used against him. Even a proper confession, by itself, will not sustain a conviction. There must be evidence, independent of the confession, to corroborate it. The restraints on the use of confessions are an attempt to curb overzealous policemen from coercing defendants into making statements that violate their rights or, in many cases, that simply aren't true.

Plea bargaining—encouraging a guilty plea by a promise of leniency in sentencing or by a reduction in the crime charged—is permissible. This practice is employed often, especially in large city court systems where time and manpower are in short supply.

Particular Crimes. The more important crimes will be defined and briefly explained in the alphabetically arranged glossary of legal terms at the end of the book.

CHAPTER TWENTY-ONE

PRACTICE IN THE COURTS: PREPARING THE CASE

The actual trial is really only a fraction of the lawyer's work. In this respect a legal case is like an iceberg—only a small part of its bulk appears on the surface. Cases can be won or lost in preparation. In this chapter we will discuss some of the considerations that go into the preparation of a case, and some of the steps that are taken to bring the parties into court for trial.

The Facts. Whether you are plaintiff or defendant, whether the case is civil or criminal, it is of the greatest importance that you give your lawyer *all* the facts. Some clients approach their lawyer as though he were the judge. They give him only those facts that they regard as favorable to them.

This can be disastrous. The layman is seldom able to discriminate between facts that are favorable or unfavorable, important or trivial.

That's why the lawyer insists on having every bit of information—even more information than the client may believe is relevant to his case. The interviews are long, and the questions put by the lawyer are searching and detailed. He wants to examine all documents, book entries, diaries and memoranda.

Don't withhold anything. The more facts your lawyer has, the more effective he can be for you. He needs even seemingly remote facts to advance your side of the story. And he needs them just as much to anticipate the arguments and the evidence that will be produced by the other side.

He needs these facts for still another reason. While you are making your explanations, answering his questions, supplying your facts in your own way, he will be estimating what kind of a witness you will make in court, how he can best use your testimony, and how to anticipate the opposing attorney's handling of it.

Your lawyer is on your side. He should have your complete confidence. If he doesn't, you aren't getting the full advantage of the lawyer-client relationship. Remember that you are protected in this relationship by an age-old immunity. Conversations and correspondence between lawyers and clients are *privileged communications*. Your lawyer can never be compelled to divulge them except with your permission.

The Pleadings. The popular notion of the lawyer's job begins and ends in the courtroom. It pictures him there, addressing the judge and the jury, examining and cross-examining witnesses. Say the word "lawyer," and one's immediate mental association is with the word "trial."

True enough, the courtroom trial is a very important phase of the lawyer's job, a vital part of his act. But it is by no means the most important. The work done before the trial, in the library and in court, requires many times the labor and time taken up by the trial itself. Usually it is the work done before the trial that determines its outcome. Very often it makes the trial itself unnecessary.

Let's examine what your lawyer does when you are the plaintiff. First he will interview you exhaustively to get all the facts. He will then decide what laws apply to them. On the basis of the law and the facts, he will draw up a document that will start the litigation.

This may be a summons to court. In most states, the attorney, as an officer of the court, may issue this himself. It has the same effect as if it were issued by the judge.

The summons identifies the plaintiff and the defendant. It requires the latter to appear in the action in the court named in the summons within a certain period of time. The time varies from court to court. Generally, the summons needn't say anything about the plaintiff's action or the relief sought. However, this information may be included with the summons.

The appearance called for by the summons is not, at this stage, an actual appearance in the courthouse. Usually what happens is that the defendant gives the summons he has received to his attorney. The latter then delivers to the plaintiff's attorney a *notice of appearance*. This signifies that the defendant will contest the action. If he doesn't, and if the nature of the action and the relief sought have been specified, a default judgment will generally be entered in favor of the plaintiff.

The import of the notice to the plaintiff is twofold: it shows that the defendant knows of the action and names the defendant's attorney, who is the one to whom all future papers should be given.

The courts vary in their rules of procedure for the serving of summonses—whether or not a copy of it should be filed in court, or whether the person serving it must make an affidavit stating that he has served it, giving the time and place.

What To Do When You Receive a Summons. What the notice of appearance signifies is that the defendant submits to the jurisdiction of the court. When you serve or file an answer, you are making what is commonly known as a *general appearance,* and the action of the court will be binding on you. In addition, you've opened yourself up to any additional cause of action that can be added to the original one.

There are times, however, when you should not submit to the jurisdiction of a court. Then you must refrain from making a general appearance.

For example, a summons from a municipal court must be served within the city. Suppose you are a resident of a suburban county and the municipal court summons was served upon you outside the city. You have the choice of ignoring the summons or denying the court's jurisdiction over you.

If you ignore the summons, you face having a default judgment taken against you which, even if you void it, could hurt your credit standing. If you decide to challenge the court's jurisdiction, you may, through your lawyer, make a *special appearance* in court for the sole purpose of explaining that you know about the suit and are there to show that the court is without power to act against you— i.e., that it has no jurisdiction over you. In some states, all this may be accomplished in the defendant's answer to the charge made by the plaintiff. Any objection to a court's jurisdiction should be raised promptly or else it might be lost.

The *complaint* is a statement of the plaintiff's claim against the defendant and the relief sought. It must be so drawn that, assuming all the facts in it to be true, it would justify a court in giving a judgment to the plaintiff under some principle of law. The items in the complaint are called *allegations,* which are based upon direct knowledge or upon "information and belief." (This latter form allows a plaintiff to begin an action if he has a good faith belief in the facts, and then use an array of pretrial devices for uncovering facts before the trial.) For the convenience of the court and of the opposing lawyer, the allegations are usually required to be separately paragraphed and numbered.

The plaintiff may have several different grounds for complaint against the defendant, or his plea for judgment against the defendant may be based on several different theories of law. Each such ground for recovery must state what the law calls a cause of action. This means, simply, a legal ground for suing the defendant.

The answer must deal with each of the allegations of the complaint. It may deny all of them—this is a *general denial*—or it may admit some and deny others.

The defendant's attorney isn't restricted to denying only the allegations of the complaint. He may set up his own allegations which, if true, would be a defense against the action of the defendant. He may, if he has cause, set up a *counter-claim* against the plaintiff, or a *cross-claim* which includes allegations against co-defendants.

Generally, silence in the answer as to any allegation is seen as an admission that it is true. However, a party can usually state that he lacks sufficient knowledge to answer the allegation, and this acts as a denial. If there's been a counter-claim against the plaintiff, he must respond—this is called a *reply*. Otherwise, no response to the defendant's answer is usually required.

Motion Practice. If a defendant's lawyer considers the complaint of the plaintiff legally defective, many courts give him the right to attack it, or to force the plaintiff to correct it. This he can do by motion—an application for an order from the court.

Motion practice occurs in a great many litigations, and much litigation is disposed of in that way. In this field of practice, the clients—the parties to the action—usually take no part except to sign papers. The lawyers exchange briefs and argue before a judge, without a jury and very often in the judge's chambers.

For example, suppose that the defendant's lawyer, when he examines the complaint, decides that it does not, as a matter of law, state a cause of action. This is another way of saying that his reaction to the complaint is, "So what? Assuming all that you say is gospel truth, the law just doesn't give you the right to a judgment against the defendant under the circumstances." Therefore he doesn't answer the complaint.

Instead, he notifies the plaintiff's attorney that he will move to dismiss the complaint on the ground that it fails to state a cause of action. In other words, he'll ask the judge to throw the matter out of court. He is prepared to show that, admitting for argument's sake all of the plaintiff's allegations to be true, he still isn't entitled to any recovery by law.

The defendant's lawyer, in such a case, generally states the legal reasons for his position in a *brief*. The plaintiff's lawyer prepares an answering brief. The issue is decided by the judge.

Remember that a proceeding of this kind doesn't try the facts of the case. These aren't decided one way or another. It's simply a matter of law—whether or not, on the facts in the complaint, the plaintiff has a case against the defendant.

You can resort to a variety of other grounds to get a motion to dismiss granted early on. There are also motions to get a clearer idea of the plaintiff's allegations, to add or drop parties, etc. These motions can be made before, during, and after a trial. They are part of the procedural law (sometimes called "adjective" law) of the state. This is a vast body of statute law that sets down the method and machinery of administering justice, and it varies from state to state. Procedural law must be followed precisely, and for that reason it is important to place your affairs in the hands of someone who is familiar with the complicated procedures.

Special Appearance. As we have seen, this is used whenever the service of a summons isn't valid or the court has no jurisdiction to act. Suppose you, a New Yorker, have a claim against a New Jersey corporation. You inform your lawyer that its president is in town on a business trip and is stopping at a local hotel. Your lawyer has a summons served upon him there.

But he isn't asked to appear, personally, as the defendant. He is served in his capacity as an officer of the corporation, in order to bring the corporation itself into the New York courts.

Is this a valid service of summons? The answer hinges on whether or not the corporation is "doing business" in New York. The fact that the corporation's president is physically in the state doesn't bring his corporation there with him.

"Doing business" is a tricky phrase, and has been troubling the courts for many years. There is still no conclusive definition of the acts and conduct that would subject a corporation to the jurisdiction of a state's courts.

In general, if an out-of-state corporation maintains an office within the state for the transaction of its regular business, keeps a bank account there, is listed in the telephone directory, etc., it is considered to be "doing business" in that state. It cannot, under those circumstances, refuse to be sued on the ground that its principal place of business is in another state.

The law provides many ways to get jurisdiction—the right of the court to proceed against a party—over a defendant. This, too, is a complex part of the law and can't be covered usefully here. Professionals will know how to apply the various legal grounds to the facts you provide them.

Other Pretrial Proceedings. We have seen how an action is started by summons, complaint, appearance, and answer. When the answer of the defendant has been served on the plaintiff's attorney, we say that the "issues have been joined." It is now possible for all the parties to know what the case is all about, and what the facts in dispute are. At this point, it is possible to schedule the action for trial, to put it on the court calendar.

But the attorneys do not stop at that, merely waiting for the day of trial to come around. What is done in this interval will determine how the trial will go. Witnesses must be interviewed. Those who can't appear at trial, because they live far away, will be traveling abroad, have become ill, or for any other reason, will have their testimony taken down by *deposition*. This is a form of sworn statement, generally in response to oral questions and subject to examination and cross-examination, in which questions and answers are reduced to writing in advance of the trial, for

use when the trial takes place. If the questions are oral, they are asked before an appropriate officer, like a notary public. A deposition can also be taken in response to written questions. This method is often used when the deponent is from out of state. The written questions have to be shown to all the other parties before they can be answered.

Examination Before Trial. In many states where the calendars are crowded, it's possible for one party to question the other in great detail before trial in order to develop facts necessary for the preparation of the case. This has the virtue of saving time in court, helps to prevent surprises, and narrows the issues that eventually have to be tried. A deposition taken before trial also "freezes" a witness's testimony—if he changes his story later, the document can be brought in to show the inconsistency.

If the information demanded can't be ascertained quickly, *written interrogatories* are submitted, and are answered after the party has a chance to check business records, fact sheets, etc.

The Bill of Particulars. In most cases the defendant, when he files his answer and notice of appearance, is entitled to demand specific details of the plaintiff's claim. So he requests a bill of particulars, which generally doesn't go through the court but directly to the plaintiff. Here's an example: If the plaintiff, in his complaint, alleges that there was a contract between the parties, the defendant has a right to know (and to have it stated in a formal document) whether the contract was in writing or oral; when and by whom it was made; whether the plaintiff claims that the defendant entered into it personally or through an agent; and so forth.

The demand for a bill of particulars may vary in length from a brief query to an extended document. Admittedly, it is sometimes used to trouble the other side. But it is also useful in discouraging "nuisance suits." These are made a little less easy by the need to assemble precise facts.

Sometimes, even if you are entitled to it,

your lawyer will decide not to make the demand. He may feel that furnishing the bill of particulars will be advantageous to the plaintiff, guiding him to some extent in the preparation of his case.

Summary Proceedings. When the plaintiff's case is open and shut, and there would appear to be no defense, most courts will allow a motion to be made for a "summary judgment." In this short-cut proceeding, the plaintiff says, in effect, "Let's not waste the time of the court and the taxpayers' money. The defendant's answer is an obvious sham. I am prepared to show the court documents in support of my claim, and the defendant is unable to resist it." The defendant can get a summary judgment, too, if the plaintiff's case is clearly without merit.

A motion for summary judgment will be denied if there are any issues at all that are in dispute and must be tried by a court. What appears to be an ironclad claim often turns out to be a lively controversy. For example, the holder of a promissory note sues the maker for nonpayment. The note appears in good form. On the face of it, there would appear to be no defense, and a motion for summary judgment is made. In opposition to the motion, the defendant submits an affidavit to the effect that his signature on the note had been forged, or that he had already paid the note. This would be enough to create issues that would prevent a summary judgment and call for a trial.

Supplementary Proceedings. After the trial and after a judgment has been rendered in favor of the plaintiff, there are procedures available to enforce payment of the judgment. If the defendant refuses to pay, claiming that he doesn't have the funds, he may be questioned after the trial regarding his property and his income. If any of his assets are found, they may be attached and sold to satisfy the judgment. In addition, there are steps that can be taken to prevent him from transferring his assets to others to defeat your claim to them.

What we have outlined here are only a few of the pretrial and posttrial procedures of which laymen are generally ignorant. Proce-

dural law is an enormously important subject all by itself. But its complexities can be avoided in some cases.

Small-claims Courts. Often, it isn't worthwhile to hire a lawyer to sue someone against whom you've got a small claim. In many states, there are simplified and speeded-up procedures in special courts which allow you to "do it yourself." These small-claims courts are often arms of the municipal or county court systems, and exist for the prosecution of claims for money (with an upper limit of from $400 to $1,000, depending on the state). The plaintiff is aided in bringing the suit by the court, even to the point that trials are scheduled after working hours in many instances. While the defendant's rights are protected, the paperwork and procedural law are streamlined. A defendant can move a suit to a regular court, but if he agrees to use the small-claims court, there is generally no right to appeal the decision. Small-claims courts are often used in consumer's suits about defective merchandise, broken contracts, padded bills, etc. Court systems that have small-claims courts encourage their use, so you should check local courts and consumer bureaus for information on how to utilize them.

Limitation of Actions. Go back, for a moment, to your first interview with your lawyer regarding your claim. He is delving into the facts, fishing for details, names, dates and places. He may, when you mention a certain date, interrupt to tell you that that changes the picture. Your otherwise valid cause of action has been outlawed by the passage of time.

In the lawyer's own language, your action has been barred by the statute of limitations. Almost every type of claim will be denied unless you act within a certain period of time. These time limitations are fixed by statute, and vary from state to state. Table 9 contains a partial list of such limitations.

CAUTION: In reading the statute of limitations table, keep this always in mind: There are many circumstances that affect the statute of limitations, so that the passage of time doesn't necessarily bar an action. For exam-

Table 9—STATUTE OF LIMITATIONS

	An Action to Recover Possession of Real Property	Contract Actions Generally*	Special Limitation for Contracts Not in Writing	Action on a Sealed Instrument	Action to Recover Damages for Personal Injuries**	Action for Wrongful Death
Alabama	10	6		10	1	2
Alaska	10	6		10	2	2
Arizona	10	6	3		2	2
Arkansas	7	5	3		3	3
California	5	4	2		1	1
Colorado	(a)	6	3		1	2
Connecticut	15	6	3	6	2	1
Delaware	20	6	3		2	2
District of Columbia	15	3	3	12	1	1
Florida	(a)	5	3		4	2
Georgia	(a)	6	4		2	2
Hawaii	20	6			2	2
Idaho	5	5	4		2	2
Illinois	20	10	5		2	1
Indiana	10	10	6	10	2	2
Iowa	10	10	5		2	2
Kansas	15	5	3		2	2
Kentucky	15	15	5		1	1
Louisiana	(a)	5			1	1
Maine	20	6	6	20	2	2
Maryland	20	3	3	12	3	3
Massachusetts	20	6		20	3	2
Michigan	(a)	6			3	3
Minnesota	15	6			2	2
Mississippi	10	6	3	6	6	6
Missouri	10	5		10	5	2
Montana	5	8	5		3	3
Nebraska	10	5	4		4	2
Nevada	5	6	4		2	2
New Hampshire	20	6		20	6	2
New Jersey	20	6		16	2	2
New Mexico	10	6	4		3	3
New York	10	6		6	3	2
North Carolina	(a)	3		10	3	2
North Dakota	20	6	6		6	2
Ohio	21	15	6		2	2
Oklahoma	15	5	3		2	2
Oregon	10	6		10	2	2
Pennsylvania	21	6	6	20	2	1
Puerto Rico	30	15			1	1
Rhode Island	6	6		20	3	2
South Carolina	10	6		20	6	6
South Dakota	20	6		20	3	3
Tennessee	7	6	6		1	1
Texas	(a)	4	2		2	2
Utah	7	6	4		4	2
Vermont	15	6		8	3(c)	2
Virginia	15	5	3	10	2	2
Washington	10	6	3		3	3
West Virginia	10	10	5	10	2	2
Wisconsin	(a)	6		20	3(b)	3
Wyoming	10	10	8		4	2

*Contracts governed by the Uniform Commercial Code have a limitations period of four years.
**Generally, there are shorter limitations periods for tortious conduct that doesn't result in physical injury.

FOOTNOTES

(a) The period within which to commence an action to recover possession of real property varies according to the factors involved. Thus, a claimant may hold off action a longer period of time if the other party has not cultivated the land, or paid taxes on his claim, or exhibited some form of deed. In effect, the more evidence of ownership by the adverse party—the party occupying the property without title—the shorter the period of time within which to commence action to eject him.

(b) In Wisconsin, the three year limitation for personal injuries applies only to injuries sustained on or after July 1, 1957. For injuries sustained prior to that date, the period of limitation is 6 years. In Wisconsin, a cause of action on a sealed instrument arising outside the state must be brought within 10 years.

(c) In Vermont, the limitation on personal injuries sustained as a result of skiing is one year.

ple, if the defendant made a new agreement to pay (in the case of a contract calling for the payment of money), the time may run from the more recent date. In some cases, the absence of the defendant from the state, or his use of an assumed name, will suspend the provision. Similarly, some causes of action only arise when the defendant learns of the wrongdoing.

In most cases, a claim isn't automatically barred by the statute—this has to be pleaded by the defendant in his answer. In other words, the case isn't just thrown out of court because it wasn't started in time; it's the defendant's responsibility to ask that this be done. The reader is cautioned not to use the table to determine for himself whether or not his claim or a claim against him is actionable. That decision is for his lawyer to make.

Statute of Limitations. Statutes limiting the commencement of legal proceedings were enacted to protect persons from lawsuits brought after evidence has been lost or witnesses have died. Complete treatment of these statutes is beyond the scope of this book. We have therefore selected six types of common legal actions and have given the time limitations affecting them throughout the United States.

It is important to remember that the time limitation may be suspended if the claimant is under some legal disability, or in some instances because of the defendant's actions.

In this table, Column One shows the time within which an action must be started in order to prevent one who has no title to property he is occupying from acquiring title to it.

Column Two shows the time limitations on commencing claims based on ordinary written contracts. This information should only be taken as a general rule, since there are numerous types of contract actions with different limitation periods. Remember: sales contracts generally have a four-year period.

Column Three indicates in which jurisdictions there is a separate limitation on unwritten contracts. Where no number appears, assume that the period appearing in Column Two applies.

Column Four shows the limitation on instruments that are sealed, although in many states the seal has lost its significance. If no number appears, sealed and unsealed instruments are treated alike.

Column Five shows the time within which to commence a personal-injury action—for example, an injury sustained in an automobile accident. This column doesn't refer specifically to other personal wrongs such as slander, libel, assault, etc., which often have shorter limitation periods.

Column Six refers to the time within which to commence an action on behalf of the estate or next of kin of one whose death was caused by some wrongful act by the defendant.

CHAPTER TWENTY-TWO

PRACTICE IN THE COURTS: JURIES AND EVIDENCE

Day in and day out the courtroom is the scene of human drama. Here the lawyer plays a vital part. He must be ready to deal with the unexpected, and bring to bear his knowledge of the law of evidence and his understanding of human beings. How are juries selected? Who has the burden of proof? What is a prima facie case? What are the different kinds of evidence?

TRIALS

Jury or No Jury. Early in the litigation, usually when he puts the case on the calendar for trial, your attorney makes up his mind whether or not to demand a trial by jury. This may not always be available. We have seen that the right to trial by jury has to some extent been curtailed in cases of minor importance. The trial is held before a judge alone, in civil cases involving the law of equity. (See definition of **equity** in glossary.)

But, assuming we have the choice, how do we make up our minds? Do we want this case to be decided by a judge, or by a jury of twelve of our equals? At whose hands will we fare better? Often it is a toss-up. Certainly it is hard to predict what a jury will do. The unknowable personal experience of each man, his prejudices and his unforeseeable individual reactions, reasonable or unreasonable, all go into the verdict.

But the judge, too, is a human being. No matter how impartial, objective and dispassionate he may try to be, he is subject to the same influences, prejudices and bents that affect the rest of us. Just as there are different kinds of men, there are different kinds of judges.

It is the duty of the judge, not the jury, to apply the law of the case. It is for the jury to decide the questions of fact. When the parties waive a jury, the judge decides the questions of fact, and also applies the laws involved.

But there are some guiding principles that help a lawyer make his choice. Juries are more likely to show sympathy for the party or the situation with which they can identify themselves. EXAMPLE: Unless they happen to be twelve corporate executives, which is highly unlikely, the jury will probably favor an individual against a large corporation. In most cases, juries will also favor a frail woman over a strong man, and a tenant over a landlord.

JURY DUTY

While on the subject of juries, it is appropriate to give some attention to the role of the citizen as a juror. The invitation to serve on a jury always seems to come at the wrong time. Every lawyer knows what it is to receive a client's telephone appeal: "I have just received a summons for jury duty. I simply can't spare the time just now. What shall I do?"

Invariably we try to persuade the caller not to seek excuses. All good citizens are busy people, and jury service is one of the duties of citizenship. If all who are busy were excused, we should have unrepresentative juries, as they would have to be, of the retired and the unemployed.

Furthermore, excuses are good only for a specified time. They merely postpone your eventual service. Judges seldom allow more than two consecutive excuses. The time when you will have to serve may then prove more inconvenient than the first time. Besides, the fact that you have served will make it easier for you to get excused on the next call.

Jury service is a right as well as a duty. The awareness of the importance of the institution of trial by jury should make every citizen a willing member of the panel.

Who Is Called? The names of jurors are drawn from tax rolls and, in some places, from the voting registers. Generally exempt from service, provided they ask to be excused, are clergymen, policemen, firemen, and lawyers. Women used to be excluded from jury duty altogether in some states, and exempt unless they volunteered for it in others. But the laws have changed, and now women are treated on the same basis as men in the majority of states. Anyone who is called and fails to attend is subject to punishment by fine.

Challenges. Jurors are subject to examination by the lawyers. They may be challenged for cause. That is, they may be excused if any interest is shown to exist on the part of the juror in the matter about to be tried, or if any relationship exists between the juror and either of the parties or their lawyers that might bias his judgment. Or they may be excused for scruples they may have regarding procedures or prescribed penalties such as capital punishment in cases involving the possibility of such sentences.

In addition to challenges for cause, each side is entitled to a certain number of *peremptory challenges*. These are challenges that either side can exercise, without giving any reason—simply because of the belief that the particular person will not be favorably inclined to the party who does the challenging.

In most state courts, the jurors are individually examined by the attorneys. In the federal courts, the questioning is done by the judge.

BURDEN OF PROOF

In civil cases it is the plaintiff, in criminal cases the prosecutor, whose duty it is to furnish evidence to establish the case against the defendant. It is never the duty of the defendant to refute facts not established by the plaintiff. It is the plaintiff (or the prosecutor) who has brought the matter into court. It is therefore his obligation to justify his complaint with proof.

If the plaintiff fails to prove enough facts to constitute a legal claim for which the court can give him a remedy, the defendant can move to dismiss even before he begins his defense. The minimum burden the plaintiff must carry is to prove what we call a *prima facie* case.

The Prima Facie Case. By this we mean a set of facts which, if not refuted, will permit a finding for the plaintiff. When the plaintiff's counsel says, "plaintiff rests," defendant's lawyer may rise to his feet and ask the court to dismiss the case because the plaintiff has failed to prove a prima facie case.

What he is saying, in layman's language, is: "Judge, there is no need for me to present the defendant's case because, even if you were to believe all that the plaintiff has presented before you, it would not justify your making a decision in his favor."

Sometimes the defendant has to assume the burden of proof. This is true in cases where he is not simply denying what the plaintiff claims, but is affirming some reason why he should not have to pay.

An example of this is a claim based on a promissory note. The plaintiff gives evidence by presenting the note itself and establishing that the signature on it is that of the defendant. The defendant does not deny the existence of the note, or that his signature appears on it. His defense is that he was forced to sign it under duress, at the point of a gun. Since this is an affirmative proposition, asserted in order to avoid the effect of what the plaintiff has proved, the burden of proof as to this proposition is on the defendant.

Preponderance of Evidence. In most civil cases the question for the court is: "After considering all of the evidence, which side do you believe?" or, "Whose evidence carries more weight by reason of its quality and quantity?" In order to give a decision to one side or the other, it is not essential that every reasonable doubt be removed from the minds of the jurors. It is only necessary that the weight of the evidence tip the scales in favor of one as against the other.

In some civil cases, the burden is greater than just a preponderance of the evidence. For example, where the plaintiff claims that the defendant committed fraud, he has to prove it by "clear and convincing" evidence.

Beyond a Reasonable Doubt. But in criminal cases it is not the preponderance of the evidence alone, or even "clear and convincing" evidence, that decides the case. The defendant has the benefit of the presumption of his innocence. He is presumed to be innocent until he is proven guilty; and his guilt must be established by evidence which removes any doubt a reasonable man might have.

EVIDENCE

Distinguished from Proof. The legal meaning of the word "evidence" includes all the means by which facts are proved or disproved. Proof is not the same as evidence; it is the *result* of evidence.

The court bases its decision on certain facts. Knowledge of the facts must come to the court through the presentation of information or "evidence." The presentation of this evidence must follow certain rules which constitute the "law of evidence."

The motion picture, the stage, the novel, radio and television have familiarized the layman with certain legal terms referring to evidence. Among them are "circumstantial evidence," "hearsay," "incompetent, immaterial, irrelevant!", "expert testimony," etc.

The Different Kinds of Evidence. Facts are brought before a court in the form of either real or testimonial evidence. When we talk about *real evidence,* we mean that the object itself is brought before the court. It may be a document, book, instrument, tool, or any other article; it may even be a human being. When we talk about *testimonial evidence,* we mean evidence given by a witness who testifies about what he actually saw and heard.

In addition to being divided into real and testimonial evidence, evidence is divided into two other classifications: direct and circumstantial. *Direct evidence* is evidence that proves the point in issue directly, without any inference having to be drawn. *Circumstantial evidence* is evidence that doesn't prove that point in issue directly, but from which an inference may be drawn that the point is true. These two classifications apply to both real and testimonial evidence.

Professor Wigmore, an authority on the subject, illustrated the different kinds of evidence by the following example. Assume that the question the court has to decide is whether an accused person has lost his right hand and wears an iron hook in its place. If a witness testified that he had seen the arm, that would be both testimonial evidence and direct evidence (since the testimony proves the point directly). If the court were shown some mark on an object that had been grasped or carried by the accused, that would be both real evidence and circumstantial evidence (since you can infer from the mark on the object that the person who grasped it wore a hook). If the court were allowed to see the arm itself, that would be both real evidence and direct evidence.

Circumstantial Evidence. It is safe to say that most of the evidence submitted to the courts, in both civil and criminal cases, is circumstantial evidence. The reason for this is that most of the acts and transactions that later become the subjects of trials are not done in the presence of witnesses.

Examples of circumstantial evidence are: the character and reputation of one accused of a crime; the physical or mental capacity, or the possession of the skill or means to do a certain act; threats, motive, habit, etc., or expert testimony.

The rules change according to the type of case in which the evidence is offered, according to the purpose for which it is offered, and according to the circumstances of the trial.

For example, as a general rule, the prosecution cannot offer evidence regarding past crimes of which the defendant was convicted. The purpose of this rule is to prevent the defendant's being tried on the basis of whether he is a good or a bad man, and to assure that the determination is made on the facts of the case alone.

But when the defendant takes the witness stand in his own behalf and introduces evidence as to his good character, he has opened the door for the prosecution to show that he has had previous convictions.

Such testimony is also admissible for other reasons. In some crimes, a necessary element is *intent*.

For example, Joe Stripes is caught passing counterfeit money. This is established by direct testimony of witnesses. We all know that it is possible for people to pass counterfeit bills innocently on occasion. But the prosecution is able to show that Joe has had six prior convictions for this crime.

This evidence is admissible, since proof has already been offered that Joe passed the fake money. His prior convictions would not have been admissible as evidence to prove that he committed the act; they were admissible only to show his intent.

Hearsay. When the evidence a witness gives is not based on his own knowledge, on what he himself observed with his own senses, but upon what someone else said, we call such evidence "hearsay." It is not good evidence and should be excluded, because the one whose words are being quoted is not himself a witness. He has not taken the oath and he is not on hand to be cross-examined.

Suppose a witness in an automobile accident case asserts that, immediately after the accident, he spoke to a bystander who said,

"that Buick was going eighty miles an hour." This would be mere hearsay, and would be excluded.

It would be different if the bystander himself were in court to tell what he saw. He would be under oath, and there would be an opportunity to cross-examine him to estimate his powers of observation and his ability to judge speeds.

There are numerous exceptions to the hearsay rule, but these are technicalities of no particular interest to the layman.

Expert Testimony. On matters too technical or special for ordinary citizens to decide, the help of experts is permitted.

To differentiate such matters from those upon which a jury can form its own opinion, let us use this example. In a case involving an automobile accident where both personal injury and property damage were suffered, the plaintiff, a merchant, calls other merchants as expert witnesses to estimate his financial loss due to absence from his business. He also brings in an auto mechanic to testify as an expert on the extent of the damage to his car.

The merchants' testimony is not admissible because, with the same available facts, the average jury can make a proper estimate of the money damage. But determination of the damage to the car is another matter. Here the expert's testimony is admissible, since the matter is a technical one.

In his direct examination of the "expert witness" he had brought in to support his case, the lawyer seeks to build up the expert's authority. He does so by asking questions the answers to which will demonstrate the expert's training and experience and satisfy the jurors that his opinion will therefore be competent and trustworthy.

On the other hand, the task of the opposing counsel is to cast doubt on the expert's ability to judge expertly on the matter in question. Experts must be well qualified if they are to retain the confidence of the jury through the questions raised during the cross-examination.

When the experts are not familiar with all the facts as they occurred, they are asked hypothetical questions which assume facts previously established in the course of the trial.

Often a considerable complexity of technical detail is involved. This demands of the lawyer that he familiarize himself with the necessary technical knowledge. Without such knowledge he would not be able to ask the expert questions that will make points for him.

Irrelevant, Immaterial and Incompetent. Actually, the rules of evidence are based on common sense. What is admissible evidence must relate to the issue under discussion, have some bearing on it, and come from a source that is believable.

When, in the course of a witness' testimony, the opposing lawyer rises to his feet and says, "I object!", he means, "What this witness is saying should not be allowed to enter into the consideration of this case." And the usual reason or reasons given by him would be that the evidence is *irrelevant, immaterial* or *incompetent,* or all three.

When he says it is *irrelevant,* he means that what is being said has nothing to do with the case. When he says the evidence is *immaterial,* he means this may have some relation to the case, but has no influence on it, one way or the other. When he says the evidence is *incompetent,* he means that this is not the kind of evidence which is acceptable in order to prove what is at issue.

For example, if the question concerns the terms of a written lease, evidence should be given by the lease itself, and not by the witness' recollections. This means that the witness' testimony about the terms of the lease is incompetent.

When the lawyer's objection is sustained, the court has agreed that the objection is a sound one and the evidence objected to will be excluded from the record. When the objection is *overruled,* the court has disagreed with the objector and the evidence is accepted.

If either of the lawyers feels that the judge's ruling is in error, and that the error will hurt his case, he takes an *exception,* so that he may later use this ruling against him as one of his grounds for appeal, if the verdict should be against his client.

Prejudice. The sense in which we use this word here is not usually one meaning "bias." From time to time something will happen at a trial that will unreasonably hurt one side and prevent a fair verdict. We say, in such a case, that the injured party's case has been *prejudiced.*

We have frequent examples of this in personal-injury cases. If the plaintiff in any way indicates that the defense is being conducted by an insurance company, this is prejudicial to the defendant and would justify a mistrial.

The reason for this is that a jury would be inclined to favor a claim against an insurance company on the theory that the business of the insurance company is to pay claims, and that it has plenty of money for this purpose. The reverse is also true. That is, if the defendant lets it be known in court that he is not insured, that is prejudicial to a fair trial.

Privileged Communications. Confidential communications between attorney and client, physician and patient, husband and wife, and clergyman and penitent are privileged. That is, they may not be disclosed on the witness stand unless the privilege is waived by the one who is protected by it.

This rule is based on the character of the relationship involved. If he were not protected by it, a client would not enter into a confidential relationship with his attorney, a patient might hesitate to call in a physician in certain cases, a husband and wife might withhold implicit trust in each other, and a penitent might be deterred from going to his clergyman.

EXAMINATION OF WITNESSES

Procedure at Trial. The jury has been seated and attorneys for both sides have made their opening remarks. Through his attorney the plaintiff, who has the burden of proof, puts his first witness on the stand. This first questioning is called "direct examination." When this has been completed, the witness is turned over to the defendant's attorney, who may cross-examine him.

This continues until all the witnesses for the plaintiff have been examined and cross-examined. After cross-examination, the witness may be called again for "redirect," usually in order to clarify some point on which doubt was cast by the cross-examination. After redirect, we have "recross-examination."

Direct Examination. This is the method by which a witness' testimony is presented to the court. It is by direct examination that an attorney must get across the facts upon which he relies to make out his case. There is a tendency, therefore, to "lead" the witness by phrasing the question in such a way that it contains the answer. This is usually allowed in the introductory questions establishing the name and address of the witness. Leading questions may also be used when the witness is a child and can't answer any other kind of question, when he needs help in refreshing his memory, and when he is being unco-operative in answering the questions put to him. Except for these circumstances, however, leading questions are improper, and a lawyer will not be allowed to use them if his opponent objects.

Cross-examination. This is one of the most effective instruments for arriving at the truth in a court of law. The real drama in a courtroom occurs when a witness for one side is turned over to the other for cross-examination. Here the widest latitude is permitted in order to show that what the witness said on direct examination should not be believed. For example, leading questions are always allowed

on cross-examination. The only limitation on cross-examination is that the questions must be related to matters that were brought out on direct examination. Even with this limitation, a cross-examining lawyer may always attack the witness' credibility, whether or not the subject was dealt with in direct examination.

So important is cross-examination considered that the testimony of a witness will be stricken completely if, because of illness or death, he should not be available for cross-examination. Therefore, depositions by witnesses who will not be available at the time of the trial will include their answers to questions put by counsel on both sides.

WHAT TO BEAR IN MIND WHEN INITIATING CRIMINAL ACTION

When you have been the victim of a wrong that is both civil and criminal, make sure of two things before going to a district attorney or magistrate.

Be Sure of Your Facts. If you are unable to sustain your complaint with the facts, you may expose yourself to a suit for malicious prosecution. You need to know more than just the fact that you've been wronged. You must be sure that the conduct inflicted on you is considered by the law to be a wrong, and you must show that all the aspects of the wrong are present in your case.

Be Prepared To Follow Through. Even if you are inclined to relent when the wrongdoer makes good, the D.A. may insist on prosecuting the case, and you may be obliged to give testimony.

CHAPTER TWENTY-THREE

CIVIL RIGHTS

The civil rights and liberties of its inhabitants are the surest indication of the degree of civilization that exists within any state. Due process of law, equal justice, the right to express dissent and disapproval, to advocate change by lawful means, are the key to the great advances made by our republic.

LAWS AND MEN

Even this little book, sketchy as it may seem to lawyers, will serve to drive home one clear idea—law means that we play the game according to *rules*. Our government is a government of laws, not of men. From time to time the rules have to be changed, but, in changing them, we again follow rules—the ones that prescribe *How the rules should be changed*.

This is in direct contrast to government by *men*. In a dictatorship the key word is power—power in the hands of men who ignore the rules. For them the laws of the land are transformed into instruments by which to exercise their dictation over other men.

The difference between these two concepts is an essential starting point for a clear understanding of civil rights.

Civil rights is a subject close to every lawyer's heart. Civil rights and civil liberties make up the foundation stone of his profession. If his clients had no civil rights, his profession would be reduced to making emotional appeals to the powers that be—pulling wires in behalf of his clients instead of asserting his clients' rights according to law.

Origin of Our Rights. Although we often change our laws (federal, state and municipal legislatures turn out thousands every year), certain fundamentals cannot be changed by simple legislation. These are the rules set up in the Constitution of the United States and in the state constitutions.

Our federal Constitution places limits on the powers of the legislatures, both federal and state, in order to establish minimum guarantees.

Neither the Constitution nor the guarantees in it were sudden, mysterious gifts handed to our founding fathers in their hour of need. The Constitution was not delivered intact to the people, like the Ten Commandments. It was the culmination of prolonged and bloody struggles of people, here and abroad, to wrest minimum rights from the hands of absolute monarchs.

The framers of the Constitution had this battle very much in mind. The original colonists were composed largely of men who had uprooted themselves to escape from governments under which their civil rights were inadequate. They were therefore suspicious of any strong central government that might have the power to override the people's rights. They accepted the formation of a federal government and constitution only after providing what they thought were workable safeguards against excessive power.

The Forces Against Civil Rights. There is always a tendency on the part of people in power to stay put and to perpetuate and extend their influence. People in the majority don't want to slip back into the minority. Unless checked, the majority may try to suppress those opposed to them; and this can most effectively be done by limiting their freedom to speak out in dissent.

FREEDOM OF SPEECH

Speech, Press and Assembly. There is nothing in the Constitution guaranteeing everyone the right to say anything he pleases. What the First Amendment to the Constitution does say is, "Congress shall make no law . . . abridging the freedom of speech, or of the press; or the right of the people peaceably to assemble . . ."

This puts freedom of speech more properly in the category of civil liberties than civil rights. However, this distinction has no particular importance for our purposes here.

In general you can express any ideas you have pretty freely. But—

You don't have freedom to perpetuate a fraud. If you tell lies, knowingly, to deceive others, the laws respecting fraud will be applied to you. It will be no defense to you to protest that your freedom of speech is being interfered with.

You don't have freedom to interfere with the fair and orderly administration of justice. If you use abusive language in a court of law, or try by irregular methods to influence the court or a jury, you may be punished for contempt of court.

Nor do you have the freedom to say or write anything that will incite others to violence or bloodshed. The government, federal, state, and local, is within its rights when it interferes with such expression as will cause riot and public disorder.

Furthermore, you can't hold public meetings intended to promote disorder, incite riots, or inflame people to violence or the destruction of property.

While society is increasingly tolerant of lewd, abusive or profane language in many situations, you still do not have absolute freedom to use such language in public. Performance, publication and sale of obscene material is restricted in many areas. Use of the mails to transmit obscene material is prohibited by fed-

eral law. (See p. 136 for a discussion of the obscenity controversy.)

These, in general, are the traditional limitations on our freedom of expression. They fall into a clearly discernible pattern. It is this: The right to express oneself may be withheld when it comes into conflict with basic rights of the community.

Under the principles that emerge, we find that people may express ideas antagonistic to the powers that be, may gripe about the government and campaign for changes in it. These, basically, were the rights our founders sought to assure for us.

But—and it is a big "but"—the application of these principles is not always simple, not always clear, and not always on the side of freedom. That is why civil liberties cases are always in the courts.

The Areas of Controversy—"Clear and Present Danger." Under the state's power to protect the community against disorder and violence, actions of one kind or another have, from time to time, been taken against organizations and individuals whose ideas offended and sometimes outraged large segments of the population and the authorities. In the past, such actions were all related to illegal acts like riots, insurrection, disturbance of the peace, violence, etc. A public meeting conducted in a peaceful and orderly fashion was not usually interfered with, even if the ideas expressed were unpopular and offensive.

During and after the First World War, however, a tendency developed to pass laws against *what* was said rather than the *effect* of what was said. A rash of so-called criminal syndicalism laws appeared under which it was a crime to "teach and advocate" the use of force or violence to effect any political change, or any change in industrial ownership, or to possess or circulate literature, or to belong to any organization which advocated any of these things.

Prosecutions under these laws have been examined by the courts and, in general, convictions have been set aside when it has been found that the particular speech, or membership, or possession of literature did not present any "clear and present danger" of violence or insurrection. The courts have required evidence that the person accused has actually and personally advocated violence or disorder.

Attempts have been made to suppress unpopular groups—communist organizations or minority religious sects like Jehovah's Witnesses. Local ordinances have required licenses before public meetings are held; meetings that would cause "alarm and consternation" have been forbidden; and the use of public auditoriums have been denied unless loyalty oaths were taken. In a series of cases arising out of such legislation, the courts have made a variety of findings:

(a) A law providing for licensing in advance of meetings in public parks was held to be a valid exercise of the state's right to take steps to preserve order and peace.

(b) An ordinance providing for an application to be made seven days in advance of a public meeting, and forbidding acts which might cause "consternation and alarm" was declared unconstitutional as being too vague to be enforced, and as interfering with freedom of speech and assembly.

(c) The courts have at times nullified convictions under such acts, not because the convictions under them were held to be discriminatory.

In general, the courts appear to pose the following questions:

Is the law controlling meetings a valid exercise of the government's right to preserve peace and order? If it is, the law is constitutional.

In denying the right to speak or hold a public meeting, did the authorities consider who was doing the speaking? If that was the standard, it is invalid. It is not *who speaks* that matters, but *what is said*. If there is immediate danger that what is said will cause violence, incite a riot, or bring about disorder in the community, the government has the right to act.

Obscenity. This is another area of contro-

versy. Even though the Constitution says that freedom of speech may not be abridged, it has often been held that obscenity may be prohibited because it isn't the kind of speech that was meant to be protected.

The laws of many states, and of the federal government, make it a crime to publish, mail or sell obscene matter. It is therefore important to find an acceptable definition of obscenity. This is a difficult task, because what is obscene to one person is innocent to another. The Supreme Court struggled for years to work out a definition of obscenity that would apply throughout the whole country, but finally it decided to leave the decision to local communities. As long as a state clearly defines what it means by "obscene," it may prohibit any work that the average person in the community would find offensive.

The law used to be that a work which had *any* "redeeming social value" could not be treated as obscene. But that rule no longer applies, and now a state can prohibit any work that, taken as a whole, lacks serious literary, artistic, political, or scientific value.

Unofficial Censorship. Active groups of vocal citizens often successfully influence the kind of publications sold by a bookseller or newsstand, the kind of entertainment shown in theaters, and other offerings to the public. They do this by protest, picketing and boycott.

These methods, although restrictive of freedom of expression, are nevertheless acts which are themselves entitled to protection. The rights to protest, to influence public opinion and to picket, when they do not come into conflict with the libel and slander laws, or with the right of the community to preserve order, are protected.

TREASON AND DISLOYALTY

An act of treason against the United States in time of war is punishable by death. Espionage statutes provide severe penalties for specific and well-defined acts of spying and sabotage.

In the Alien Registration Act of 1940,

known as the Smith Act, espionage and sabotage laws were made applicable in time of peace. Also included in the Smith Act is the well-known provision making it a felony to advocate the overthrow of government by force, or to conspire to do this, or knowingly to be a member of any organization advocating or conspiring the overthrow of government by force.

On test in the courts this law was upheld as constitutional, although it seemingly represented a departure from the previous position that acts, not advocacy, are criminal and punishable. Later, however, the Supreme Court reaffirmed the principle that a state cannot forbid advocacy of the use of force or advocacy of law violation unless the advocacy is directed to inciting, and is likely to incite, imminent lawless action. The Supreme Court states that the Smith Act is constitutional because it embodies this principle.

FREEDOM OF RELIGION

The First Amendment to the Constitution states: "Congress shall make no law respecting an establishment of religion, or prohibiting the free exercise thereof . . ." This amendment makes it impossible for Congress to abridge freedom of religion.

All of the states have similar provisions in their constitutions. The Fourteenth Amendment effectively prevents the states from adopting an "established" or official religion, or interfering with the practice of any religion or sect.

The problem of the separation of church and state often comes to the attention of the courts because, from time to time, state legislatures enact laws to assist and promote religious participation and instructions. State legislatures often assist religious schools because they know that the public school systems would have a greater financial burden to carry if religious schools had to close for lack of funds. However, assistance which entangles the state government too closely with the religious institution will not be allowed.

Examples of the kinds of assistance that have been allowed are: construction grants for church-related colleges, releasing children from classes for religious instruction so long as the instruction is not conducted in public school classrooms, and bus transportation programs and loans of textbooks directly to private school students, on the theory that such programs benefit the students rather than the schools.

On the other hand, a state may not reimburse a religious school for the cost of books used in its classes, even where the classes are not in religious subjects. It may not supplement the salaries of teachers at religious schools, whether or not they teach religious subjects. And it may not lend films, laboratory equipment, or counseling and testing services to religious schools, even when the material lent is not of a religious nature, since that would be assisting an institution with a religious purpose.

Freedom To Observe Religion of Choice. There is practically unlimited freedom to observe and practice any religion, to preach it, try to win converts and even to disparage other religions. In the case of the latter, however, the same limitations apply as in the case of expression in general.

A religious gathering that causes disorder can be stopped. A statement that is defamatory can be the subject of a suit for damages, and it will be no excuse that the slanderer was practicing his religion.

Cases have arisen in states where it is compulsory for schoolchildren to salute the flag. Certain religious sects forbid this. The courts have held that a child cannot be dismissed from school when it is his religion, and not disrespect, that makes him refuse to salute.

DUE PROCESS OF LAW

When we speak of "due process of law," we mean certain safeguards which are designed to protect the individual from arbitrary government action against him. What the founding fathers had in mind when they provided these safeguards were despotic practices such as: searching a man's home, in the name of the king, without a warrant or reasonable cause; seizing persons or property, denying counsel, bail, the right to be faced with accusers or to cross-examine them; denial of trial by jury; denial of the right to question the legality of one's detention (habeas corpus); and inflicting cruel and unusual punishment.

The original Constitution, which was ratified in 1787, did not have all of these safeguards, and some of the states signed it with reluctance. As a result, a set of proposals for constitutional amendments was introduced at the first session of Congress. When these proposals were approved in 1791, they became the first ten amendments to the Constitution, often referred to as the Bill of Rights.

The Bill of Rights is binding on the federal government but not on the states. However, the Fourteenth Amendment, which was added to the Constitution after the Civil War, specifically applies to the states, and forbids them to "deprive any person of life, liberty, or property, without due process of law."

The meaning given to "due process of law" in the Fourteenth Amendment is not necessarily the meaning given in the Bill of Rights. It has been held to be a requirement that civilized standards be applied, and that the standards adopted for the whole community be available to each defendant. In many cases these standards are the same as the specific standards imposed on the federal government by the Bill of Rights, but in some cases they are different. Some of the important differences will be pointed out in the discussions of the individual safeguards which follow.

Searches and Seizures. The Fourth Amendment prohibits "unreasonable searches and seizures" of persons or property. Evidence that has been obtained through an illegal search or seizure cannot be used in court against the person whose rights have thus been violated, since the guarantee would be meaningless otherwise. This "exclusionary rule," as it is called, applies in both federal and state courts. However, it does not apply to grand juries, which decide whether or not to indict someone who is charged with a crime. This means that illegally obtained evidence may be used as the basis for an indictment, even though it may not be used at the defendant's trial.

Since the exclusionary rule applies only to illegally obtained evidence, the line between "reasonable" and "unreasonable" searches is very important. Of course, where the police have obtained a search warrant from a judge before making a search, the requirements of the Fourth Amendment are satisfied. But even warrantless searches are sometimes considered reasonable. For example, if a policeman sees someone behaving suspiciously and has reason to believe that the person may be armed, he may stop and frisk that person, and any weapons he finds may be used as evidence. And whenever someone is arrested and taken into custody, any incriminating evidence found on him may be used against him whether or not it is related to the crime for which he was originally arrested.

Trial by Jury. The Sixth Amendment guarantees the right to a trial by jury to defendants in all criminal prosecutions in federal courts. If a defendant in a state court is charged with a crime that would entitle him to a trial by jury in a federal court, then he has a right to a jury trial in the state court. However, the jury in the state court does not necessarily have to have the traditional number of twelve people on it, and its verdict does not have to be unanimous.

It is not enough that the defendant be tried by a jury. The jury must be impartial. More due process cases have arisen on allegations that the jury was not impartial than because of the denial of jury trial. While due process does not require that persons of the same race or sex as the defendant be included in the jury, it is a violation of due process if the panels from which juries are drawn specifically exclude persons of a certain race or sex.

The right to a trial by jury may be waived

by the defendant. In many state courts it is waived simply by his failure to assert it.

In addition to guaranteeing the right to trial by jury, the Sixth Amendment guarantees defendants the right to a speedy trial and the right to confront the witnesses against them. Both of these guarantees apply in state courts as well as in federal courts.

Right to Counsel. Whenever a defendant is charged with a crime that may lead to a jail sentence, he has the right to the assistance of counsel at his trial. If he cannot afford it, the court must appoint a lawyer to represent him. This rule applies in both federal and state courts. It applies whether the crime the defendant is charged with is a felony or a misdemeanor, as long as there is a possibility he may be sent to jail for it.

Whether or not a suspect has a right to counsel before trial often depends on whether he has been formally charged with a crime. For example, a suspect who has not yet been charged does not have an automatic right to counsel during police interrogation. Either the suspect or his lawyer must demand the right to consult with each other. On the other hand, a suspect who has been formally charged with a crime may not be interrogated by the police unless his lawyer is present, whether or not he requests it.

The rule about lineups is similar. Before a suspect has been charged with a crime, he may be exhibited before witnesses for identification in the absence of his lawyer. But once he has been formally charged, his lawyer must be present at the lineup or the identification evidence will be inadmissible at the trial.

Testifying Against Oneself. The privilege against self-incrimination is contained in the Fifth Amendment. Under the Fourteenth Amendment, it applies in state courts to the same extent as in federal courts. It means, simply, that no one is required to answer questions or give evidence that might incriminate him.

The privilege is derived from the fact that the power of the state and its vast resources are so enormous in contrast with the individual that, if it were legal to do so, the government could obtain confessions from individuals of acts of which they were not guilty. Under our system of law, evidence of a man's guilt must be found elsewhere than in his own words.

The Fifth Amendment was the basis of the famous *Miranda* case, in which the Supreme Court held that a person who is taken into custody by the police must be given certain warnings before he can be interrogated. He must be warned: (1) that he has the right to remain silent; (2) that any statement he makes may be used as evidence against him; (3) that he has a right to the presence of a lawyer; and (4) that if he cannot afford a lawyer, one will be appointed for him if he desires.

A defendant may waive these rights and make a statement if he wants to. If he doesn't waive his rights, or if the warnings are not given, any statements he makes may not be used to prove his guilt. However, they may be used to attack his credibility as long as the jury is instructed that it may not consider them as proof of guilt.

The privilege against self-incrimination means that a defendant in a criminal prosecution doesn't have to testify at all if he doesn't want to. If the defendant chooses not to testify, the court may not make any comment to the jury about his failure to do so. This rule applies in both state and federal courts.

A significant fact about the privilege against self-incrimination is that it can be waived or surrendered by the person under interrogation. The surrender need not be intentional or expressed. The privilege may be waived unwittingly by the witness. The courts have held that if he answers any questions at all pertaining to the subject matter of the inquiry, he may not later claim the privilege.

Although the value of this privilege against self-incrimination is universally recognized, it has been argued that it is a serious obstacle to investigators. Legislation has been passed that gives the government power to grant witnesses immunity from prosecution, so that they cannot refuse to testify on the ground that their own words would incriminate them. Such laws are in effect in various states and are effective as a means of inducing criminals to give information concerning their associates.

Since the granting of immunity is such a great power, and subject to many abuses, there is always debate as to who shall have the right to exercise it. Under the federal law, immunity can be granted only by the court.

Double Jeopardy. No person can be tried more than once for the same crime. This rule is observed by the federal government by virtue of the Fifth Amendment, and, in most of the states, by similar articles in their own constitutions.

A defendant is considered to have been placed in jeopardy once if a jury has been sworn in and the trial has begun. If there is a mistrial because a key witness is missing, or because evidence upon which the prosecution bases its case is not admitted by the court, the defendant cannot be retried on the same charge.

The test of whether or not a defendant is being placed in jeopardy a second time (double jeopardy) is whether or not the evidence required to prove the second charge is the same as that required to prove the first. Thus, even if the technical name of the crime in the second proceeding is different, the second prosecution will be barred if the acts involved and the evidence offered are the same.

But when new conditions so alter the whole significance of the act as to change the nature of the crime, a second trial will be permitted. An example is a prosecution for a criminal assault, followed by another prosecution for homicide. This is possible where the victim of the assault dies of his injuries.

Traditionally, the rule against double jeopardy was understood to mean that the acquittal of a defendant was final. The prosecution was not permitted to appeal even though the defendant, if convicted, could appeal. However, the Supreme Court recently held that, even if the defendant had been acquitted, appeal by the prosecution would not violate the double jeopardy clause so long as the appeal didn't constitute a new trial.

EQUAL PROTECTION OF THE LAW

Section One of the Fourteenth Amendment reads as follows: "All persons born or naturalized in the United States, and subject to the jurisdiction thereof, are citizens of the United States and of the state wherein they reside. No state shall make or enforce any law which shall abridge the privileges or immunities of citizens of the United States; nor shall any state deprive any person of life, liberty or property without due process of law; nor deny any person within its jurisdiction the equal protection of the laws."

The Equal Protection clause prohibits discrimination by the states, not private discrimination. Nor are all discriminatory state laws prohibited. For example, a state law that discriminates against welfare recipients with large families is constitutional so long as there is a rational basis for it, such as encouraging employment.

But a rational basis alone is not enough to justify certain kinds of discrimination. For example, where a law discriminates on the basis of race or national origin, the state has a heavier burden of justification. This burden is usually expressed by saying that the state must prove that the discriminatory law promotes a compelling state interest. Applying this test, the Supreme Court has struck down laws segregating public facilities and prohibiting interracial marriages.

The constitutionality of laws that discriminate on the basis of sex is a currently unsettled question. The Supreme Court has struck down a state law giving preference to men over women where individuals of different sexes were otherwise equally entitled to administer a decedent's estate. On the other hand, it was held that it is not a denial of equal protection for a state disability insurance system to exclude pregnancy from the list of disabilities covered by the system.

The law in this area will probably remain

unsettled until the Equal Rights Amendment is disposed of, one way or another, by the states. This proposed amendment to the Constitution, which would prohibit all sex discrimination by the federal and state governments, was passed by Congress in 1972 and submitted to the states for ratification. Like all constitutional amendments, it requires the approval of thirty-eight states.

Another controversial question involves programs that give preference to members of minority groups in hiring and in admission to colleges and graduate schools. These programs, which are sometimes called "affirmative action" programs and sometimes called "reverse discrimination," are intended to remedy the effects of past discrimination against minorities, but have been attacked on the ground that they unfairly discriminate against white applicants. As of this writing, the Supreme Court has not ruled on the constitutionality of such programs.

The Civil Rights Act of 1964. Civil rights can be affected by statutes as well as by constitutional provisions. The most well-known federal statute dealing with civil rights is the Civil Rights Act of 1964.

One part of the Act makes it illegal for places of public accommodation (such as hotels, restaurants, and theaters) to discriminate on the basis of race, color, religion, or national origin. (Sex discrimination is not covered by this part of the Act.) In order for a place of public accommodation to be subject to the Act, it must affect interstate commerce, since the federal government has no authority to regulate purely local commerce. However, this requirement has been broadly interpreted by the courts, and it is a rare enterprise that will not be found to have some effect on interstate commerce.

Another part of the Civil Rights Act of 1964 (known as Title VII) makes it illegal for employers to discriminate against employees (or applicants for employment) on the basis of race, color, religion, sex or national origin. Unions are also prohibited from discriminating against their members on those bases.

CHAPTER TWENTY-FOUR

LABOR AND MANAGEMENT

Collective bargaining between labor and management is so vast and has so great an impact on our economy that no one is really untouched by it. The great number and variety of disputes and controversies in this field have made necessary the development of special laws, agencies and techniques to settle conflicts and bring some stability to industry. This chapter includes a brief history of labor-management legislation and an explanation of the everyday application of the aspects of the law with which we are most likely to come into contact.

LAWS AFFECTING LABOR AND MANAGEMENT

The early days of labor-management relations were marked by bitter conflict. Strikes, violence and disorder were common. The use of professional strikebreakers, labor spies, the militia and the legal weapon of injunction by anti-union employers were all part of an era of unregulated struggle. The country's vital transportation was threatened by this turbulence. To bring labor stability to the railroads, the *Railway Labor Act* was passed in 1926. It established the right of railway employees to bargain collectively with the railroads, through union representatives of their own choice, and adopted methods of handling disputes and negotiations in an orderly and peaceful atmosphere. This act is still very much in use and has been extended to include the multitude of airline employees that have come into being since the act was passed.

Of great significance was the passage of the *Norris-LaGuardia Act* in 1932. This act limited the rights of federal courts to issue injunctions in labor disputes. Some judges treated striking and picketing as the lawful exercise of rights guaranteed by the Constitution. Those judges protected such action even if it caused inconvenience and loss of business to employers. But many other judges issued injunctions against union activities such as picketing. The injunction was an especially effective way of controlling union activities, since someone who is charged with violating an injunction has no right to a trial by jury. Very often this practice prevented unionization and caused the imprisonment of union organizers who disregarded the injunction mandate. For this reason the Norris-LaGuardia Act was a landmark which greatly improved the atmosphere of organized labor.

Another provision of the Norris-LaGuardia Act put an end to the "yellow dog" contract. This was a contract made with a new employee in which the employee agreed not to join a union under penalty of losing his job.

The Norris-LaGuardia Act, like all the other laws included in this chapter, is a federal law. As such it applies to businesses and employees engaged in interstate commerce. Purely local businesses which neither buy nor sell substantial amounts of goods over state lines are subject to state laws. These differ considerably depending on the state's policy toward organized labor. New York and other states have passed legislation similar to the Norris-LaGuardia Act.

The *Wagner Act* of 1935 was the most important and far-reaching piece of labor legislation ever enacted in the United States. It firmly established the rights of employees to organize or join labor unions, to bargain collectively with their employers through a representative of their own choosing, and to take part in "concerted activities," including picketing and strikes. If an employer interfered with the exercise of any of those rights or refused to bargain collectively with the employees' chosen representative, it committed an unfair labor practice. The NLRB (National Labor Relations Board) was given the power to prevent and remedy unfair practices by the employer and to conduct secret elections to determine the choice of the employees as to which, if any, union they desired to represent them.

The Wagner Act was so favorable to unions that membership doubled in about two years after its enactment. Before it was passed, a truly determined employer with enough resources could prevent the unionization of his plant without regard to the wishes of his employees. After its passage the opposite sometimes occurred: the employer was placed in a situation where he signed a contract with a union even if a majority of his employees did not wish it.

Reaction on the part of industry and Congress to this favorable labor legislation was slowed down by World War II, when special controls on wages and prices put a check on union demands. After the war, however, Congress, under the leadership of Senator Taft, amended the Wagner Act for the purpose of bringing the powers of labor and management into balance. The *Taft-Hartley Act* was passed in 1947. It created a set of union unfair labor practices to balance the employer unfair labor practices the Wagner Act had created. One of the activities that it made illegal was the secondary boycott, which involves bringing pressure on one person to make him stop doing business with another person.

The Taft-Hartley Act also made the "closed shop" illegal. This means that it is unlawful for a labor contract to stipulate that the employer must hire only union members. An em-

ployer subject to the federal law is free to hire any applicant whether or not he is a union member, but most contracts have a "union shop" clause, which requires that a new employee must become a member of the union after thirty days or lose his job. Federal law allows the "union shop" clause, but it also provides that states may ban it if they want to. Several states have taken advantage of this opportunity to pass so-called "right-to-work" laws, under which employees cannot be fired if they refuse to join the union.

Under another provision of the Taft-Hartley Act, the federal government can apply for an injunction to end strikes that endanger the health or safety of the country.

The Wagner Act was further amended by the *Landrum-Griffin Act* in 1959. This law, known as the Labor-Management Reporting and Disclosure Act, is largely the response of Congress to the sensational disclosures of the Senate Rackets Committee. It sets up a "Bill of Rights" for members of labor unions. It guarantees the rights of individual members with regard to taking part in union meetings, expressing themselves on union business and voting for officers and on proposals for increased dues in secret elections. Other provisions of the law require the bonding of union officials who handle money, the filing of regular reports by employers, by labor relations consultants and by labor unions, all intended to compel the disclosure of money transactions of a kind that may indicate fraud, collusion or overreaching.

Public Employees. The pro-labor legislation of the 1930s, discussed above, did not extend to the employees of federal, state and local government. The prevailing view at the time was that there is no right to public employment, and that anyone who didn't like the restrictions placed on public employees should seek private employment instead.

In the last twenty years, however, the rights of public employees have been greatly expanded. This development is due in large part to the growing importance of public employment (more than 15 per cent of the national labor force is employed by government).

Most states now give public employees the right to organize and require public employers to negotiate with their employees. Strikes by public employees are still prohibited in almost all states on the ground that such strikes are harmful to the public. The effectiveness of the laws against strikes by public employees is open to question, but such laws are likely to remain in force even though they are often violated.

THE NATIONAL LABOR RELATIONS BOARD

The NLRB is the government agency which has primary responsibility in the field of labor-management relations. It was originally created by the Wagner Act, and the various amendments to this act have modified and extended its authority. The Board has its headquarters in Washington, with regional offices throughout the country. Each regional office has a director and legal and administrative personnel to process the cases which arise in its geographical jurisdiction. The Board has the authority to receive complaints, investigate them, conduct conferences and trial hearings before trial examiners (who function as judges), make decisions, issue orders, and apply to the courts for judicial decrees to enforce its orders.

Jurisdiction. The Board, and only the Board, has the right to deal with cases affecting interstate commerce. The various state agencies were restricted to purely local matters until the passage of the Landrum-Griffin Act in 1959. This act gave the state boards the right to deal with cases, even those involving interstate commerce, which the Board would not process because they did not meet the standards which the Board had set up. Its refusal to take certain cases in interstate commerce was based on its inability to process all of the cases which came to it. Since the state boards had authority only in intrastate matters, the result was a "no man's land" of cases

which got no attention at all. The Board periodically fixes its own jurisdictional standards. It refuses to take any cases involving certain industries, because the industries don't have a strong enough effect on interstate commerce. Other industries must meet "dollar volume" standards before the Board will agree to take cases involving them. For example, the Board refuses to take cases in which the employer did less than $500,000 of retail business in interstate business in a year. In nonretail business, the Board will accept jurisdiction if the employer shipped at least $50,000 worth of goods or services to out-of-state destinations or received at least $50,000 worth of goods and services from out of state.

Representation Proceedings. One of the main functions of the NLRB is to determine what union, if any, has the right to be the collective bargaining representative of a group of employees. The procedure may be started in one of the Board's Regional Offices by the union or by the employer. Sometimes more than one union may be contending for the right to represent a plant. In such a case, the union or employer who starts the case is required to name the competing unions in the petition which is furnished by the Board. A typical case is one in which a petition is filed by a union which has been organizing a certain group of employees in a plant. It completes the form of petition supplied by the NLRB, naming the employer, describing his business and specifying the particular unit or group of employees the union claims to represent. The Board will not, as a rule, process the petition unless the union can prove, by showing authorization cards signed by employees, that it represents a substantial number of the group. (The Board usually considers 30 per cent or more to be a substantial number.) If, after a hearing, the Regional Director decides that a question of representation exists, that the group of employees (or "unit," as it is called) is appropriate, and that an election can be held to reflect the free choice of the employees, he will order an election by secret ballot under the supervision of one of his staff.

If a majority of the employees vote for a particular union, it is certified as the bargaining representative of the unit. No matter who wins the election, at least a year must pass before another election can be held. This means that a union which wins an election remains the collective bargaining representative of the group for at least a year, even if the employees change their minds and decide they prefer some other union or no union at all.

Under the Landrum-Griffin Act, it is now possible for an employer to obtain a quick election if the union has picketed for more than thirty days and hasn't filed a petition. However, the picketing must be for the purpose of forcing the employer to recognize or bargain with the union, or for organizing the employees into the union. If none of those purposes is involved, the employer can't get a quick election even if the picketing goes on for more than thirty days without a petition being filed by the union.

UNFAIR LABOR PRACTICES

The law sets up two lists of unfair labor practices—one for unions, the other for employers.

Employer Unfair Practices. Employers are not allowed to interfere with or restrain any of their employees in their right to form, join or assist labor organizations. Employers are not permitted to exercise domination or control over a union or give it financial support. Employers are not allowed to discriminate against employees in any way for the purpose of encouraging or discouraging membership in a union. An employer is not allowed to discipline an employee for filing charges with the Board or for testifying as a witness in a Board case. An employer is not allowed to refuse to bargain with a union which is the certified representative of his employees.

The above items are stated in general terms. There are a great many activities which constitute unfair practices without being specifically described as such in the law. For example, if an employer, upon learning that

his men are thinking of joining a union, raises their pay or promises to do so, or gives them any benefits at all for the purpose of influencing them, it is unfair labor practice. Discharge of employees because they are active in union organization is, of course, an unfair labor practice, and the employer can be ordered to reinstate the discharged employee and give him back pay for time lost. The law specifically provides that an employer has the right to express his views or opinions, but such expression must contain "no threat of reprisal or force or promise of benefit." Since it takes an expert to come up with a message from an employer to his organizing employees that can measure up to this standard, employers should get advice of counsel before going to the printer.

Union Unfair Practices. A set of unfair labor practices by unions was added to the law for the first time by the Taft-Hartley Act.

Labor unions may not restrain or coerce employees in connection with their rights to join or not to join a union. An exception to this is the right of a labor organization to include, in a collective-bargaining agreement with an employer, a union shop clause which provides that after thirty days of employment a new employee is required to become a member of the union and pay the regular dues and initiation fees as a condition of his continued employment. In other words, a new employee who refuses on the thirty-first day of his employment to become a member of the union may be discharged at the union's request.

It is an unfair labor practice for a union to cause an employer to discriminate against any employee, refuse to hire him, discharge him, or fail to give him the work he may be entitled to by virtue of seniority for the purpose of encouraging or discouraging membership in any labor organization.

It is an unfair labor practice for a union itself to discriminate against an employee on any ground other than his failure to pay the dues and initiation fees that are regularly required as a condition of membership. This means that an employee who is out of favor with the union for any reason—as, for example, disregarding a union picket line or making a deal with an employer to accept wages or working conditions which are less than those established in the union agreement—cannot be deprived of his employment or of his seniority standing or in any other way discriminated against. It is also an unfair labor practice for a union to refuse to bargain collectively with an employer once the union has been designated as the representative of the employees.

Secondary Boycotts. One of the unfair labor practices most often talked about is the picketing by a union of a firm or company which is not directly involved in the labor dispute, as a means of exerting pressure on the company with which the union actually has the dispute. For example, if there is a dispute between the management of a retail store and its employees, the union may wish to persuade a wholesale establishment not to deal with the retail store. Picketing the wholesale establishment for such a purpose would be an illegal secondary boycott.

The prohibition against secondary boycotts has teeth in it, as we shall see from the exceptional way in which such cases are processed.

Board Procedures. Usually the processing of an unfair labor practice charge is a rather long-drawn-out affair. It begins with a charge made by someone who claims to have been the victim of the unfair practice. This is followed by an investigation by staff agents of the Board. If the investigator finds that the charge has substance, he recommends to the General Counsel of the Board that a formal complaint be served on the offender. The complaint must be answered, after which a formal hearing is held before a trial examiner. Witnesses are heard and all of the proceedings are taken down by an official reporter. The hearing is in all respects like a trial in court without a jury. After considering the matter and studying the record, the trial examiner makes his decision, which is called an "intermediate report,"

based on findings of fact and conclusions of law.

If the trial examiner finds that an unfair labor practice was committed, he makes specific recommendations as to what the remedy should be. If any of the parties disagree with the trial examiner's findings or recommendations, exceptions are filed with the NLRB in Washington, and the matter is automatically transferred to the Board for final decision. The Board may reverse or modify the decision of the trial examiner. If the Board adopts the decision and makes a final determination that the accused is guilty of an unfair labor practice, the matter does not necessarily end there. In order for the Board's decision to be enforced, an order must be obtained from a U. S. Court of Appeals. This is generally applied for by the Regional Director of the NLRB. In the Court of Appeals, the one found guilty by the Board has the opportunity to have the whole matter reviewed. He need not wait for the Board to take the matter to the Court. He may himself petition the Court to review the decision of the Board.

It may take anywhere from six months to two years to complete the procedure thus described. In contrast to this, the procedure for dealing with secondary boycotts is streamlined and fast. To begin with, the regional offices of the Board are instructed to give priority to secondary-boycott cases over all others. The purpose is to give immediate relief to a company that may be tied up by a strike when that company is neutral and is wholly unconcerned in the labor dispute. In such cases, the Board agents make an accelerated investigation and immediately apply to the U. S. District Court for a temporary injunction to stop the secondary activities until the Board has conducted its full-hearing procedure and has arrived at a final decision.

Related to the illegal secondary boycott is the so-called "hot cargo" clause, under which an employer agrees not to handle any goods received from or going to an establishment where there is a labor dispute. Before 1959, unions used "hot cargo" clauses to get around the ban on secondary boycotts. They did this by getting employers to agree to practices that would be illegal secondary boycotts if the unions did them alone. However, this loophole was closed by the Landrum-Griffin Act, which made "hot cargo" clauses illegal, except in certain cases involving the construction industry and the garment industry.

SENIORITY RIGHTS OF EMPLOYEES

Generally speaking, union agreements provide that the first to be hired shall be the last to be discharged and that senior employees have preference in promotions, overtime work, preferential shifts, etc.

The Board feels that the matter of seniority is something peculiarly within the knowledge of the employer. The employer's records should contain accurate information as to when the individual employees were hired and the seniority rank of each one. It is the feeling of the Board that when the employer leaves such matters to the exclusive discretion of the union, such discretion will be used for purposes of unfair discrimination.

As we saw in Chapter 23, the Civil Rights Act of 1964 makes it illegal for an employer to discriminate against his employees on the basis of race, color, religion, sex, or national origin. A minority employee who has been discriminated against by his employer may have lost valuable seniority rights as a result of the discrimination. To remedy this problem, the employer may be required to give the employee retroactive seniority. However, the date to which retroactive seniority is given cannot be earlier than the date the Civil Rights Act of 1964 became effective (July 2, 1964). And an employee who was not discriminated against after that date is not entitled to retroactive seniority even if he suffered discrimination before that date. The Supreme Court so ruled in a recent case, despite the employees' argument that the decision would perpetuate the effects of discrimination that was legal when it was committed but that has since been made illegal.

DISPUTES AND GRIEVANCES

Without machinery for dealing with disputes peaceably and amicably, industry would be disrupted by countless strikes, lockouts, work stoppages, walkouts, etc. Such needless work interruptions are prevented by the provisions of the collective-bargaining agreements which employers enter into with the unions representing their employees. It is a rare agreement these days that does not contain a "no strike, no lockout" clause together with a provision for the arbitration of all disputes that may arise under the agreement. This means that during the term of the agreement the union will not resort to strikes and the employer will refrain from locking out his employees. Such disputes and disagreements as may arise and which cannot be settled by other means are dealt with by arbitration.

There are thousands of disputes which never reach the state of formal arbitration. Traditionally, even without unions, an employee who had a complaint—let us say he objected to a supervisor's order as being unreasonable—would take the matter up with management directly. Union members will usually, in the first instance, bring their grievances to the union shop steward, who is a fellow employee designated by the union to represent the employees on a particular job. In many cases the shop steward, dealing with his opposite number in management, either a supervisor, plant manager, or personnel manager, can settle the dispute. If the shop steward does not succeed in resolving the matter, it is usually referred to a business agent of the union, who, in turn, will take the matter up with a higher company official. It is only when these intermediate steps are unsuccessful that the matter is carried to mediation or arbitration.

Mediation. A mediation involves bringing in an impartial third party who will try to reconcile the positions of the union and the employer. A mediator does not have the power to decide or determine anything. He merely tries to conciliate the parties and effect a settlement by compromise. Mediation is not always resorted to by the parties, but if it is and is unsuccessful, the next step is generally arbitration.

Arbitration. The collective-bargaining agreement usually provides that the parties must first try to settle disputes by discussion and negotiation. A representative of the employer meets with a representative of the union. If they should fail to iron out their difficulties, they must then proceed to arbitration following the method specified in the agreement. The agreement may actually name an impartial arbitrator acceptable to both sides. More often, the agreement provides for a method of selecting an impartial arbitrator from a list of names or a panel submitted by the Federal Mediation Service or the American Arbitration Association or the State Board of Mediation. Whatever method the parties have specified in their agreement, it must be followed to conclusion. State laws require that parties who have agreed to arbitration must follow the arbitration procedure, and they are bound by the arbitrator's award just as if it were the judgment of a court of law. In fact, after the arbitrator has made his award, either of the parties may go to court and have the award "confirmed." This gives it the same force and effect as if it were a judgment. Unless it is specifically provided for in the labor agreement, there is usually no appeal from an arbitrator's award. Even when a court thinks an arbitrator's decision is wrong, it will let it stand so long as the labor agreement gave him the authority to make it. Of course, if it can be shown that an arbitrator was not truly impartial, that he was dishonest or had a personal interest in the result, the award can be set aside.

How Arbitration Works. Assume that an employee has been discharged for arguing with his supervisor and walking off the job. The employer's personnel manager and a business agent of the union attempt to settle the matter. The personnel manager insists the man was properly discharged. The union delegate supports the man and insists he should be reinstated at once. Both cling stubbornly to their positions with the result that the union gives notice in writing of its intention to arbitrate in accordance with the terms of the agreement. An arbitrator is agreed upon and a date for the hearing is fixed. On the appointed date, the employer and the union appear before the arbitrator with their witnesses. The employer has with him the personnel manager and the supervisor who was involved in the argument. The union business agent is present with the discharged employee, who is called the "grievant." The atmosphere is informal. The parties sit around a table with the arbitrator at the head. Sometimes a stenographer is present to take down the testimony, but this is rare. Often the parties are not even represented by their attorneys. The first thing the parties must do is to agree upon the exact language of the question to be given to the arbitrator for determination. This is called the "submission." In this case, the parties agree on the terms of the submission as follows: "Was the discharge of the employee John Doe for just cause? If not, what should the remedy be?"

The union then advises the arbitrator that it is seeking reinstatement of the employee in his job with full back pay. The union contract is offered in evidence. It may provide that no employee can be discharged without just cause (this is not the same as a layoff for lack of work), and that the employer may not discharge anyone without advance notice to the union and a grievance procedure except for two causes: drunkenness on the job and dishonesty. Then the employer is called upon to explain the circumstances of the discharge and why he thinks it is justified. After the employer's witnesses have been heard, the union gives its side of the story. With all of the facts before him, the arbitrator usually reserves his decision, which is called an "award." After a short delay, he delivers the award in writing.

In general, arbitrators will uphold the right of employers to discipline employees who are guilty of some actual breach of duty or a clear violation of reasonable rules established by the employer. However, they regard dismissal or discharge as a drastic form of discipline. A frequently used phrase to describe discharge from a job that provides a man's livelihood is "economic capital punishment." Arbitrators consider that the offense or breach of duty by the employee must be serious in order to justify dismissal. Sometimes they rule that the employer was justified in meting out some form of discipline but that discharge was too severe. Often they award reinstatement, but if the employee was to some degree at fault they may deny all or part of his back pay.

CHAPTER TWENTY-FIVE

THE LEGAL PROFESSION

The word "jungle" is a common synonym for a lawless state. The opposite of the jungle is the highly developed community in which men live, work and conduct their complex affairs in an orderly, smooth and harmonious manner, with the maximum of individual liberty, according to law. It is because law is both an instrument and a standard of civilization that the legal profession occupies such a respected place.

PROFESSIONAL REQUIREMENTS

Law, as a profession, is a very demanding discipline. It requires long years of formal schooling, and continuous study during its practice as well. No libraries are as much used as are law libraries, or kept as up-to-date or complete. You will find lawyers there in the evening hours doing research after a full day of courtroom practice or work in the office.

It used to be common, and it is still possible (although rare) in some states, for a lawyer to be admitted to the bar after apprenticeship in the office of another lawyer. However, the greater number of our present-day lawyers are graduates of law schools, which they enter after receiving an undergraduate degree.

Regardless of how they acquire their preparatory education, prospective lawyers must pass stiff bar examinations given by each state in which they intend to practice. Furthermore, they must be approved for admission by a committee on character and fitness.

After admission, a lawyer can survive in the profession only by proving his merit. This demands a variety of qualities not generally required in other callings.

A lawyer must be adept at investigating facts. He must, of course, also know the law and be familiar with sources of special knowledge. He must be skillfull and persuasive as negotiator and advocate. He is called upon to advise his clients, to represent them and to fight their battles. He must be able to gain and hold their confidence. So he must develop an insight into human psychology and behavior.

Professional Ethics. In his professional life, the lawyer is bound by rules of ethics that call for an extremely high standard of behavior. If he fails to adhere to those standards, he can be disbarred.

Traditionally, a lawyer never advertises his services or solicits clients. However, the Supreme Court has overturned bans on advertising, so that prospective clients can shop around for lawyers with the expertise—and prices—that they desire. Lawyers must never betray the confidence of their clients. The information they obtain from clients can never be used by them in any way that will prejudice the clients' interests. And this applies even after the relationship of lawyer and client has ended. If this were not so, a client might balk at being honest with his lawyer.

Lawyers must avoid situations where there is even the possibility or appearance of impropriety. In New York, for example, the bar associations have held that it is improper for a lawyer who previously represented two men who were partners, to act for one of them in a dispute with the other. The reason is that, while acting for both of them, he acquired confidential knowledge from each. Acting for one against the other might involve the use of such knowledge, and this would be prejudicial to the former client.

HOW TO CHOOSE A LAWYER

Practically everybody knows a lawyer in his community—if not through business, then in some social connection. Yet recent reports have uncovered many instances in which a lawyer's assistance could have solved a problem, but wasn't resorted to. The person involved either was unaware that his problem was a legal one, didn't know where to turn for legal help, or was afraid of the expense.

People who have no contact with lawyers usually ask someone they trust to refer them to a lawyer. Today, many unions, employers and other groups have plans offering low-cost legal aid, or even free legal help, to those who participate in the plan.

It is recommended that those in need of legal services get in touch with the local bar association. Many local associations have set up legal referral services to help those who don't know a lawyer or aren't sure they have a legal problem. Through these services, such a person can get an interview with a skilled and experienced member of the bar.

If it turns out that the person has a legal problem he will be referred to a lawyer experienced in that particular kind of problem, and the fee will be reasonable. In this way, those with no previous contact with lawyers can get legal help at a low cost.

Legal Aid Societies. For those who can't afford to pay even a small fee to a lawyer, there are Legal Aid offices in most large cities in the United States. Some Legal Aid offices have staff lawyers, while others maintain a list of volunteers who give their services free to applicants, who must show they are eligible— that is, they must prove their inability to pay.

The local societies are largely supported by private contributions and are independent of one another.

In criminal matters, the state will appoint counsel for any person charged with an offense, if he so requests. This is required under the United States Constitution. And remember, for small matters, it is often possible for you to "do it yourself" in small-claims courts.

Attitudes Toward Lawyers. People may stay away from lawyers because they don't know they have a legal problem. More often it is because they don't wish to get involved in what they fear will be heavy expenses. This may lead to trouble.

Instead of going to a lawyer with his problem, the confused person often takes it to a layman he thinks is "in the know" or to some organization not permitted to practice law. The usual result is that he is left without the protection of the lawyer-client relationship, as well as without its benefits. In the end, his costs are often greatly in excess of the legal fees he would have incurred. However, many in the legal profession have voiced concern that lawyers have priced themselves "out of the market" for ordinary legal affairs.

Lawyer Stereotypes. The lawyer is sometimes depicted, in a stereotyped way, as a fee-grabber, as a spellbinder, as the mouthpiece of shady characters, or as a manipulator. One reason why such misrepresentation goes without reply is the legal profession's high and restrictive standard of ethics.

Lawyers generally may not advertise—they may not market their services either individually or as a group. They sponsor no public-relations campaigns to boost the lawyer in the eyes of the community, although admittedly some public-interest work that lawyers do is done in an effort to improve the image of the profession.

Role of Bar Associations. Lawyers generally are not very active in promoting themselves. There are numerous bar associations, but you will find that the extent of their activities *for the benefit of their members* is to maintain libraries and to sponsor further legal education for lawyers. Their chief activities serve the public in general, and members of their profession only incidentally. Bar associations maintain committees to hear grievances against, and to discipline, their own colleagues. Their findings rarely favor a lawyer over a client. The associations also study and propose new legislation—not just legislation affecting the interests of lawyers, but all legislation affecting the public. They are constantly pushing for faster, cheaper and more efficient court procedures.

Legal Expenses. Fortunately, popular misconceptions regarding lawyers are not shared by those who have occasion to make regular use of their services. Few business firms of any size are without legal counsel on regular retainer.

But the average salaried man or woman doesn't usually include legal expenses in the annual budget. When they become necessary, legal expenses are resented as a burden. This is true, too, of small businessmen who have only occasional need of legal help. The expense is unforeseen and, therefore, the tendency is to be grudging about fees.

The man who pays thousands for a major operation will grumble about paying a much smaller fee for a document requiring hours of research, drafting, and the application of sober judgment, foresight, and experience. Yet both jobs require years of study and preparation to do properly. Legal fees may be high, but it is worth it to have a job done properly. Efforts are being made to stop the rising costs. For instance, it is felt that if lawyers advertise their fees, there will be competition in price that will benefit the consumer.

LAWYERS ARE SUBJECT TO DISCIPLINE

In law, as in every profession or calling, there are always some practitioners whose methods and conduct are subject to criticism. But the very nature of legal procedures, as well as the traditions and organization of the profession, holds down the number. The vast majority of lawyers maintain high ethical standards.

These standards are so high that conduct tolerated in almost any other field is considered misconduct in lawyers. A craftsman who fails to do a job for which he has been engaged need not be paid, or may be made to refund the money paid him. But he will not lose his license. A lawyer who neglects the work of a client may, however, be suspended or disbarred. And these high standards extend beyond the job a lawyer takes on. Several Watergate defendants were disciplined for conduct unrelated to their work as lawyers.

Because of the highly confidential nature of the lawyer's work and because he is trusted implicitly by his client, the lawyer is expected to guard his client's interests with the greatest diligence. The responsibilities assumed by lawyers in caring for the matters, documents, property and money entrusted to them are often onerous.

In New York and elsewhere, the conduct of attorneys is policed by the Bar Association. Members investigate complaints against attorneys. If the complaints are well founded, they institute proceedings in court to disbar or suspend the lawyer guilty of misconduct.

The attitude of the courts may be summed up in the following words, taken from the opinion of the court in a case involving an attorney: "Membership in the bar is a privilege burdened with conditions. A fair private and professional character is one of them. Compliance with that condition is essential at the moment of admission, but is equally essential afterwards. Whenever the condition is broken, the privilege is lost."

Disbarment. In most states, lawyers found guilty of a crime will be disbarred. This applies even where the crime has nothing to do with the lawyer's practice or professional conduct.

There are also many noncriminal acts for which a lawyer may be disciplined. Disloyalty to clients or former clients, ambulance chasing, splitting fees with nonlawyers, disclosing confidential information, are others. Nonpayment of bills can draw formal censure upon a lawyer.

Disbarment and suspension are drastically severe measures, especially in view of the years of preparation leading up to admission to the bar. But it is fair to say that it isn't the fear of these measures that makes the lawyer adhere to the high standard of conduct required of him. Most lawyers, early in their professional life, come to learn the value of mutual trust between lawyer and client, lawyer and lawyer, lawyer and judge. They realize that without this kind of confidence, the usefulness of the lawyer to society would be drastically reduced.

THE FAMILY LAWYER

The businessman profits by having a lawyer on retainer who gets to know the operation of his business intimately enough to grasp problems quickly when they come up, and to anticipate and prevent difficulties. Similarly, it is worthwhile for a family to have a lawyer acquainted with its members, their interests and their problems.

Family lawyers were once as common as the family doctor. But now, as families are more scattered, the family lawyer is a rarity. There is a further tendency to turn to specialists in the various fields of law for help with specific business and special legal problems.

It remains a good idea, however, to be guided in legal matters by the lawyer with whom a relationship is established over the years. When it becomes necessary to have a legal specialist for a particular problem, it's advisable to have the specialist called in by your own attorney. More often than not, a special legal matter involves other points with which your attorney is already familiar.

LEGAL LANGUAGE—IS IT NECESSARY?

The language used in legal documents is often technical and difficult for the layman to understand. Even when it contains no technical terms, the language seems cramped, awkward and redundant. Need this be so?

One often hears the accusation that lawyers stick to their special language to confuse the layman, or as a means of reserving for the lawyer, as his "trade secret," what would otherwise be simple techniques that any layman could apply. This is not true.

The fact is that legal terms have meanings that have been tested and interpreted over and over again. They are used to ensure accuracy and precision—and to prevent trouble arising afterwards. This is not to say that every word is always necessary or clear. Some states are seeking to streamline legal terminology (in leases and contracts, for example) to make it more understandable to the layman.

Because of their background, lawyers have a special sensitivity to language and a better-than-average command of it. Words are a tool they like to use. Awkward phrases and long, redundant paragraphs displease them more than they annoy the layman. Simple caution, however, dictates a sacrifice of readability and style for the sake of exactness of meaning. When a lawyer draws up a document, he is doing it for a client with a specific end in view, not for an audience delighting in verbal effects. He is protecting his client's interests and not his own reputation for stylistic elegance.

An immediate example is this book you are reading. To make it readable for laymen, it was necessary to discard phraseology that lawyers find useful in conveying precise ideas to each other and to judges. As a result, there will be many parts to which lawyers will take exception because points have not been stated with the exactness to which they are accustomed. We have taken this risk in the hope that it will be justified by contributing to a better general understanding of the lawyer and his function.

The glossary of legal terms that follows contains words that have other meanings than those given here. Since this is not a general dictionary, we will confine ourselves to the legal meanings.

GLOSSARY OF LEGAL TERMS

Abandonment—The act of leaving a husband or wife. *See* DESERTION, *p. 109*. Besides being grounds for separation or divorce, this act in many states is also a crime.

Abatement—Lessening, decrease. *See* ABATEMENT OF LEGACIES, *p. 73*.

Abduction—The illegal taking away by force or enticement, usually of a female, for purposes of prostitution, concubinage or marriage. The definition varies in the different states. *See* KIDNAPING.

NOTE: In the State of New York, a parent or guardian may be guilty of abduction if he consents to the unlawful seizure or detention of a female under the age of eighteen by any person for the purpose of prostitution or sexual intercourse.

Abortion—The act of procuring the miscarriage or premature delivery of a pregnant woman.

Abstract of Title—A statement or report giving the history of the title to real property.

Acceptance—The completing part of a contract. A contract is made complete when an offer is accepted. Also the obligation to pay a draft or bill of exchange.

Access—The physical possibility of sexual intercourse. The child of a married woman is presumed to be legitimate and the issue of her husband, except on proof of "non-access." Evidence that husband and wife were so remote from each other at the time of conception that intercourse between them would not have been possible, would constitute such proof.

Accessory After the Fact—One who helps a criminal to elude or evade arrest or capture. The one who performs the criminal act is called the "principal."

Accessory Before the Fact—One who counsels, induces or encourages another to commit a crime. In New York and elsewhere, an accessory before the fact is a principal and may be tried and convicted as though he himself had committed the criminal act.

Accord and Satisfaction—An agreement or a document settling a claim or a suit.

Account Stated—A sum of money agreed on as the amount due from one person to another.

Acknowledgment—A declaration before a person qualified by law to administer oaths, that a document or a deed is the act of the person who signed it.

Acquittal—The absolution from guilt of a party accused of a crime. Acquittal follows a finding of "not guilty."

Act of God—An accident which could not have been foreseen or prevented, such as those caused by earthquakes, severe storms, etc.

Action—A proceeding in court.

Actionable—Subject to or affording grounds for action. A claim or a complaint which can be taken to court, is actionable.

Ademption—The cancellation of a legacy by reason of some act of the testator. *See p. 76*.

Adjective Law—The branch of the law which deals with the rules of procedure.

Adjudication—The determination of a judge.

Administration—The management and distribution of the property of a decedent. *See p. 78*.

Administrative Law—The law governing procedure before the various agencies of the government.

Admiralty—The branch of the law and the courts which deal with vessels and navigation.

Admissible—Acceptable evidence which is permitted to be introduced as being pertinent for consideration in deciding issues in court, is called "admissible."

Admissions—Declarations or voluntary acknowledgements of facts made by one of the parties in a suit.

Adoption—The legal act by which a person takes into his own family and treats as his own, the child of another. This is a purely statutory proceeding. In most cases adopted children have the right of inheritance; but the statutes should be consulted on this point. Similarly, if an adopted child dies, the adopted parents generally get preference over the natural parents in settlement of the estate. *See p. 101*.

Adultery—Voluntary sexual intercourse between a married person and one who is not the wife or husband.

Adverse Possession—The occupancy or enjoyment of property in spite of, and in defiance of, someone else's legal title. If such possession continues for twenty years, legal title can be claimed by the one in possession. Adverse possession must be actual possession, continuous, visible and hostile to the one who has legal title. *See pp. 44, 127*.

Advocate—A term generally used to describe a lawyer in his role as pleader in a courtroom.

Affidavit—A statement in writing, and sworn to before a notary or other officer authorized to administer oaths.

Affirmance—The judgment of an appellate court confirming a judgment of a lower court.

Alias—(Latin) "Another," or "otherwise." Often used in connection with names to signify that they are assumed.

Alibi—(Latin) "Elsewhere." In criminal cases alibi signifies proof that an accused person was not at the scene of the crime at the time it was committed, the implication being that he could not physically have committed the crime. A good defense when the jury is satisfied as to its truth.

Alienation of Affections—Any act or course of action leading to withdrawal of affections from one to whom it is due, such as a husband or wife or a fiancé or fiancée. Alienation of affections was formerly a ground for action for the recovery of damages; but, in New York and a number of other states, it has been ruled out as an actionable issue.

Alimony—The allowance ordered by the court to be paid by the husband for the support and maintenance of his wife, after separation.

Alimony Pendente Lite—The allowance ordered by the court to be paid by the husband to his wife while a divorce action is pending. This is distinguished from permanent alimony, which is the allowance ordered after the conclusion of the suit.

Amicus Curiae—(Latin) "A friend of the court." Usually applied to one who intervenes in a lawsuit, although not a party to it, in order to assist the court in its deliberations.

Annul—To cancel or make void.

Antenuptial Contract—A contract made by husband and wife prior to their marriage. *See p. 98.*

Appraisal—A valuation of property; the opinion of an expert as to the true value of real or personal property.

Arbitration—Often included in contracts as a means agreed upon by the parties to settle controversies between them; the investigation and determination of a dispute by one or more persons, called arbitrators, who are named by the parties themselves.

Arraignment—The calling of a person accused of a crime before the court, to be advised of the charge against him, and enable him to make his answer.

Arrangement—A term used in bankruptcy proceedings for reorganization plans, under which the creditors agree to compromise all or part of their claims, or to defer their claims.

Arrest—To restrain a person or deprive him of his liberty. *See p. 117.*

Arson—A crime; originally the willful and malicious burning of the house of another person. The various states have different definitions and different degrees of this crime.

In New York, a person is guilty of arson in the *first degree* if he intentionally damages a building by causing an explosion when another person who is not a participant in the crime is in the building

at the time and the defendant is or should be aware of his presence.

He is guilty of arson in the *second degree* if he intentionally damages a building by starting a fire when another person who is not a participant in the crime is in the building at the time and the defendant is or should be aware of his presence. (Thus, the only difference between first and second degree arson is whether the damage is caused by explosion or by fire.)

He is guilty of arson in the *third degree* if he intentionally damages a building by starting a fire or causing an explosion. This is the highest degree of arson a defendant can be charged with if the building was empty or if he had no reason to know anyone was in it.

He is guilty of arson in the *fourth degree* if he recklessly damages a building by intentionally starting a fire or causing an explosion. The difference between this and the other degrees of arson is that a defendant can be found guilty of arson in the fourth degree even if he had no intention of damaging the building.

The punishment for arson in New York is imprisonment: for arson in the first degree, a term of fifteen to twenty-five years; in the second degree, not exceeding twenty-five years; in the third degree, not exceeding fifteen years; and in the fourth degree, not exceeding four years.

Assessment—The determination of the value of property for the purposes of fixing a tax. The term is also used to denote a special tax on property based upon benefits to the property itself.

Assets—Property; real assets would be real property, personal assets, personal property.

Assignment—The transfer of rights from one person to another.

Attachment—The taking into custody of property belonging to a person involved in a proceeding. A property attachment is sometimes the beginning of a lawsuit against someone who is not within the state, but whose property is within the jurisdiction of the court.

Attestation—The witnessing of a document in writing. *See* ATTESTATION CLAU.E, *p. 72.*

Attorney—One who acts in the place of another.

Attorney-at-Law—A lawyer who has been admitted to the bar and may be hired to represent a litigation party in court. Since admission to the bar makes him an officer of the court, he has the right to issue summonses for court appearances.

Attorney-in-Fact—One who is appointed, in writing, to perform a specific act for and in place of another.

Bail—A guarantee that a defendant will appear in court. More accurately, the Bail is the person who guarantees the appearance of the defendant and whose bond requires that he will forfeit a certain amount of money if the defendant fails to appear.

Bailee—This term has no connection with bail as defined above. A bailee is one to whom property is entrusted for any reason. A warehouseman is a bailee;

so is one who borrows property, or receives property to repair it. The contract that arises is called a *bailment,* and the person whose property is delivered to the *bailee* is called the *bailor.*

Bailiff—In the past a magistrate or a sheriff's officer or deputy. Now, most commonly, a court attendant.

Bankrupt—An insolvent person, one whose total property is not sufficient to pay his debts. *See p. 61.*

Barratry—In maritime law, an act by the captain of a ship (or the crew) against the interests of the ship-owner.

Bastardy Proceedings—Action against the father of an illegitimate child to compel support for the child.

Battery—Beating or other physical violence.

Bench—A way of referring to judges collectively, i.e. "members of the bench."

Bench Warrant—An order for the arrest of a person issued by a judge.

Beneficiary—(1) One who receives the profits or rents of a transaction. (2) One who receives the proceeds of an insurance policy. (3) One who receives the income or profits from a trust fund.

Bigamy—Having two living spouses; a crime in all states.

Bill of Exchange—A negotiable instrument; an order drawn by one person (the drawer) upon another (the drawee) requiring the drawee to pay a certain sum to order of the bearer. *See p. 26.*

Bill of Particulars—A statement of the details of a claim or counterclaim. *See p. 124.*

Bill of Rights—The first ten amendments to the Constitution of the United States. *See pp. 134ff.*

Blackmail—Extortion of money, etc., by threat of legal prosecution, bodily harm, public disgrace, etc. A felony.

Bona Fides—(Latin) "Good faith."

Bond—A written and sealed obligation to pay a sum of money. The one who is obliged to pay is called the "obligor"; and the one to whom the money is to be paid is called the "obligee."

Breach of Contract—A violation by one of the contracting parties of an obligation or duty under a contract signed by him or in his name. This usually excuses the other party from performing his contract obligations.

Breach of Promise of Marriage—The breaking of an engagement to marry. Some states, including New York, have abolished this as a cause of action. *See p. 97.*

Brief—A statement prepared by a lawyer of the case of his client. This usually contains allegations of the facts, the questions at issue and a discussion of the legal points involved.

Broker—One who arranges transactions involving real or personal property for others. A broker does not usually have possession of the property, nor does he buy or sell for his own account. His commission (brokerage) is earned when he has brought together a seller, ready and willing to sell, and a buyer, ready and willing to buy.

Burden of Proof—The duty of producing evidence to prove disputed facts. *See p. 129.*

Burglary—The breaking and entering into a house for the purpose of committing a crime. In many states this crime is divided into several degrees, depending upon whether the one who commits the act is armed or unarmed, whether the crime is committed during the day or night; whether or not the house is occupied by a human being at the time of entry. In New York State criminal statutes the degrees of burglary are defined in the following terms:

First Degree: A person who, with intent to commit some crime therein, breaks and enters, in the nighttime, the dwelling house of another, in which there is at the time a human being:

1. Being armed with a dangerous weapon; or,
2. Arming himself therein with such a weapon; or,
3. Being assisted by a confederate actually present; or,
4. Who, while engaged in the nighttime in effecting such entrance, or in committing any crime in such a building, or in escaping therefrom, assaults any person, is guilty of burglary in the first degree.

Second Degree: A person who, with intent to commit some crime therein, breaks and enters the dwelling house of another, in which there is a human being, under circumstances not amounting to burglary in the first degree, is guilty of burglary in the second degree.

Third Degree: A person who:

1. With intent to commit a crime therein, breaks and enters a building, or a room, or any part of a building; or,
2. Being in any building, commits a crime therein and breaks out of the same, is guilty of burglary in the third degree.

Bylaws—The rules by which a corporation conducts its business.

Capital—The fund of money or property available to an individual or a firm for the conduct of its business.

Capital Crime—A crime for which the punishment is death. (From Latin, caput—*head.*)

Capital Punishment—Death.

Carnal Knowledge—A phrase customarily used in connection with the crime of rape, sexual intercourse.

Carrier—Transporter of passengers or goods, from one place to another. *Common carriers* offer their services to the general public. *Private carriers* operate under special contract with individuals or firms.

Case Law—Decision law (judgments previously rendered on legal issues) as distinguished from statutory law.

Cause of Action—Facts which give the right to one party to bring a lawsuit against another.

Caveat Emptor—(Latin) "Let the buyer beware." *See p. 94.*

Certificate—A written statement concerning facts which are usually within the knowledge of the officer who executes it, or based upon records or documents in his official custody.

Certified Check—A check upon which the bank has

stamped an indication that the money has been appropriated from the account of the maker.

Certiorari—A review procedure started in a higher court to examine the determination of a lower court or of some government official or agency.

Chambers—The judge's private room in the courthouse.

Chancery—*See* EQUITY.

Charter—A grant by a state giving a corporation the right to exist. Otherwise known as "certificate of incorporation," or "articles of incorporation."

Chattels—Articles of personal property as distinguished from real property given as security for a loan.

Check—A bill of exchange drawn on a bank and payable on demand. *See p. 27.*

C.I.F.—A designation in an invoice or a contract of sale, signifying that the price includes *cost, insurance and freight.*

Civil Action—Generally used to distinguish an action to recover money, property or rights, by one person from another, from *criminal action,* an action by the state against a person for violation of the criminal laws.

Civil Commotion—A riot not amounting to a rebellion. When used in insurance policies, its usual purpose is to exempt from the coverage losses which may occur in a "civil commotion."

Civil Rights—Rights secured to the citizens of the United States by the Constitution. *See pp. 134ff.*

C.O.D.—A designation in an invoice or a contract of sale signifying that the person who delivers the goods is to *collect* the sale price *on delivery.*

Codicil—An amendment or addition to a will.

Coercion—The use of force or compulsion to make a person act against his will.

Cognizance—Acknowledgement or recognition of a fact.

Collateral—Incidental; something that is additional to, or an offshoot of a matter which is being discussed.

Collateral Security—Property pledged to guarantee the performance of an obligation.

Collusion—Joint action by two or more persons to commit a fraud.

Color of Title—The appearance of validity in an imperfect title to property. A faulty deed or other written instrument which gives apparent title, is said to give "color of title."

Comity—Courtesy; the rule under which courts recognize the decisions of other courts, and courts of one state give force and effect to the laws and judgments of other states.

Commercial Paper—A term used to include all negotiable instruments, notes, drafts, etc., received in the ordinary course of business.

Commitment—The order directing the taking into custody of a person by an officer; the actual sending of a person to a prison or to an institution for the mentally ill.

Committee—(1) One or more members of a body (usually a legislative body) designated to carry out certain prescribed duties.

(2) A guardian appointed to take care of the person and the property of one adjudged to be incompetent.

Common Law—Case law or precedent law established by court decisions, as distinguished from statute law enacted by legislatures; also used to distinguish the system used in England and the United States from those used elsewhere.

Community Property—Property owned in common, or together by husband and wife. *See p. 100.*

Competency—Used in connection with witnesses or evidence, this term means fitness to furnish testimony useful for ascertaining the truth. In other senses the term signifies the ability of a person to conduct himself without the supervision of a guardian.

Competency Proceeding—A judicial proceeding to determine whether or not one is mentally able to manage his own affairs.

Complainant—One who makes a complaint.

Complaining Witness—In a criminal trial, in which the plaintiff is the state, the one who has complained of the offense to the state authorities.

Composition—An agreement between a debtor and his creditor, or a group of them, settling the debts for less than the actual amount due.

Compound Interest—Interest computed on interest previously earned.

Compounding a Crime—An agreement with a criminal, for a reward of some kind (such as the return of stolen property), not to prosecute. Compounding a crime is itself a crime. Helping a criminal escape prosecution in any way renders one liable to prosecution as an accessory to the crime.

Concealment—The fraudulent hiding of material facts from one who should be told.

Condemnation—A judgment affecting or confiscating property; a ship may be condemned as unsafe; food as impure; real property as needed by the state. In international law, a ship is *condemned* as a prize by one belligerent as the property of another.

A conviction or an unfavorable judgment.

Conditions of Sale—The terms under which an auctioneer will conduct a sale.

Condonation—Forgiveness; most often used in connection with adultery of a spouse. If husband and wife continue or resume cohabitation after one is known to have committed adultery, the offense is forgiven or condoned by the other, and may not be used as grounds for action. *See pp. 108–9.*

Confession—A voluntary admission of guilt or responsibility. *See p. 120.*

Confidential Communications—Statements or conversations which are protected against investigation by the courts. *See p. 132.*

Conflict of Laws—The clash between differing laws where more than one state has jurisdiction over the parties to a dispute, or over the matter in litigation. The outcome of the case then will depend on which jurisdiction prevails. A special branch of law.

Confrontation—The bringing of the accuser into the presence of the accused.

Connivance—Aiding in the illegal act of another, and thereby indirectly consenting to it. Where a husband brings about a situation in which his wife is led to commit adultery, his connivance will prevent his use of the fact as grounds for divorce.

Consideration—Something of value which induces a person to enter into a contract. The promise to do something must be in exchange for some act or thing of value which is the *consideration*. This is a necessary element in a contract.

Consolidation of Actions—A combination of several lawsuits, affecting the same matters and the same parties, into one action, on order of the court.

Conspiracy—A combination of two or more persons to perform an unlawful act; or to use unlawful means to carry out a lawful act.

Constabulary—A body organized by a government to preserve public order.

Constitution—An established government for any organized group; the fundamental law of a state.

Contempt of Court—Willful disobedience of the rules and orders of a court. A judge may punish from the bench one who is guilty of a contempt committed in his presence. When this offense is committed out of court, as when one disobeys a court order (like an injunction), a proceeding is usually held to impose punishment.

Contingent—Depending upon the occurrence of some uncertain future event.

Contract—A voluntary and lawful agreement between two or more parties to do, or not to do, something.

Contributory Negligence—A defense in an action for negligence; conduct on the part of the plantiff which is held to be partly responsible for his injury.

Conversion—A civil wrong; appropriation to one's own use of the property of another. EXAMPLE: if the wife of a tailor wears a dress that has been left with him to be repaired, that is conversion.

Conveyance—A transfer of title.

Conviction—A verdict finding the defendant guilty.

Copyright—The exclusive ownership of and right to publish literary or other artistic works. *See pp. 65–66.*

Co-respondent—Most commonly used to designate the partner in adultery of a defendant in a divorce action. Its larger meaning includes persons called upon to answer a complaint or a petition.

Corporation—An artificial person or entity created by law for a specific purpose. *See pp. 36ff.*

Corpus Delicti—(Latin) Literally, "the body of the crime"; proof that the crime has actually been committed. In the case of homicide, death must be proved by evidence of someone who has inspected the body.

Counter-claim—A claim set up by the defendant against the plaintiff, connected with the same matter, the effect of which would be to establish a basis for reducing the judgment against the defendant or granting him judgment against the plaintiff.

Covenant—A contract; a deed; a contract contained in a deed, the obligations of which are transferred, along with the property, from one owner to the other.

Credibility of a Witness—Worthiness of belief in his testimony. Whether or not a witness is credible is a question for the jury.

Creditor—A person to whom a debt is due by a *debtor;* a *judgment creditor* is one who has obtained a judgment entitling him to attach property of the debtor for repayment of the debt.

Crime—An act in violation of public law punishable by the state. *See p. 116.*

Cross-examination—*See p. 133.*

Curtesy—The right of a husband, upon the death of his wife, to an interest in the property she leaves. *See p. 100.*

Damages—The sum claimed by a plaintiff as a loss to him sustained through the act, or failure to act, of the defendant.

Debtor—One who owes a debt; a *judgment debtor* is one against whom a judgment has been obtained permitting attachment of his property for payment of the debt.

Decedent—One who is deceased.

Decree—The decision of a court of equity; a decree *nisi* (unless) or an *interlocutory* decree is a temporary decree which becomes final after a certain period of time, unless, in the interval, something occurs to change the decision of the court.

Deed—An agreement or instrument in writing and under seal; most often used to designate the instrument by which real property is conveyed by one to another.

Defamation—Injury to a person's reputation. When in writing, called *libel;* when spoken, *slander.*

Default—The failure to perform some duty or obligation; the failure to appear in court when the case is called.

Defendant—The person sued by the plaintiff, or the accused in a criminal case.

Deposition—A sworn statement in writing containing the testimony of a witness to be used in a trial.

Descendants—Those who stem or issue from a person—his children, grandchildren, great-grandchildren, and so forth.

Devise—The giving of real property by will. *See p. 70.*

Dictum—An expression of opinion contained in the decision of a court upon some matter related to the subject of the decision itself. It does not have the force of a decision but may be cited in later legal arguments on issues on which the dictum bears directly.

Directors—Those who are elected by the stockholders to manage the affairs of a corporation.

Disbarment—The removal of an attorney from the bar; revocation of his right to practice. *See pp. 152–53.*

Dissent—Disagreement; a dissenting opinion is one which differs from the majority.

Distribution—*See p. 77.*

Divorce—Legal dissolution of a marriage. *See pp. 108ff.*

Docket—A court's official record of its proceedings.

Domicile—The home; the place which is the permanent and real home of a person; where he intends to live permanently. This differs from his *residence*, where he may be for the time being.

Dossier—A file; a collection of papers on a particular subject.

Dower—The right of a widow to an interest in the real property of her husband. *See p. 100.*

Due Process of Law—According to the law of the land. *See pp. 137ff.*

Duress—Force, compulsion; threat of force, violence or loss of liberty.

Earnest Money—A deposit; a token sum, the payment of which constitutes a binder; an indication of an intention to go through with a deal.

Easement—A right to pass over or through the property of another.

Ejectment—An action to repossess real property unlawfully held by another.

Emancipation—Release of a minor from the control of his parents. A child who is deserted by his parents is "emancipated," and may work for others and keep his earnings.

Embezzlement—Appropriation of the property of another, after possession has been obtained by lawful means. Differs from larceny in that the latter is illegal possession from the beginning whereas, in embezzlement, the property was originally entrusted to the embezzler.

Eminent Domain—The right of a government to take private property for public use. This right exists everywhere in the world and is based on the obligation of the government to act for all the people in the interests of public need or safety. Where this right is exercised by the state, the person whose property is confiscated has a right to be compensated.

Encroachment—In real property, use of the property of another. Building a house whose porch extends beyond the building line into the public street, or planting shrubs that grow over the property of a neighbor, are typical "encroachments."

Encumbrance—A right in real property which diminishes its value but does not prevent its transfer from one person to another. Examples are leases, liens, easements, rights to crops or timber, etc. Such rights are generally held by third persons (not the grantor or the grantee) and the deed can be taken, subject to them.

Entirety—The phrase "by the entirety" describes the ownership of *all* of a piece of real property by two or more people, on such terms that it cannot be divided between them. Upon the death of one, the whole property goes to the other. This is commonly the way in which property is owned by husband and wife.

Equity—Literally, the word means "justice." In practice a separate system for the administration of justice. An outgrowth of the English Chancery system by which courts were set up by the king to give relief in cases where the courts of law were inadequate. Today, courts of equity are usually merged with courts of law, and the same judges hear equity cases as law cases. The distinction exists, nevertheless, and application of the principles of equity is a distinct branch of the law. One resorts to a court of equity for the purpose, usually, of getting other relief than payment of money. Injunctions, accountings, rescis-

sion or cancellation of contracts, specific performance of contracts, are all *equity* actions. They are heard by a judge without a jury.

Equity of Redemption—The right of a mortgagor to regain his property after he has lost the legal right to it by failure to make payment in time. *See p. 50.*

Escheat—An ancient word, used in feudal times. It denotes some act causing land to revert to the feudal lord instead of passing on to the owner's heirs. Today the term signifies the return to the state of property to which no heirs can be found.

Escrow—An arrangement by which a deed, or any other instrument or property (sometimes a sum of money) is entrusted to a third person (called the escrowee or escrow agent) to be delivered by him to one party or the other, upon the fulfillment of conditions stated in the agreement. For example, a deed to real property may be executed by the grantor and entrusted to a bank as escrow agent with instructions that, upon payment of a certain amount of money, the deed is to be delivered to the grantee.

Estoppel—A doctrine of law which prevents (estops) or precludes a party from making a claim or a statement, by reason of some action previously taken by him or by a court. Example: If Jones, the true owner of a property, is present when Brown sells it as his own to Smith, and allows Smith to believe that Brown is the owner, Jones will later be *estopped* from claiming it back from Smith.

Et Alius—(Latin) "And another." Usually found in the abbreviation "et al."

Eviction—Removal from possession of real property; a dispossess. This is not necessarily accomplished by legal process, nor does it always compel removal. A *constructive eviction* occurs when a landlord deprives the tenant of the use of the property by some act such as obstructing the entrance, failing to supply water or elevator service, etc. This gives the tenant the right or a cause to move; but if he stays, he must pay the rent.

Evidence—The word includes everything that may be considered by a court in order to settle a question of fact. *See p. 130.*

Ex Contractu—(Latin) "From contract." Used to describe a cause of action arising out of a contract or a contractual relationship.

Ex Delicto—(Latin) "Out of wrong." Used to describe a set of facts or a cause of action which follows a crime or a tort. Often used to distinguish such a case from an *ex contractu* case.

Ex Parte—(Latin) "From one part." Used to describe a proceeding in which only one of the litigating parties appears before the court.

Ex Post Facto—(Latin) "After the fact." An "Ex Post Facto law," forbidden by the Constitution, would be one that fixes a punishment for an act after it was committed; or which changes the penalty for an act after it has been committed.

Execution—(1) The completion of a document such as a deed or contract.

(2) The complete performance of an act, duty or obligation.

(3) Punishment by death in accordance with the sentence of a criminal court.

(4) The method of collecting a judgment debt.

(5) The management of an estate by an executor under a will.

Executor—The one who has the responsibility of carrying out the terms of a will. The feminine equivalent is *Executrix*.

Executory—That which remains to be done. An executory contract is one that provides for an act to be done in the future.

Extradition—The proceeding whereby fugitives from one state or country are returned for prosecution by the state or country in which they are found. The United States will surrender fugitives only in accordance with treaties with other nations. The usual test applied in extradition is whether the act of which the fugitive is accused is a crime in both the place that has him and the place that wants him.

Fee—In real property, the ownership of land or the land itself.

Felony—A serious crime, punishable by imprisonment in a penitentiary. *See pp. 116–17.*

Fiduciary—Describing relationships of high trust and confidence. Guardians, trustees, executors, administrators and the like, are fiduciaries.

Fine—A punishment calling for the payment of money.

Fixture—An article attached to real estate. *See p. 40.*

Flagrante Delicto—(Latin) "In the act of doing wrong"; loosely, "caught red-handed."

F.O.B.—Free On Board. A term meaning that the shipper will assume responsibility and all costs until the goods are placed on the carrier. *See p. 20.*

Foreclosure—A proceeding against a property owner who has failed to meet the obligation of a mortgage loan or other liens like tax liens. This is the method used to force a sale of the property to pay the debt. *See p. 48.*

Foreign Corporation—A corporation organized under the laws of another state.

Foreign Judgment—A judgment obtained in an out-of-state court.

Forensic—Connected with legal proceedings. Forensic medicine is the relation of medical facts to legal principles. Testimony given by doctors as expert witnesses in a trial, is an application of forensic medicine.

Forgery—A crime; making or altering a document for an illegal purpose. It is not the false signature alone that constitutes forgery. Alteration of a document or even its misuse may be a forgery, even if the signature is genuine.

Forum—In legal sense, a tribunal, a court of law.

Frauds, Statute of—A statute providing that certain transactions, in order to be enforceable in the courts, shall be in writing.

Future Estate—A right in property (usually created by will or trust) which will begin at some future time or upon occurrence of some future event, like the death of a life tenant.

Garnishee—One who has possession of property (or money) belonging to a judgment debtor; or who will owe the debtor money. An employer is a garnishee of an employee whose salary has been attached. Proceedings to attach the salary of an employee are called garnishee proceedings; the sheriff or marshal addresses himself to the employer or other garnishee for the collection of the judgment debt. *See p. 57.*

General Assignment—The transfer by a debtor of all of his property to an assignee for the benefit of creditors. *See p. 60.*

Good Will—As applied to business, this is its custom, trade and reputation; the value of intangibles belonging to a business as distinguished from its capital assets or property.

Grand Jury—A body of citizens (the number differs from state to state) to whom facts are presented by the district attorney. If the jury finds sufficient evidence, in the facts presented, that a crime has been committed by the one accused, an indictment is returned. *See p. 118.*

Guardian—One who is legally appointed to manage the affairs of a minor. He can be guardian of the property, or of the person, or both.

Guardian ad Litem—One who is appointed by the court to protect the interests of a minor in a lawsuit. He is empowered to act in the child's behalf until the case is concluded.

Habeas Corpus—(Latin) "That you have the body." A court order (writ) requiring one who imprisons or detains another to produce the prisoner at a certain place and time where the legality of his detention can be inquired into. *See p. 138.*

Hearsay Evidence—Evidence from a testifying witness of what he was told by another, rather than what is within his own knowledge. Such evidence is usually incompetent to prove anything, since the credibility of the one to whom the statement is attributed cannot be judged, because he is not in court. *See p. 131.*

Heirs—Those who have the right to share in the estate of a deceased person. *See p. 70.*

Holding Company—A corporation which conducts no business operations except to own, buy and sell the stock of other corporations.

Holdover—A tenant who retains possession after the expiration of his term without the consent of the landlord.

Holograph—A document written entirely in the handwriting of the one who makes it, as a holographic will.

Homicide—The taking of human life. This general term includes all form of killing, from accident to deliberate murder.

Hostile Witness—A witness openly unfriendly to the side that calls him. When such hostility appears, the witness may be cross-examined by the party who called him to the stand.

Ignorance of Law—Lack of knowledge of the laws covering a given situation. The well-known maxim that ignorance of the law is no excuse is only partly true.

Mistakes can be rectified by the courts. One who parts with money or property under a mistake, when there is no just reason why the mistake should be held against him, may often recover it. But ignorance of the law cannot be a good answer when a crime has been committed or a wrong done.

Illegal Consideration—When a contract is made providing for some illegal act, such as the commission of a crime or prostitution, it will not be enforced in the courts.

Immaterial Evidence—Evidence that cannot help to decide an issue or that is unnecessary and unimportant in deciding a given question before the court.

Immunity—In criminal law, protection of a witness or informer against prosecution based on the information which he gives. A means of compelling testimony of one who otherwise could, under the Fifth Amendment, refuse to do so on the ground that he might incriminate himself.

Impeachment—In government, an accusation against a public officer; in legal practice, an attack upon the credibility of a witness by evidence of contradictory statements, by citing his reputation for not telling the truth, etc.

In Pari Delicto—(Latin) "In equal guilt." When both parties are equally at fault, as when they enter into an illegal contract, the courts will help neither.

In Personam—(Latin) "Against the person." This is distinguished from *In Rem* "against the thing." An action *in rem* is one directed against a specific piece of property, or a ship, rather than against its owner.

Incompatibility—Inability to exist together. In domestic relations, inability to live and get along together; in some states grounds for separation and divorce.

Indemnity—A sum of money or an undertaking given to a person to protect him against loss or damage. EXAMPLE: If a stockholder should lose his stock certificate, the corporation may issue a new one to him provided he agrees to *indemnify* it against the loss it might suffer if a claim is made on the original certificate.

Independent Contractor—One who does work for another without being his employee. The test of independence is generally whether or not the contractor is under the control of the employer as to the details and methods of his work. If the performance is left to the contractor's discretion and he is able to hire and fire his own workmen, he is independent. The question is important to determine liability for negligence, for workmen's compensation, payroll taxes, etc.

Indictment—An accusation of a crime drawn up by a grand jury after its investigation of the facts. *See p. 118.*

Infant—One who is legally a minor, not of full age.

Information—In criminal law, an accusation made by a law officer rather than by a grand jury. *See p. 117.*

Infringement—In patent and copyright law, the unauthorized use of an invention, literary or artistic work in violation of the rights of the patent holder or copyright owner; a violation.

Injunction—A court order prohibiting or restraining the defendant from doing or continuing to do certain acts. Generally used to protect rights of persons who could get relief in no other way. EXAMPLE: To restrain the erection of a structure that would violate a building restriction or a zoning law; to prevent a corporate officer from wasting the assets of the company; to restrain a husband (or wife) from starting out-of-state divorce proceedings; etc.

In Rem—*See* "IN PERSONAM."

Insanity—In civil law, the mental state disabling a person from managing his own affairs. In criminal law, incapacity to have a criminal intent. In general it must be examined in relation to the particular act under inquiry by the court. The question is whether the defendant had the mental capacity to know what he was doing, to comprehend the meaning and consequence of the act, and to control the doing or not doing of it.

Insolvency—Lack of means to pay one's debts.

Interlocutory—*See* DECREE.

Intestate—Without a will. One who dies without having made a will, or whose will is not legally drawn, has died *intestate*. *See p. 77.*

I.O.U.—A memorandum of an indebtedness. It is not a promissory note unless it contains additional language that would make it so. But it can be used as evidence of an agreed statement of account.

Irrelevant Evidence—Evidence not related to the issue under examination by the court. *See p. 132.*

Jeopardy—Risk; when a defendant has been properly brought into court upon a legal information or indictment, and the court has power to try him, he has been in jeopardy. The case must then proceed to a verdict unless postponed with the defendant's consent, or by an imperative cause like the death of a juror or severe illness of a witness, juror or the judge, which makes it necessary to hold a new trial. If there has been no such consent and no such imperative cause, the defendant cannot again be tried for the same offense. *See p. 118.*

Judgment—The decision of the court.

Judicial Notice—A method by which the court accepts certain facts without requiring evidence. EXAMPLE: The court may be asked to take judicial notice of the laws of the state, of historical or geographical data, or of commonly known facts such as that railroads run on rails, gasoline is combustible, etc.

Jurat—The certification by a notary, or authorized officer, that an affidavit has been sworn to. It usually reads, "sworn to before me this . . . day of . . . . , 195. .

John Jones, Notary Public"

Jurisdiction—Authority, or scope of authority. The jurisdiction of courts is limited by law in many ways. EXAMPLE: CIVIL JURISDICTION—power to decide noncriminal matters; CRIMINAL JURISDICTION—power to try criminal cases. LIMITED JURISDICTION—power to try cases of a specified nature or those involving no more than certain sums of money; ORIGINAL JURISDICTION—is the court that first tries a case, while APPELLATE JURISDICTION is the power to review the decisions of other courts. CONCURRENT JURISDICTION is the power in several courts to try the same case. A court may have jurisdiction over the parties to an action because of their place of residence or the location of the subject matter of the case, because an event (tort, crime) took place in its territory, or a contract was made there.

Jury—A body of twelve persons sworn to try the facts of a case. The right of trial by jury is guaranteed in the federal Constitution. In many states it is somewhat abridged by laws permitting certain minor cases to be tried by a judge alone. In certain courts juries of six are permitted. The parties may waive their right to a jury trial; in some places it is waived when not demanded. The jury that tries the facts of a case is technically known as a *petit jury*, to distinguish it from *grand jury*, which is assembled and sworn to investigate facts and accusations for indictments against persons accused of crimes. *See pp. 128, 138–39*, also glossary definition of GRAND JURY.

Kidnaping—A felony, punishable by heavy jail sentences. One is guilty of this crime who willfully abducts or detains or imprisons another, or takes another person out of the state against his will or, under New York law, abducts a child under sixteen, for theft or for ransom; or who brings a kidnaped person into the state. When state lines are crossed in the course of the crime, the federal law applies, and federal enforcement officers have jurisdiction.

Laches—A defense against a claim. Neglect to do a thing at the proper time; undue delay in asserting a claim. Not necessarily measured in time or by the statute of limitations, but by the effects upon the rights of others caused by neglect or delay.

Landlord—One who owns land which he rents to others. For LANDLORD AND TENANT, *see pp. 52ff*.

Larceny—A crime; the wrongful taking of the property of another. In many jurisdictions this offense is divided into *grand larceny* and *petty larceny*, depending upon the value of the property taken.

Law—The established rules of a community by which the conduct of its members is regulated.

Leading Questions—Questions put to a witness in such a way as to extract a desired answer. *See p. 133*.

Lease—A contract for the use, possession or occupancy of land for a period of time. *See pp. 52ff*.

Legacy—A bequest; a gift of property by a will. One who receives a legacy is a *legatee*. *See p. 70*.

Lessee—A tenant; one who has a right in land by virtue of a lease.

Lessor—A landlord; one who grants a right in land by virtue of a lease.

Letter-of-Credit—Much used in international commerce, and to some extent in domestic business. A document addressed by a bank in one place to its correspondent in another requesting that advances be made to a third person. A letter-of-credit usually states the terms and conditions to be met before funds are made available to the beneficiary. Ex-

porters who have had no previous dealings with foreign purchasers usually demand, before accepting an order, that the letter-of-credit in their favor be irrevocable and confirmed. This means that the funds have been made available to the originating bank and will remain available for the period of time stated in the letter-of-credit.

Letters-of-Administration—The authority to act granted to the administrator of an estate.

Levy—Literally, to raise; in common practice, a seizure by a sheriff to raise the money to satisfy a judgment.

Libel—(1) A legal proceeding. Suits in admiralty, cases affecting ships, are usually called libels especially when the ship is seized.

(2) A tort; a defamation in writing or printing; a written or printed statement having no justification or excuse, which is injurious to one's character, reputation or livelihood, and may be grounds for an action for damages.

License—Permission; a right to do something granted by one in authority.

Lien—A claim on the property of another resulting from some charge or debt. *See p. 59*.

Life Estate—or *Life Tenancy*. A right to the use of real property terminating on the death of the user; or of the one by whose life the tenancy or estate is measured.

Limitation of Actions—*See* STATUTE OF LIMITATIONS. *pp. 125–27*.

Limited Liability—A risk of loss measured by the amount of investment in corporations and limited partnerships. *See pp. 35, 38*.

Liquidated Damages—A sum of money, agreed upon in advance, to be paid in the event of a breach of contract.

Lis Pendens—(Latin) "Litigation pending." A term used to describe the notice filed as a warning to prospective purchasers of property that it is the subject of litigation and within the control of the court.

Literary Property—The property interest that an author or his heirs has in his work.

Litigation—Suit; a contest in court.

Livery of Seisin—An ancient expression for the ceremony by which real property used to be conveyed. *See p. 43*.

Magistrate—A public officer. The President is the chief magistrate of the country; the Governor, of the state; the Mayor, of the city. More commonly, the term is used to describe judges of lower criminal court. *See p. 117*.

Majority—The years after infancy or minority when a person is legally responsible for all his actions. *See pp. 8, 10*.

Maker—The promissor to pay a note.

Malfeasance—An act wrongful in itself or which the doer had no right to do. Distinguished from *Misfeasance*—the doing wrongly of an act which is lawful; and *Non-Feasance*—the failure to do an act which one is required to do.

Malice—Evil intention.

Malicious Mischief—Willful or reckless injury to person or property.

Malicious Prosecution—The bringing of a civil or criminal action without probable cause.

Mandamus—(Latin) "We command." Applied to a court proceeding to compel a public officer to carry out the duties of his office.

Manslaughter—The taking of a human life but without malice or intention to do so.

Marketable Title—A title to real property that a reasonable purchaser would accept. One that has no defects restricting or reducing its use or value.

Marriage—A contract between a man and a woman to live together as husband and wife, one that involves the status of the parties. *See pp. 97ff.*

Merger—Of corporations—the absorption of one by another.

Misdemeanor—A crime or offense not amounting to a felony.

Misrepresentation—A statement contrary to fact; when made with intent to deceive, it is fraud.

Moot—Unsettled; in dispute. In the term "moot court", the word has another sense. A moot court is a mock court conducted by students for practice.

Moral Turpitude—Criminality; moral corruption in fields affecting society in general. Crimes involving moral turpitude are those considered basically evil in man's relations with his fellow men as distinguished from those forbidden by regulatory statutes. Thus, stealing is a crime involving moral turpitude; gambling is not.

Mortgage—Grant of a right in real or personal property as a pledge for the repayment of debt. *See pp. 48ff.*

Motion—An application to the court. When made by one party with no opportunity for the other party to oppose it, it is called an *Ex Parte* motion. When it is to be argued or defended, it is called a *Motion on Notice.*

Mutiny—Any act against the authority of the officers of a ship.

Names—The law recognizes only one full name for a person. Ordinarily, unless done to escape punishment or defraud others, a person has the right to adopt any name he chooses. The adopted name is said to become the real name *by reputation.* Names can be changed legally by court proceedings which usually provide for some method, such as publication in a newspaper, of giving notice to the world of the change. Business names are also acquired by reputation. When the business name is not the name of the individual or individuals who own it or conduct the business, it is usually necessary to register the name, so that the public will have some means of associating the trade name with the individual. Names of corporations appear in the corporate charters granted by the state. They can be changed upon appropriate application.

Naturalization—The granting of citizenship; the proceeding by which an alien becomes a citizen of the United States.

Necessaries—The things necessary for the support and maintenance of a person. In domestic-relations proceedings the definition of what constitutes necessaries varies with the financial circumstances of the parties.

Negligence—Failure to act like a reasonably prudent person to protect the interests of others. *See p. 82.*

Negotiable—Transferable from one person to another by assignment, endorsement or delivery. Negotiable instruments include checks, notes, drafts, bills of exchange, and sometimes bonds and securities. *See pp. 24ff.*

Next of Kin—Nearest relatives. These are defined in the law relating to the inheritance of property in the various states.

Nolle Prosequi—(Latin) "I do not wish to prosecute." This is a choice by a district attorney or a plaintiff not to go ahead with an action, or part of an action. It does not have the effect of closing the matter for all time; it can be taken up and prosecuted in the future.

Nolo Contendere—(Latin) "I do not wish to contest." Similar, but not exactly the same as a plea of guilty. It is accepted in some courts, usually as meaning, "I throw myself on the court without specifically admitting my guilt."

Nominal Damages—Damages awarded to plaintiff as a token of the court's finding in his favor, when wrong has been committed against him by which he has suffered no real damage.

Non Compos Mentis—(Latin) "Of unsound mind." Used to indicate insanity, temporary or permanent, or any condition, like intoxication, which deprives one of knowledge of the meaning or consequences of his acts.

Notary (Notary Public)—An officer of the state with authority to administer oaths and accept acknowledgments of documents. In some places the authority extends to taking depositions, etc.

Nuisance—Use of one's property in such a way as to cause damage, annoyance or inconvenience to another. It is a *private nuisance* when it affects only one or a few persons; a *public nuisance* when it affects the community. EXAMPLES: Keeping dangerous animals, making loud noises, smoke, obnoxious odors, etc. Maintaining a public nuisance is a misdemeanor in New York and other jurisdictions. In many places individual nuisances are described and penalized. Civil actions may be maintained to restrain nuisances and to recover damages caused by them.

Nullity—That which has no legal meaning or effect.

Oath—A solemn pledge. It is a religious act calling upon God to witness and to punish if the truth is not spoken. When administered in court or other official appearances, false statements made after administration of the oath are punishable as perjuries. The manner in which oaths are administered to witnesses varies from place to place. Usually it is just a matter of raising the right hand while repeating certain words.

Obligation—A duty by the *obligor* owed to the *obligee*.

On Demand—Immediately due; a note payable on demand matures as soon as it is made and delivered. An action may be started on it at once.

Par Value—The face value of a share of corporate stock.

Pardon—An act by the executive (the Governor or the President), relieving a convicted person from punishment.

Parol Evidence—Evidence given verbally by a witness.

Parole—The release of a prisoner on his word to abide by the law.

Partition—Division of property into separate parts by co-owners; also an action to divide real estate into shares when one (or more) of the joint owners, or owners in common, desires his separate share.

Partnership—A business relationship between two or more persons who join together to contribute to the capital of the enterprise, and share the profits and losses. *See pp. 33ff.*

Party Wall—A wall constructed between two adjoining pieces of property, and used in common by both owners.

Patent—The grant by the government of an exclusive privilege. *See pp. 63–65.*

Per Capita—(Latin) "By the head." A phrase used in wills meaning by the number of descendants regardless of degree. *See p. 72.*

Per Curiam—(Latin) "By the court." A decision handed down by the whole court, all the judges acting unanimously.

Per Stirpes—(Latin) The opposite of "Per Capita," above. Used in wills to mean that children take, as a class, the share which their parent would have received if he were alive. *See p. 72.*

Perjury—A false statement willfully made under oath, material to some matter being investigated in a legal proceeding; false testimony. Perjury is a crime.

Personal Injury—An injury to the body.

Personal Property—Everything capable of being owned except real property. Also known as *Personalty* as distinguished from *Realty*.

Plaintiff—One who, in a court action, complains of another, who thereby becomes the defendant.

Pleadings—The documents of a case in court; the complaint and the answer together constitute the pleadings.

Pledge—A deposit of property to assure payment of an obligation; a promise.

Police Power—The power which a government has to act for the general welfare of the community.

Polygamy—A crime; marrying a third wife when two former wives are living.

Post Mortem—(Latin) "After death." An examination of a corpse to determine the cause of death. Except when death occurs by violence, or under circumstances indicating the probable commission of a crime, a *post mortem* can be made only with the permission of the one who has the right to have the remains for burial—husband, wife, parents or child.

Precedents—Former decisions used as guides or models for judicial action.

Preferred Stock—Shares of stock in a corporation which entitle the owner to some advantage over the owners of common stock. This may differ according to the charter of the corporation by which the classes of stock are created. Often dividends must be paid on preferred stock before they are declared on common.

Preliminary Examination—A hearing before a magistrate, of one accused of a crime, to determine whether there is sufficient evidence to sustain the accusation and justify holding him for trial.

Premeditation—In criminal law, an intent formed in advance to commit the act; a plan or design.

Preponderance of Proof—Evidence that outweighs that given by the opposing party.

Presumptions—Inferences drawn from certain established facts. A presumption of law is a rule binding on everyone, like the presumption of legitimacy.

Prima Facie—(Latin) "At first sight." Evidence which proves a case or a fact unless it is rebutted.

Principal—1. The more important of several persons;
2. The one on whose behalf an agent acts;
3. In crime, the chief wrongdoers, who may be assisted by an "accessory".
4. The capital of an estate or trust.
5. Money that draws interest.

Privileged Communications—Those communications which cannot be made the basis for recovery of damages in a libel or slander suit because of the relationship of the parties involved, to each other or to the subject matter of the communication. EXAMPLE: Statements made during the course of a lawsuit by the judge, counsel, witnesses or parties to the action. Statements made by members of a legislative body in the course of their duty. A fair report by a newspaper of a judicial or legislative proceeding is also privileged. But if hostility or real malice is shown, such statements are not privileged. CONFIDENTIAL COMMUNICATIONS (*see* glossary definition) are also privileged.

Pro Forma—(Latin) "As a matter of form."

Probable Cause—In Criminal Law, the basis for arrest or the commencement of proceedings; good reason to believe that a crime has been committed by the person accused. *See p. 117.*

Probate—Proof that a document offered is the genuine last will and testament of a deceased person. *See p. 70.*

Probation—Relief from all or part of a prison term, on condition that the convict conduct himself respectably; a means of encouraging good behavior in and out of prison.

Process—The summons, subpoena, warrant or other document used to compel a party or a witness to appear in court. If process, or the manner of service is defective, appearance can be made *specially* for the purpose of attacking it. *See* SPECIAL APPEARANCE, p. 122.

Promissory Note—An unconditional promise, in writing,

to pay a certain sum of money to a person, to his order (anyone whom the *payee* names) or to the bearer. *See p. 25.*

Prosecutor—State attorney, district attorney; the one who represents the people of the state as the plaintiff in an action.

Prospectus—A statement of facts circulated among prospective purchasers of stock, describing the corporation, its property and its operations for the purpose of inducing persons to become stockholders. Misrepresentations in a prospectus can be made the basis for an action in fraud.

Protest—In negotiable instruments, a document drawn by a notary public, giving notice to all interested parties that the note, draft, etc., was presented for payment and refused. Notice of protest as a formality is not generally necessary in order to hold prior endorsers responsible.

Public Administrator—In New York and elsewhere the official who will act as administrator of the estate of a deceased person when no one else entitled to act is found or is qualified.

Public Policy—The general principles of good and evil which prevail in the state. Contracts which are against the public policy, gambling contracts, contracts which attack the institution of marriage, etc. are against the public policy of many states.

Purchase Money Mortgage—A mortgage loan providing a purchaser with the money necessary to buy property.

Quantum Meruit—(Latin) "According to what he deserves." When there is no agreement as to the amount to be paid for services, the law implies an obligation to pay the reasonable value of such services.

Quiet Enjoyment—An obligation (covenant) in a lease that the tenant will enjoy peaceably his possession of the property.

Quit Claim—A kind of deed to real property which is no more than a release of whatever rights the grantor may have.

Rape—Sexual intercourse by man with a woman who is not his wife, without her consent. It is not necessary that physical force be proved. If resistance is overcome by fear, or prevented by drugs or intoxicants or weakness of mind, the offense is still a rape. Sexual intercourse by a man with a woman under 18, not his wife, is what is known as statutory rape (in New York, rape in the second degree). The fact that she consented to the act does not affect the crime, since, as a minor, she is presumed incapable of consent. When the accused is under fourteen, there must be independent proof of his physical capacity.

Ratification—An act or an agreement by which something previously done is confirmed or adopted, as when a principal ratifies the act of his agent, or an adult ratifies a contract made by him as a minor.

Real Property—Land and everything growing or erected on it, including things permanently attached to it. *See p. 40.*

Rebuttal—Reply; evidence given to counter what was produced by the other side.

Receiver—An officer, appointed by the court to take charge of the property of a debtor, usually insolvent, for the benefit of creditors. In other proceedings, an officer appointed by the court to protect substantial interests, as for example, when the property of a corporation is being wasted or mismanaged, etc.

Receiver of Stolen Goods—When one receives goods knowing them to have been stolen, he is punishable as a principal in the crime.

Recital—Statement of facts. In contracts, the preliminary "whereas" clauses frequently used are recitals, and the facts stated in them are binding on the parties.

Recording—The filing in a public place of deeds, liens, mortgages, bills of sale, etc., as prescribed by law as a means of giving notice to interested parties.

Records—Written reports of judicial or legislative acts; books, etc. of a corporation.

Referee—A person, usually an officer of the court, to whom a matter is referred by the court for decision. The proceeding is called a reference and, in some cases, the finding of the referee is final; in others, his decision, in the form of a report, is subject to confirmation by the court.

Reformation—In equity, a proceeding to change the form of a written instrument so that it will reflect the terms the parties originally intended, but due to mistake or error, failed to achieve in the document itself.

Release—A discharge of a claim; giving up of a right or a claim; a satisfaction piece. Settlement of a claim should invariably include releases of each party by the other.

Relevancy—The relationship or logical connection of evidence to the disputed issue.

Renunciation—Giving up a right; in New York, a document signed by persons who have the right to letters of administration of a decedent's estate, surrendering the right in favor of another.

Replevin—An action to recover the actual possession of personal property, rather than its value.

Reports—(Law Reports) Official collections of case decisions.

Reprieve—A delay in execution granted by the same authorities as have the right to pardon; or by the court, when the delay is necessary to settle some legal question.

Res Ipsa Loquitur—(Latin) "The thing speaks for itself." A doctrine often applied in negligence cases where proof of the accident itself is sufficient to establish the negligence of the defendant. Thus, when the instrument or apparatus like a train or a bus is under the exclusive control of the defendant and the injured person is without fault (contributory negligence), the occurrence of the accident itself creates the inference of negligence.

Res Judicata—(*Latin*) "The matter has been decided." One is barred from suing on a matter when a competent court has previously ruled on the same matter between the same parties.

Rescission—Cancellation. The parties to a contract may rescind it by their own agreement. An action to rescind may be maintained when there has been a mistake or ignorance as to material facts by both parties, or by one who was taken advantage of by another.

Residence—The place where a person physically lives. This differs from his "domicile" (see definition). The laws of the various states set up different requirements as to period of residence for different purposes—as, for example, to maintain a divorce action.

Respondent—The one required to answer; the defendant in certain proceedings; the one required to answer an appeal from a judgment.

Resulting Trust—A trust relationship not expressed in any document, but arising from the acts and intentions of the parties. EXAMPLE: When the title to a piece of real estate is taken in the name of A and the purchase price is paid by B—who is in no way obligated to A—a trust *results* in which A holds the property as trustee for the benefit of B.

Retainer—An arrangement with a lawyer to represent a client in a legal matter; a *general retainer* is one in which the client receives the right to the lawyer's services, when called upon, and the lawyer is not to accept a fee from another against the interests of his retainer.

Reversion—The return of real estate to the original owner or his heirs, after the termination of some temporary grant. EXAMPLE: By will, the testator gives property to his sister for her life. When she dies, the property *reverts* to his estate.

Riparian Rights—The rights of owners of land adjoining a stream.

Salvage—A word used to denote the compensation given in maritime law for services rendered in rescuing a ship, its cargo or passengers. Also used to describe the property saved.

Seal—A measure, dating from ancient times, by which a person, by stamping an impression of a particular design in wax, at the end of a document, identified the act or instrument as his. Seals are still used by government offices and by corporations, etc., to make acts official. The seal is not necessary for that purpose unless specifically required by law. A contract under seal creates the presumption of consideration. In some places the distinction between sealed and unsealed documents has been abolished. Where it still exists, no special device is required where individuals are concerned. The word "seal" or the initials "l.s." next to the signature is enough.

Search Warrant—A warrant addressed to an officer, authorizing him to search a place for stolen goods, illegal drugs, etc. Warrants must be issued only on reasonable cause and must contain a description of the place to be searched and the property to be seized. *See p. 138.*

Security—A means of assuring payment of a debt or the doing of some act; a person who binds himself to pay a debt if someone else fails to pay it. *Security for Costs* is provided by law in certain cases where the court is shown that the plaintiff in an action is a nonresident; or that the action is unfounded and will put the defendant to heavy expense.

Seduction—Inducing a female by deception or enticement to consent to sexual intercourse. In New York, the right to recover money damages for seduction was abolished in 1935 by the so-called Heart Balm Act, which also abolished the causes of action for alienation of affections, criminal conversation (seduction of a married woman), and breach of contract to marry. The legislature abolished those causes of action because it felt that they gave rise to too many groundless suits designed to extract a settlement through the threat of publicity. To ensure that the Heart Balm Act would be effective, the legislature made it illegal for anyone to bring suit for, threaten to bring suit for, or receive money in settlement of, any of the abolished causes of action.

Self-defense—Action to prevent harm to one's person, family or property. The law permits the use of as much force as may be necessary, in defense against assault, even to the point of killing the attacker when the circumstances warrant. There must be belief by the defender, and reasonable ground for such belief, that he or his are in immediate danger.

Separation—Living apart by husband and wife by agreement, or in accordance with a court decree. *See pp. 106-7.*

Sheriff—A state officer. The sheriff's duties vary in accordance with state law. The duties include law enforcement, custody of prisoners, service of process, execution of judgments, conduct of sales to satisfy executions, etc.

Signature—A signed name or a symbol on a document to identify the maker. In general, unless otherwise prescribed by law, the signature need not be witnessed or notarized, need not be in ink, need not be written out in full, nor correctly spelled. It can be in print, as in a telegram or typescript; it can be a mark, if the signer cannot write; it can be written by another for him; or the name signed can be a fictitious one. The important thing is the identity of the signer, the fact that *he* signed or caused someone to sign for him. But he who signs a document is presumed to know its contents.

Silence—The saying "Silence is consent" is not uniformly true. Silence can only be held against a person when the circumstances require him to speak.

Slander—Spoken defamatory words which are false and injure the reputation of another. Truth of the words is a good defense, even if the reputation is damaged. If reputation is poor to begin with, damages may be minor.

Sodomy—A crime; sexual intercourse against nature, between two persons (perverted sexual intercourse) or between a person and an animal.

Specific Performance—Obligation to carry out an act stipulated in a contract, when a breach of contract cannot be compensated in money. In such cases, it is within the discretion of the court to issue an order compelling performance. Most frequently this remedy is applied to contracts for the sale of real property, since such property is unique. When personal property and personal services are so special and unique that money damages cannot replace or compensate for them, there may be grounds for a demand for *Specific Performance.*

Spendthrift Trust—A method of placing a principal fund of money out of the reach of one who, if he had access to it, might squander it.

SS—Abbreviation of the Latin *scilicet*—"Let it be known." Often used in affidavits and other legal documents.

Stay—A delay or suspension of legal proceedings. *Stay of Execution* in civil actions is granted, pending appeal or a court order. EXAMPLE: Execution of a judgment can be *stayed* pending the outcome of an appeal.

Sterility—Lack of capacity to bear or beget children. This is distinguished from impotency, which is lack of capacity, in the man, to perform the sexual act.

Stipulation—An item in a contract; an agreement between attorneys in connection with a court proceeding.

Stockholder—One who owns a share or shares in the capital of a corporation.

Subpena (or **subpoena**)—(Latin) "Under penalty." A command to appear and testify in court. A *Subpena Duces Tecum* is a subpena commanding the witness to bring papers which are in his care into court.

Subrogation—Substitution of parties. The right to take over the position of another. EXAMPLE: Insurance policies often include a provision that, in case of accidental damage, the company will pay the insured, but will have all the rights of the insured to sue the one responsible for the damages.

Substituted Service—Service of process on a person other than the one named in the paper. Under certain circumstances, when the party cannot be found, the court will order service upon someone else.

Summary Proceedings—Shortcut proceedings to do away with the delays incidental to regular trial practice. These are generally permitted in actions to dispossess tenants for nonpayment of rent, etc.

Summons—*See* PROCESS.

Supplementary Proceedings—Proceedings after judgment and execution. Allowed by statute in order to locate property which may be used to satisfy the judgment.

Suretyship—An agreement on the part of a person or organization (the surety) to be responsible for the debt, default or wrongdoing of another (the principal). Similar to guaranty. If the principal does not perform a certain obligation, his *surety* is bound to. A surety company is one that engages in the business of issuing surety bonds, or becoming surety for trustees, guardians, executors, administrators, employees, etc. If any of these should be unfaithful to his trust and make away with property, the company makes good the loss.

Tax Sale—A sale at auction, for nonpayment of taxes. The deed given is called a tax deed.

Tenant—Technically one who has possession of land or space in a building by virtue of ownership or any other kind of right. Popularly, one who temporarily, and on certain conditions, possesses the property of another. *See pp. 52ff.*

Tender—A formal offer of money or property as fulfillment of an obligation in a transaction. A tender of the sum of money due before the foreclosure of a lien will serve to stop the sale. EXAMPLE: Under a contract for the sale of real property, the buyer is required to pay the seller $10,000 on December 1. When December 1 comes around, purchaser *tenders* the $10,000. The offer, or tender, is made by the buyer as performance of his obligation even if, for some reason, the seller is not ready to go through with the deal.

Testamentary Capacity—The mental ability sufficient to make a will.

Testimony—Oral evidence given by a witness under oath.

Title—The right of ownership. For title search, closing of title, marketable title. *See pp. 42ff.*

Tort—A civil wrong or injury. *See p. 82.*

Trademark—A design, symbol, combination of letters or words identifying a product with its manufacturers. *See pp. 66–67.*

Transcript—A copy of a document or a record.

Traverse—A denial or contradiction. In some courts a traverse is a proceeding to settle questions that arise before trial, such as whether or not process was correctly served, or whether or not a party is properly within the jurisdiction of the court.

Trespass—An unlawful act against another in violation of his rights and causing him injury; an entry without permission on the property of another.

Trial—An inquiry by a court into the facts for the purpose of deciding the issue or issues brought before it. *See p. 128.*

Trover—An action to recover the value of property wrongfully taken by another; more commonly called an action for conversion.

Trust—An obligation upon a person (the trustee) arising out of the terms of a special grant, to hold and apply property according to those terms, for the benefit of others (the beneficiaries). The trust relationship implies a very high degree of confidence in the trustee, and he is required to discharge his duties with extreme care and faithfulness.

Ultra Vires—(Latin) "Outside the powers." Used to describe acts by corporations not authorized by their charters.

Unjust Enrichment—A form of action to recover money paid to another for a purpose which has not been achieved. The principle is used when the contract relationship is not clear. Its meaning simply is that it is unjust for one to enrich himself at the expense of another.

Usury—Charging interest at a rate higher than that prescribed by law. The *legal* rate in most states is 6 per cent (In New York, where the Banking Board has the authority to adjust the rate periodically in response to economic conditions, the legal rate is currently 8 per cent. In addition to the legal rate, there is a statutory rate of interest known as the *contract* rate, which is the maximum rate of interest that parties to a contract can agree on. This rate is usually somewhat higher than the legal rate. The states have devised various means of discouraging usury, from requiring the forfeiture of the excessive interest to voiding the entire contract.

Vacate—In court practice, to cancel or make an act void. A court order may *vacate* or cancel a prior order such as a judgment.

Value Received—These words often appear on negotiable instruments (notes, drafts, etc.) to indicate that the paper has been given for some consideration. But when the instrument is negotiable, according to the definition in the Negotiable Instruments Law, these words are not necessary.

Venue—The place where the cause of action arose or took place; the court that has jurisdiction over the subject matter and the parties; the geographic jurisdiction of a court.

Verification—A certificate under oath that a written statement is true.

Vital Statistics—Public records of births, marriages and deaths.

Void—Having no effect. The word is often confused with *"Voidable."* *"Void"* signifies that something has been empty of meaning from the very beginning, like a contract to commit a crime. *Voidable* is something that has effect until some act is done. A contract that has for its purpose to defraud creditors is good until it is voided by the action of the creditors.

Voting Trust—An arrangement to control the management of a corporation by placing in the hands of one person or a group of persons the right to vote the stockholders' shares.

Waiver—The intentional abandonment of a right.

Ward—A minor (infant) who is legally in the care of a guardian.

Warrant—An order issued by a judge, justice of the peace, magistrate or other authorized official directing the arrest of a person accused of a crime. It is both a command and an authorization for the arresting officer to act. *See pp. 92, 138.*

Will—A disposition of property to take effect after death. In order for a will to be valid and enforceable it must be drawn and executed in conformity with state law. *See pp. 69ff.*

Witness—(1) One who testifies as to what he himself knows.
(2) One who is present at some event and observes the proceedings, as witnessing a will, the signing of any document, a wedding.

Workmen's Compensation—A method provided by law in most of the states for the payment of compensation to employees for injuries sustained in the course of their employment. Most laws provide for compulsory insurance. A basic feature is that the injuries must have resulted from or during the employment. The awards are usually fixed according to the nature of the disability—so much (in terms of days' or weeks' earnings) for a broken arm, so much for a leg, etc. No suit is necessary, nor is it necessary that the negligence of the employer be proved.

Writ—A court order.

INDEX